Afterlives of the Rich and Famous

Afterlives of the Rich and Famous

Sylvia Browne

with Lindsay Harrison

HarperOne
An Imprint of HarperCollinsPublishers

HarperOne

This book is metaphysical and philosophical in nature. Nothing herein is intended to imply an endorsement of the book, author, or publisher by any of the persons mentioned herein, including the deceased celebrities and their families.

AFTERLIVES OF THE RICH AND FAMOUS. Copyright © 2011 by Sylvia Browne. All rights reserved. Printed in the United States of America. No part of this book may be used or reproduced in any manner whatsoever without written permission except in the case of brief quotations embodied in critical articles and reviews. For information, address HarperCollins Publishers, 10 East 53rd Street, New York, NY 10022.

HarperCollins books may be purchased for educational, business, or sales promotional use. For information, please write: Special Markets Department, HarperCollins Publishers, 10 East 53rd Street, New York, NY 10022.

HarperCollins website: http://www.harpercollins.com
HarperCollins®, 🏫®, and HarperOne™
are trademarks of HarperCollins Publishers

FIRST HARPERCOLLINS PAPERBACK EDITION PUBLISHED IN 2012

Designed by Level C

Library of Congress Cataloging-in-Publication Data
Browne, Sylvia.
Afterlives of the rich and famous / by Sylvia Browne.
p. cm.
ISBN 978–0–06–196680–4
1. Celebrities—Death. 2. Future life. I. Title.
CT105.B755   2011
129—dc23   2011029022

12 13 14 15 16   RRD(H)   10 9 8 7 6 5 4 3 2 1

From Sylvia and Lindsay:
For you, Steve—
we truly hope you've found
everyone you're looking for
over there

Contents

Introduction

This book is about current events in the lives of celebrities who've passed away, as reported by a "resident expert" on the Other Side whose name is Francine. Two obvious questions probably leap to mind: "Who's Francine?" and "Since these celebrities are dead, doesn't that pretty much mean they're doing nothing?" Believe me, if I didn't have good answers to those questions, this book wouldn't exist.

As for the first question, Francine is my Spirit Guide. Like your Spirit Guide and everyone else's, she's been with me all my life. You'll find a complete definition of Spirit Guides and what they do for us in the glossary, so for now I'll just tell you about her.

I was born psychic, with an inherited ability to "tune in" to the spirit world of the Other Side. At first, starting when I was five years old, I was only clairvoyant—that is, able to see spirits (and I wasn't exactly thrilled about it, believe me). But then one night when I was eight, I discovered with an equal lack of glee that I was also clairaudient, or able to *hear* spirits, as well, when a chirpy, high-pitched voice came crashing into my bedroom and announced, "Don't be afraid, Sylvia. I come from God."

My beloved, brilliantly psychic Grandmother Ada explained, after prying her terrified granddaughter from around her legs, that the voice was simply my Spirit Guide introducing herself, that we all have Spirit Guides, and that they're around to gently help us navigate our way through these brief trips away from Home. And so, tentatively at first, I began communicating with Francine. Throughout our sixty-five years together she's never lied to me, never betrayed me, and never steered me wrong (I took care of that on my own). She's also been a fascinating, invaluable source of volumes of information about the afterlife.

It's a requirement of all Spirit Guides that they've incarnated—otherwise, our problems, worries, and missteps on earth would be incomprehensibly trivial to them, living as they do in the blissful perfection of the Other Side and seeing everything that happens through the perspective of eternity. Francine (who introduced herself as Ilena, which I apparently didn't like and promptly changed to Francine) only chose to incarnate once, as an Aztec-Incan woman who died at the age of nineteen, in 1520, saving her infant daughter from a spear during the Spanish invasion of Colombia. She's accompanying me through this lifetime as a result of a mutual agreement we made at Home, before I decided to come to earth again for the fifty-secondth and last time.

I've communicated with Francine every day of my life since I was eight, and I love everything about her but her voice. Like everyone in the spirit world, she lives on a plane that exists on a much higher frequency than ours, with the result that when she talks, she sounds like a tape recording played on fast-forward. I intend no disrespect—I'm deeply grateful for her guidance and for the fact that I can hear her—but it took me a while to even be able to understand her, and after just a few short sentences, listening to her can be downright irritating.

When I was in my late teens, I began wishing that other people could hear the wealth of wisdom she had to offer without subjecting myself to hours of that annoying, chirpy, Alvin-and-the-Chipmunks voice. She came up with the perfect solution: with my permission, she could borrow my body and my vocal cords and, instead of talking to me, she could talk *through* me. In other words, by going into a trance and essentially "stepping aside" temporarily, I could channel her, for as long or short a time as I wanted, with no risk to me whatsoever. I wouldn't have any memory of what she said while I was "gone," but she could give talks and lectures without driving me or others crazy, and people could record her on tape if I wanted to check out what went on in my absence.

I wanted no part of it when she first suggested it—I wasn't about to turn over control of my body and voice to anyone, thank you, not even to someone I trusted as much as I had come to trust her. But I finally agreed to try it, if only to prove her wrong, find out I hated it, and determine never to let it happen again.

As always, she was right. It was so harmless that there was nothing about it for me to hate, and I've been routinely channeling Francine ever since, going through the simple process of announcing her impending arrival, closing my eyes, and letting my spirit "take a break" from my body, so that she can "come in." Her voice is mine, of course, but her speech pattern is slower, her vocabulary and knowledge far exceed mine, and as a resident of the Other Side she's able to give eyewitness accounts of everyone and everything that goes on there.

Throughout the years she's given countless lectures to groups ranging from ten people to thousands, and she's provided an inexhaustible amount of extraordinary, profound information for any number of my books. She doesn't participate when I give readings, largely because she usually responds to earthly problems (including mine) with the accurate but unhelpful assurance, "Everything will work out as it's meant to." It frustrates me, so I can only imagine how it would frustrate my clients.

For decades now, after certain celebrities have passed away, I've had calls from the press asking for my psychic input on anything those celebrities might have to say or any information I had to offer about their lives or transition to their afterlives. Francine contributed an enormous amount of that information. And I don't mind admitting that over the years I've checked with Francine many times about "deceased" celebrities I especially loved (or, in one case in particular, especially didn't). Slowly but surely, with an emphasis on "slowly," it occurred to me that a book about celebrity afterlives might be of interest to a wide variety of people, from their fans to their families. I began assembling brief biographies, and those were fascinating enough all by themselves—even while putting together biographies of celebrities whose lives I would have sworn I knew all about, I kept thinking, "I didn't know that."

And then, while my friend and assistant, Linda, sat beside me with a tape recorder running, I channeled Francine and let Linda ask question after question, late celebrity after late celebrity. What you'll find in this book, then, is a collection of biographies and Francine's comments, transcribed and edited from the tapes of those trance sessions, as much or as little as she had to say about each name that came up, unless it was too indiscreet to include. (Francine has no filters when it comes to answering questions.) I'm not kidding about "as much or as little as she had to say," either, believe me. When she was finished talking about someone, she was finished, no matter how many more questions Linda asked her, sometimes because that's all there is and sometimes because, frankly, apathy might set in on Francine's part. "We all love each other here," she explained more than once, "but that doesn't mean we all find each other interesting." In fact, there were a few names Linda brought up (after I'd spent hours gathering information for their biographies, I might add) to which Francine simply replied, "No." That's it. Just "no." She didn't even care to discuss why she was saying no, and I didn't blame Linda one bit for leaving it at that and moving on.

Francine also asked me to clarify what might be a misimpression in reading her comments. Several of her discussions include other celebrities with whom the celebrity in question socializes, works, or performs, and she doesn't mean to imply that celebrities on the Other Side only hang out with other celebrities. For one thing, the whole concept of celebrity is meaningless at Home, where everyone is of equally admired status. For another thing, she thought it would be more interesting to us here on earth to limit her observations to names with which we're probably familiar. The way she put it was, "I could tell you that one of your celebrities enjoys horseback riding with John Smith or taking guitar lessons with Susie Jones, but would anyone care?" I had to admit that no, we probably wouldn't. So please don't be misled by her genuine efforts to edit herself on our behalf. All things considered, I'm sure she did us a favor.

As for the second obvious question about this book—doesn't the word "dead" tell us all there is to know about what someone's doing?—the answer is a resounding, comforting, "Not even close." God's promise to us, as part of our birthright from the moment He created us, is that the death of our bodies doesn't mean we cease to exist. We always were, and we always will be. We all have eternal lives to look back on and to look forward to. Not eternal nothingness, or an eternal vacuum, or an eternity of floating around like blobs of vapor playing harps. Eternal *lives*, vital and productive, each of us on our own progressive journey toward our spirit's greatest potential.

Eventually (as you'll learn in the course of this book, it just takes some of us longer than others to get there) we all spend eternity in a place called the Other Side, a place every bit as real as earth, but without its flaws. The Other Side is our real Home. It's where we came from for our brief visits here, and it's where we'll return after we've accomplished our carefully planned intentions this time around. And when we get there, we'll joyfully resume our busy lives where we left off, farther ahead than we were before because of all we learned from our latest incarnation.

It's true for you. It's true for me. It's true for celebrities, both the famous and the infamous.

That's why the question, "What are these celebrities doing now?" is just as relevant after their "death" as it was when they were here on earth. Just as everyone you've known, loved, and temporarily lost through the illusion of death is somewhere doing something at this very moment, including visiting you, the same can be said for everyone you've ever heard of, wondered about, had a crush on, admired, or loathed.

But before we start exploring the celebrities one by one, it's worth taking a look at exactly what happens when our bodies die and the variety of places our spirits might go from here.

Death . . . and Then What?

Even as a child in Catholic school I was frustrated by how vague everyone was about this "life after death" thing. There seemed to be general agreement that our spirits survive after our mortal bodies give out. It was the "and then what?" part that inspired a lot of throat clearing and hazy, halfhearted answers; I often got the feeling it was the one question the nuns et al. were hoping no one would ask. From what I could piece together, when we die, some sort of tunnel apparently drops down from the sky like a big sparkling megaphone to kind of inhale our souls up to heaven. Alternately, we were offered a lot of lovely imagery about our souls floating away from our dead bodies and disappearing beyond the clouds. But after one or the other or something else happened, our immortal souls either ended up in heaven, which looked like who knows what, to live happily ever after with God, doing who knows what, or we were sent to hell for an eternity of fiery damnation—by a God who was always described as all-loving and all-forgiving.

Looking back, it's no surprise that I wasn't satisfied with those answers, or lack of them, particularly the ones that made no sense. But finally, between Francine's generous, articulate expertise, a lifetime of study, including a degree in theology, and my own near-death experience at the age of forty-two, I learned the truth about "and then what?" and it's far more sacred and exquisite than anything my imagination could have created.

There is a very real tunnel, it turns out, and it doesn't drop down from the sky when our bodies die. Instead, it rises up from our own etheric substance, or energy field, angles across our body at about a twenty-degree angle, and delivers us to the Other Side, which is actually just three feet above our ground level, but in another dimension whose vibrational frequency is much higher than ours. It's a perfect mirror image of the natural topography of our planet—our continents, our oceans, our mountains, our rivers, our forests, our deserts, our coastlines, every single feature of earth as it once existed before pollution, erosion, and human destruction came along. Because time doesn't exist on the Other Side, nothing ages, nothing corrodes or erodes, and everything is eternally, perfectly new.

As we move through the tunnel we feel weightless, free, and more thrillingly alive than we ever felt for a moment in the finite, gravity-challenged bodies we left behind. No matter what the circumstances of our death, there's a pervasive sense of peace in the awareness that we're on our way Home, and we quickly see the legendary white light ahead of us, indescribably sacred, God's light.

No matter where on earth we take our last breath, all tunnels lead to the same entrance to the perfect paradise of the Other Side: a breathtaking grassy meadow filled with flowers whose colors seem magnified a thousand times beyond anything we'll ever experience here. Waiting in that meadow to joyfully welcome us are loved ones from all our lifetimes on earth and at Home as well as every animal we've ever loved from those same lifetimes. (Would it be paradise if there were no animals?)

Once we've experienced our reunions in the meadow, we proceed to the triumvirate of buildings—yes, there are buildings—that create the "hub" of the Other Side. You'll read more about their specific purposes in the glossary of terms that follows, without which some of Francine's celebrity comments will just be confusing, but for now, in brief, the first three buildings we see when we return Home are:

- The Hall of Wisdom: a Romanesque structure of gleaming white stone adorned with statuary and surrounded by fountains and fragrant flowers in constant bloom. Its most stunning feature is the infinite expanse of marble steps that lead to its countless entrances.

- The Hall of Justice: a pillared Greco-Roman building with a massive white marble dome. Standing guard at its entrance is a magnificent statue of Azna, the Mother God. Surrounding the Hall of Justice are its exquisite Gardens, impeccably designed and extending for as far as the eye can see, filled with sparkling waterfalls and fountains, meditation benches, towering trees and canopies of Spanish moss, crystal streams rushing through carpets of soft green grass, lush forests of ferns, and endless walls of jewel-tone bougainvillea.

- The Hall of Records: a vast edifice with spectacularly carved columns and a dome of sparkling gold. It is constantly bustling with "locals" and spirit visitors from earth alike. Inside stretch an infinite number of aisles, lined with an infinite number of shelves filled with an infinite number of scrolls, books, documents, maps, artwork, blueprints, and such, every shelf in perfectly kept order. One of the functions of the Hall of Records is to house every historical, literary, and artistic work ever written, drawn, drafted, sketched, or painted since time began, and it is revered as the sacred home of the Akashic Records, which are the complete written body of God's knowledge, laws, and memories.

There are also the Towers, two identical monoliths of blue glass, glistening from the hushed waterfalls that flow down their facades and mist the forest of jasmine that lines the path to the Towers' etched gold doors.

Through this "formal" entrance we resume the lives we chose to briefly interrupt for a trip to earth, in the divine world of the Other Side. And they don't call it paradise for nothing. The weather is constantly calm and clear with a temperature of 78 degrees, except on the highest elevations, where the 30 degree temperature maintains a perfect snowpack. There is no day or night—no time at all, in fact, beyond an eternal "now." The sun, moon, and stars are not visible, and the sky is always the pastel blend of a summer dusk.

The landscape is rich with magnificent libraries, research centers, schools, houses of worship of every denomination, concert halls and museums, not to mention stadiums, golf courses, tennis courts, and ski resorts—in fact, every noncontact sport is enjoyed on the Other Side.

Since money is nonexistent and unnecessary, there is no commerce and no reason to work for a paycheck. Most of us do work, though, for the sheer joy and passion of it. We also socialize, as much or as little as we choose, and because we have no need to eat or sleep, we literally have an uninterrupted eternity to seek out anyone and everyone we care to know, explore anything and everything we've ever wanted to see, research and learn about any and every subject and activity that's ever intrigued us, attend every party, concert, play, and sports event that interests us, and generally bask in the bliss of limitless possibilities in a heaven of sacred universal love, respect, and peace.

We're free of the earth's limitations of space and gravity and the laws of physics. We have houses if we want, wherever we want, and we create the homes we want by simple thought projection, just as we travel wherever we want by simply thinking ourselves there.

And how's this for something to look forward to: not only is our physical and mental health perfectly restored once we're Home again, but on the Other Side all of us are thirty years old. Why thirty? As my Spirit Guide, Francine, replied when I asked her that question, "Because we are." Mind you, the transitions to thirty and to perfect health are usually processes after we've arrived, rather than an instantaneous "Poof! You're thirty!" effect the moment we emerge from the tunnel. And when we visit loved ones on earth, we're easily able to take on whatever appearance will make us recognizable to them. After all, if we passed away as an infant or a very elderly person, how comforting would a spirit visit from a thirty-year-old really be?

I could go on and on about the joy that awaits us after we leave this world—the same joy we temporarily interrupted to come here for what I like to call "boot camp." In fact, I *have* gone on and on about it, in a book called *Life on the Other Side,* so I'll leave it at that for this discussion in the hope that these brief "highlights" will help Francine's descriptions of the current lives of the celebrities in this book make much more sense.

But there are other available options for our spirits when our earthly bodies die, most of them the result of our own choices during our lifetimes, and since a few of the celebrities we'll be discussing made those choices, we should briefly explore those options as well.

THE LEFT DOOR

Despite what most of us (including me) have been taught since we were children, there is no such thing as hell. The threat of hell implies a God so vindictive and unforgiving that He could turn His back on us and banish us to an eternity away from Him, and not for one minute is that a God I believe in. The God I believe in, worship, and have committed my life to is all-loving, all-knowing, all-compassionate, and all-forgiving; He would *never* turn His back on a life He created.

Sadly, we don't have to spend much time on earth to learn that there are those who choose to turn their backs on God. And "choose," by the way, excludes anything to do with mental illness or physiological chemical imbalances, which are completely involuntary. I'm talking about people who, given a choice between contributing light to this world or contributing darkness, opt for darkness—the deliberately cruel, amoral, remorseless sociopaths who view the rest of us as props for their amusement, to be used, manipulated, and in some form or other destroyed, either physically, mentally, or emotionally. Darkness can't exist where there's light, after all, so the Dark Side, as I call this segment of society, feels perfectly entitled to the destruction it inflicts. Its devotees know right from wrong. They just don't care. Unlike the misguided or the genuinely lost among us, residents of the Dark Side can't be rehabilitated—without a conscience to begin with, they have no conscience to be guided back to. They can feign charm, compassion, love, generosity, and often a devout faith in God, not because they mean a word of it, but because they know how seductive those qualities can be, and it's so much easier to destroy someone whose guard is down.

There's no such thing as action without consequence, for better or worse, and that's as true for the Dark Side as it is for the rest of us. Remember, these dark entities have chosen a path that keeps their backs turned squarely away from God, and that arrogant rejection of Him prevents them from experiencing the perfect bliss and love of the Other Side when they die. Instead, they head straight to a nightmare called the Left Door (which my granddaughter Angelia used to refer to as "mean heaven" when she was a child).

The Left Door is the entrance to a joyless, godless world of nothingness, an abyss through which dark spirits briefly pass before heading right back in utero for another incarnation that's likely to be as destructive as the one they've just completed. So when you come across those in this book who've gone through the Left Door, know that within a few months of their death they were born again on earth with a whole new identity, a whole new incarnation to live out, with no more of a conscious memory of their past lives than you and I have, and another opportunity to finally choose light over darkness.

And by the way, just as God doesn't condemn any of His children to an eternity of hell, He also doesn't condemn any of us to an eternity of recycling through the Left Door and back to earth again and again and again. Sooner or later (which in the context of eternity might mean hundreds of years), the spirits on the Other Side will retrieve a dark soul in that instant before it reaches the Left Door and return it to the healing peace of Home, where God's unconditional love is always available, even to those who don't reciprocate.

THE HOLDING PLACE

There's a kind of anteroom to the Left Door, a desolate gray expanse filled with lost souls who've been separated from their faith, hope, and joy by oppressive depression. They shuffle silently around in no direction, heads down, eyes empty and lifeless, never acknowledging each other or the hopelessness that's trapped them there.

The Holding Place is like the purgatory I learned about in parochial school, and it's sometimes, but not always, the temporary destination of spirits whose death was caused by suicide. It's simply not true—in fact, it's a cruel lie—that all suicides lead to eternal damnation. Again, God would never inflict such vindictive judgment on any of His children. Some suicides are inspired by revenge; others are an ultimate mean-spirited demand for attention or an act of self-centered cowardice (the latter typical of murder-suicides). And those particular suicides can look forward to a quick trip through the Left Door and another immediate incarnation without enjoying a moment of the blissful peace of Home between lifetimes.

But as we all know, some suicides are the result of mental illness or untreated chemical imbalances that create severe, crippling, mind-altering depression, and in the perfection of God's universal laws no one is held accountable for actions that aren't their fault. (Injustice is strictly a human invention.) A great many of these blameless, unplanned, despair-induced suicides, I promise you, make it straight through the tunnel to the Other Side. Others, often confused throughout their lives on earth about their faith in God and their occasional attraction to the Dark Side, find themselves in the Holding Place, where, if they can overcome the desolation around them, they can still choose between the doomed cycle of the Left Door or Home, where God's embrace will always be waiting for them.

GHOSTS

And then there are those who, when their bodies die, refuse to acknowledge the tunnel or see it and reject it. This leaves their spirits stranded here, outside of their bodies, stuck between the lower vibrational level of earth and the much higher vibrational dimension of the Other Side, not one bit aware that they've died. And that's how ghosts are created.

Ghosts, or earthbounds, are tragic, fascinating beings. As far as they're concerned, they're every bit as alive as the rest of us, and everything is exactly and perpetually as it was at the moment of their death, from their surroundings to their age, health (or lack of it), and scars, wounds, or visible signs of injuries that might have killed them. The one thing that's changed, which often makes them desperately confused, if not downright cranky, is that because they've changed vibrational frequencies without knowing it, the people around them suddenly seem to act as if they don't exist.

There's nothing haphazard about some spirits' determination to remain earthbound. Ghosts stay behind for a variety of misguided reasons—to care for a loved one, to protect a home or land they're deeply connected to, to seek revenge, or, with sad frequency, to avoid facing God out of fear that He'll turn them away (which is an impossibility).

No ghost is ever trapped on earth for eternity. Some of them are sent to the Other Side by people who are compassionate and educated enough, when they find themselves in the presence of an earthbound, to simply say, "You're dead. Go Home." (Sometimes that works, and sometimes it doesn't, but it's worth a try.) Many more of them are eventually rescued by residents of the Other Side, who are well aware of them and can be counted on to perform persistent interventions for as long as it takes to pull these trapped, confused souls into the tunnel and on to the joyful peace that's waiting for them in God's outstretched arms.

Glossary

You'll come across several terms in Francine's comments that could easily leave you scratching your head and saying, "Huh?" Rather than take the time to interrupt what she has to say by explaining each term as it comes up, I'd much rather give you these reference pages to turn back to and let you read any and all definitions that happen to pique your curiosity.

Astral Travel

Astral travel is the means by which loved ones on the Other Side come to visit us and we go to visit them. It's also our means of transporting ourselves from place to place at Home, free of these cumbersome, gravity-challenged bodies we're currently housed in. Astral travel brought us here from our real lives in paradise when our spirits entered their chosen bodies, and astral travel will take us there again when these incarnations are through.

Astral travel comes as naturally to us as breathing, whether we're conscious of it or not. It's a skill we were given when our souls were born an eternity ago, and that skill is ours no matter what dimension we happen to be living in, including earth. You and I travel astrally while we sleep—an average of two or three times a week, in fact. Astral travel is the truth behind some of our most vivid and memorable "dreams." And we can thank astral travel for the fact that while victims of comas and severely debilitating illnesses are struggling physiologically, their spirits are joyfully darting from place to place, dimension to dimension, and loved one to loved one.

You'll read more about the specifics of the Other Side's visits to us in the discussion of spirits in this glossary. For now I just want to focus on our own astral travel and how we routinely take trips that, among other comforts, allow us to initiate reunions with an unlimited number of people and places we miss. And since our most frequent trips take place while we're asleep, it's natural for us to mistake them for dreams. But there are some simple ways to tell the difference:

- Dreams of flying without benefit of an airplane or other external means aren't dreams; they're astral travels, perfectly real, neither dreams nor your imagination. Not all astral travel "dreams" involve flying, though. Like everyone else, including you, I astrally travel to the Other Side several times a month while I sleep, and to the best of my knowledge I've never had a dream in which I'm flying on my own power.

- Astral trips unfold in a logical sequence of events, just as our waking experiences do, rather than in that haphazard jumble of images, people, and locations that are so common in dreams.

- Any dream you're not only part of, but actually view yourself in, isn't a dream; it's astral travel. We've all heard about or experienced the phenomenon of people watching themselves during surgery, deep meditation, unconsciousness, or a coma.

The same thing can happen during astral trips for exactly the same reason—during those moments the spirit and the body are two separate entities. And take it from someone who's been there, there's a certain curious fascination in finding yourself able to look at yourself from outside your body as an objective observer. I don't happen to love that feeling, and I much prefer limiting my astral travel to those hours when I'm sound asleep and my cluttered conscious mind isn't ready to leap in and interfere.

So next time you have a pretty, peaceful "dream" about a departed loved one that unfolded in logical, sequential order and "seemed so real," please know that it *is* real, and go right ahead and enjoy every bit of the comfort it gives you.

Cell Memory

You'll find a reference or two in Francine's comments about something called cell memory, or when a celebrity reacts during the most recent incarnation to an experience he or she had in a previous life. And since cell memory isn't reserved exclusively for celebrities, but is common to all of us, it's even more worthy of a brief discussion.

Cell memory is the cumulative body of knowledge our spirits have gathered during all our lifetimes on earth and at Home, and it is accessed by every cell in the body the moment we "take up residence" in the fetus. It's what lies behind countless health problems, phobias, psychoses, chronic pains, and so much other supposedly unexplainable "baggage" we arrive with when we're born.

The basics of cell memory go like this:

- Our bodies are made up of billions of interacting cells.

- Each of those cells is a living, breathing, feeling organism, responding literally to whatever information it receives from the subconscious mind.

- It's in the subconscious that our spirit minds live, eternally intact and with total recall, no matter how healthy or unhealthy our conscious minds might be.

The instant our spirit minds enter our physical bodies for a new incarnation, the familiarity of being in a body again triggers all the memories and sensations our spirits have retained from every past life we've ever lived. It's not unlike an experience you've probably had when you returned to a place that holds powerful memories for you—your childhood home, maybe, or the site of your first school dance—and been stirred both physically and emotionally by the impact of the present colliding with the past. On a larger, more significant level, that's exactly what our spirits feel when they find themselves in a body again. Like all the other information our subconscious minds transmit, our billions of cells are instantaneously infused with an eternity of memories and sensations and physiologically react to them as part of their reality.

Through regressive hypnosis, I've helped thousands of clients access those cell memories and learn to recognize them as part of lives and deaths that have long since come and gone. But make no mistake about it, we, and the celebrities you'll read about, are unavoidably impacted by cell memories from other lifetimes, for better or worse, some of us more strongly than others.

And just to clarify an important point that some people find confusing: please remember that living several lifetimes doesn't mean that in the course of eternity we become several different people. We're always the same spirit, always ourselves, on one infinite journey, growing and learning along the way, no matter how many different bodies we might inhabit. For an effective analogy, think of your journey in this lifetime alone, every step of which led to who and where you are at this moment. From birth, through infancy, through potty training, through kindergarten, through high school, through whatever stage of adulthood you've reached now, you've gone through countless changes, physically, mentally, and emotionally, but you've always been *you*, the sum total of everything you've experienced so far. The eternal journey of our souls works exactly the same way. Through all our incarnations that temporarily take us away from Home, all our physical, mental, and emotional variations during our time on earth, and our exquisitely busy lives on the Other Side, we always have been and always will be no one but *us*, utterly unique as God created each of us, constantly learning and growing and becoming wiser through experience, whether we're at Home or here, in this rough school away from Home that we've elected to attend.

The Chart

It's worth repeating as often as it takes: earth is not our Home. The Other Side is our Home. We had joyful, busy lives there before we came here, and we'll return to those lives after we leave here. We make these brief trips to earth to learn, the hard way, through hands-on experience, for the growth and progress of our spirits along the path of their eternal journey. It's a completely different kind of education than we have access to at Home, because on the Other Side everything is infused with God's perfection. And as Francine has rhetorically asked me a million times, "What have you learned when times were good?"

We choose to come here, as rarely or as often as we decide we need to, and we choose what we're interested in learning and working on this time around. There's nothing haphazard about our incarnations. Just as we would never head off to college without having decided which school would serve us best, what courses we'll need, where we'll live and with whom, and countless other details to maximize our odds of accomplishing our goals, we wouldn't dream of coming to earth unprepared.

And so, before we come to earth for a new lifetime, we go to a vast room in the Hall of Justice and write an exhaustively detailed chart of our upcoming incarnation. From the broad strokes to the most trivial moments, we leave nothing to chance in pursuit of our goals.

I don't know any individuals, including myself, who can imagine having deliberately chosen some of the unpleasantness, ugliness, and tragedy in their lives. But again, our sole reason for incarnating is to learn to overcome challenges, negativity, and despair, none of which even exist on the Other Side, for the advancement of our souls. And then there's the fact that we write our charts in the blissful euphoria that is our constant state of mind on the Other Side. We're fearless there, we're utterly confident, we're our most loving selves, and we're surrounded by nothing but unconditional love from each other and from God. There's nothing we feel we can't handle, nothing we're reluctant to take on in our pursuit of spiritual growth. I guarantee you, no matter how challenging your life is, you were in the process of planning something even more astonishing for yourself until your Spirit Guide and the Council convinced you to tone your chart down to something a little more realistic.

And so, hard as it may be to believe, before you came here, among countless other details you chose your parents, your siblings, and every other family member; every aspect of your physical appearance; the exact place, date, and time of your birth; your friends, your lovers, your spouses, your children, your bosses, your co-workers, your casual acquaintances, and even your enemies; the cities, neighborhoods, and houses you'll live in; your preferences, weaknesses, flaws, sense of humor (or lack of one), skills, talents, and areas of incompetence; every minor and major injury and illness you'll experience; and even your hobbies, interests, passions, and private little quirks that no one else might know about but you.

Not that our charts deprive us of free will once we're here. We actually arrive on earth with countless choices surrounding every detail we've designed. If, let's say, one of those enemies you charted, maybe even someone you knew in a past life, shows up as you planned for, it's your choice whether to avoid that person like the plague, be polite but keep your distance and watch your back, or engage him or her and suffer the inevitable consequences. Or if you charted yourself to catch a cold when you're twenty-two, it's your decision whether to take care of yourself and get over it or to keep pushing your luck and run the risk of letting it develop into pneumonia. A charted life is absolutely a life filled with options, and beyond that it's proof that the success of our souls isn't measured by the obstacles we face, but by how we handle them when they come along.

And just to give you an idea of exactly how unimaginably vast the Hall of Records really is, I should add that every chart of every incarnation of every person who's ever lived on earth is carefully preserved and catalogued there, handwritten by us on scrolls of parchment, for our own review when we get Home and for others to study when and if the need or curiosity strikes them. I'm on my fifty-second and final incarnation, so I'll leave it to you to do the math on how many charts are housed there among the countless other treasures I mentioned earlier.

Cocooning

Cocooning is a compassionate, loving, expertly devised and executed process that takes place in one of many designated chambers in the Hall of Wisdom. It's reserved for those spirits who aren't able at first to make a peaceful transition from earth to the Other Side for a variety of reasons. Some spirits, even when long illnesses would seem to have given them time to prepare for their lifetimes to end, arrive Home deeply troubled, confused, and unable to find comfort in the blissful Homecoming rituals of reunions, the Scanning Machine, and a return to their perfect lives. It's an especially common experience for victims of Alzheimer's disease, dementia, substance abuse and addiction, and such severe mental afflictions as schizophrenia and psychosis, that is, any disorder that separates the spirit from its God-given identity and its clear awareness of reality.

When a spirit returns to the Other Side in need of the intensive care of cocooning, it's taken by a team of brilliantly trained medical and psychological experts to begin the restorative procedure: twilight sleep, constant care and reassurance, and whatever other healing treatments are necessary to peacefully and safely guide the newly arrived spirit through the "withdrawal" period of leaving earth. The spirit is cocooned for as long as it takes to be completely healthy, whole, and joyful again. And on very rare occasions, as with one of the celebrities you'll read about, a second cocooning will take place if the spirit emerges from it too soon.

But never does cocooning fail in the long run—which, in the eternity of Home, amounts to no more than a heartbeat or two. Eventually, every spirit on the Other Side is euphorically happy and healthy again, more alive than ever in God's sacred embrace.

The Council

The Council is its own phylum of eighteen highly advanced male and female spirits whose function is essentially to be God's voice on the Other Side. Their wisdom is revered, and because they're their own species, never incarnating and appointed for eternity, they're exempt from the rule of everyone at Home being thirty years old. The men of the Council wear identical white or silver beards, and the women have long white or silver hair. They dress in long flowing robes and preside at a gleaming white marble U-shaped table in a massive white marble room in the Hall of Justice.

The Council isn't a governing body, since government and laws are unnecessary on the Other Side. Instead, they're entrusted by God with a variety of responsibilities that profoundly affect our lives, both on earth and at Home.

For example, one of the last steps we take in our process of incarnating is to present the "rough draft" of our chart for their divine guidance, advice, and modifications. They walk us through each and every detail of our intentions and purposes for our upcoming life and how each aspect of our chart will serve or obstruct our goals, and we never leave Home without their final sacred blessing.

And as you'll discover, in the case of those rare, special, highly advanced spirits called Mystical Travelers, it's the Council and only the Council that gives them the next divine assignment God has in store for them.

Exit Points

As I said, the chart we write for a new incarnation is highly detailed, and we design it with an awareness of what a grueling challenge life on earth can be. So we never complete our charts without weaving in five possible "escape routes," or five separate ways and means to declare ourselves finished here and head Home. These five self-devised bailout scenarios are called Exit Points.

Exit Points are circumstances we prearrange that, if we choose to take advantage of them, can result in the end of an incarnation. Scheduling five of them into our chart doesn't obligate us to stick around until the fifth one comes along. We might decide on our first, or our third, or our fourth Exit Point that we've accomplished quite enough this time around, and we rarely space them out evenly when we create them. We might write two Exit Points to come along in the same year, for example, and then not find ourselves confronted with another one until twenty or thirty years later.

The most obvious Exit Points include critical illnesses and surgeries and potentially fatal accidents and assaults. Whether we survive against all odds or pass away despite an optimistic prognosis is actually just a question of whether or not we choose to take that particular Exit Point.

Other Exit Points are so subtly designed that we might not even recognize them: deciding "for no reason" to drive a different route than usual to work, "trivial" delays that keep us from leaving the house on time, a last-minute change in travel plans, or canceling a social commitment because we suddenly "just don't feel like it." Countless seemingly meaningless decisions and incidents are often the subconscious memory of the arrival of an Exit Point that we scheduled into our chart, but decided not to take advantage of after all.

We've all been through the grief of loved ones who died in spite of the most heroic efforts possible and the most fervent, desperate, heartfelt prayers we can offer. It's natural to wonder how and why we failed, how and why it wasn't enough. Please take comfort in knowing that in the end, Exit Points are decisions made between each of us and God, taken or rejected for reasons we'll all come to understand sooner or later, and all the efforts and prayers in the world won't delay a chosen Exit Point or create one that wasn't scheduled yet.

Five choices, then, ours to make, of when and how to get ourselves Home. I happen to find the fact of Exit Points to be very empowering, and I hope you do too.

Infused Knowledge

Infusion is the way in which information or knowledge is transferred from one being to another without the use of any of the five physical senses. The mind on the receiving end of infusion is given information it had no knowledge of before, with no conscious awareness of where it came from or how it was received.

Infusion is one of the most common means of communication between the spirit minds on the Other Side and the spirit minds we all possess here on earth. Remember, our lives at Home are busier, more stimulating, and more productive than our current lives can begin to compete with, and we have an unencumbered eternity to invest in our greatest passions. From medical and scientific research to exploring breakthroughs in technology to pursuing every form of the creative arts, not to mention working side by side with the brilliant minds who've already come and gone from this world, we devote ourselves at Home to learning, teaching, discovering, inventing, and creating and then infusing the results of our work into the minds of those on earth who can implement them most effectively.

The constant collaboration between earth and the Other Side is a powerful interdependent partnership in which work in both dimensions contributes equally to its success. This world can thank the divine inspiration of infused knowledge from Home for some of our greatest inventions, medical and technological breakthroughs, music, art, and literature. And those on the Other Side are equally grateful to their "receivers" here for putting practical form and function to the results of their efforts.

Infused knowledge, then, is the silent miracle through which we on earth continue to benefit from the ongoing works of Albert Einstein, Leonardo da Vinci, Amadeus Mozart, Michelangelo, Duke Ellington, William Shakespeare, John Lennon, Claude Monet,

Abraham Lincoln, Madame Curie, and every other gifted spirit whose lifetime on earth made a profound, lasting impact.

Kindred Souls

When you read the definition of soul mates, you'll discover that it's an almost guaranteed exercise in futility to race around in search of yours, since you and your soul mate are highly unlikely to even be on earth at the same time. A few of you who've cherished the dream of finding your soul mate might be momentarily disappointed, and you'll wonder who in the world you can dream of meeting instead.

The answer is, dream of meeting your kindred soul—or, more precisely, your kindred *souls*, since unlike soul mates, there are many of them, and they're every bit as significant in their own way. Kindred souls are spirits you've known in one or more past lives. It's that simple. I'm sure you've experienced the occasional feeling of instant familiarity, good or bad, that happens upon being introduced to a complete stranger. Instead of saying, "Nice meeting you," you have to restrain an impulse to say, "Oh, there you are. It's about time you showed up."

Sometimes that instant familiarity is the springboard for another earthly relationship as friends, lovers, spouses, family members, or business associates. Other times it should be the springboard for you to run like the wind, as far away as your legs will carry you. I have a client who married a man she was sure she recognized in a past life. She was right—in a past life he was her drunken, tyrannical, abusive father. As his wife in this life, she's still trying desperately to win his approval, and he's still playing the role of dictator in their relationship, while the rest of the world treats him with the disregard he deserves. On her behalf, and on behalf of any of you who are locked in a struggle with a kindred soul with whom your past life experiences were probably difficult, a bit of advice: it's almost a guarantee that you charted that person into this lifetime to learn to finally dispose of his or her power over you. That's not "turn the tables on" or "get revenge for." That's "dispose of." Walk away. The ultimate dismissal isn't continued attention; it's apathy. Keep engaging that person in any way in this lifetime and you can count on having to deal with him or her again next time around. It's up to you how many incarnations you intend to waste on someone who very probably isn't worth another moment of your time.

On the other hand, there can be great joy in recognizing and reconnecting with loving, positive kindred souls, no matter what role you've charted for them in this lifetime. It's not just that small unexpected flame in your spirit you feel when a stranger seems oddly familiar. It's not just the rare luxury of getting to skip that awkward "getting acquainted" phase, because somehow you know you took care of that several decades or centuries ago. It's the reminder, too often lost in the translation, that every time you meet a kindred soul from some past life, you're shaking hands with absolute proof of your own eternity. In fact, you'll find that many of the celebrities Francine discusses have reunited at Home with kindred souls they knew and loved on earth, just as all of us will.

Life Themes

Another of the "broad strokes" we design into our chart for an upcoming incarnation is the specific purpose that defines our intended goal for that lifetime. That purpose is known as our *life theme*. We actually select two life themes to make sure we get the most out of our brief trip away from Home—a primary theme, which is essentially who we plan to be, and a secondary theme, which is another aspect of ourselves we'll find ourselves dealing with along the way.

To give you an example, my primary theme is "Humanitarian." It's who I am, it's my passion, and it's as essential to my life as breathing. But my secondary theme is "Loner." Conflict, or what? And I admit it, there are times when I resent having to sacrifice the strong "Loner" part of me and wish I could just disappear with my husband to some small tropical island with no cell phones and lots of great books. The interesting challenge of my secondary theme, though, is to learn to recognize it not as an obstacle, but as an aspect of myself that I handpicked and then find ways to embrace and express it without compromising my primary theme in any way.

There are forty-six life themes. As you read them and their descriptions, I think you'll be fascinated by the positive and negative potential in each of them, depending on how they are handled. I think your spirit will resonate when you recognize your own primary and secondary themes, and I also think you'll get some surprising insights into those celebrities whose life themes Francine mentions.

Aesthetic Pursuits. Those with the Aesthetic Pursuits theme are driven by an innate need to create some form of artistic beauty—music, drama, writing, sculpture, painting, choreography, crafts, and so on. This drive can lead to fame and privilege, which is enjoyable if the secondary theme is compatible, but tragic if the secondary theme is in direct conflict.

Analyzer. Those who need to scrutinize the intricate details of how and why everything works. Analyzers are invaluable in scientific and other technical areas. But their fear of missing or overlooking something can make it difficult for them to relax, trust their instincts, and stand back far enough to see the bigger picture.

Banner Carrier. Banner Carriers are on the front lines of battles against what they perceive as injustices. Banner Carriers will picket, demonstrate, and lobby, whatever it takes to fight their idea of the "good fight." Their challenge is to learn that they can make their point more effectively with tact and moderation than with divisive fanaticism.

Builder. Builders are the "wind beneath the wings" of society, the often invisible but essential cogs that keep the wheels of accomplishment turning. Builders are not those who march across a stage to accept a trophy; they are those who played a major part in constructing the stage itself. They can feel unappreciated for not getting the credit they rightfully deserve, but they need to remember that the rewards for gracefully mastering the Builder theme lie in the accelerated advancement of the spirit, which is far more valuable than any trophy could ever be.

Caretaker. The Caretaker theme is closely related to the themes of Rescuer and Humanitarian, but it goes even deeper. Those with this theme take people into their homes, give hands-on care to the elderly, and house those who've found themselves on the streets. They form foundations for the poor and infirm, they join groups to travel overseas and help the impoverished, and they go to prisons, mental facilities, and anywhere else they're needed as "foot soldiers" on the front lines for the sake of the disadvantaged. Their challenge is to learn to take care of themselves while they're so busy caring for everyone else.

Catalyst. Those with the Catalyst theme make things happen and mobilize inaction into action. They are energetic and enthusiastic and seem to excel in stressful circumstances. On the downside, they struggle with feeling empty and depressed without a goal to tackle.

Cause Fighter. If there is not a social issue to take on, Cause Fighters will create one. They're the generals who command the Banner Carriers—vocal, active, and passionate about their efforts toward a better world, sometimes at the expense of their own and others' safety. At their most undisciplined, Cause Fighters run the risk of vying for a bigger spotlight on themselves than on the cause they're promoting.

Controller. At their most successful, Controllers are brilliant at taking charge of every task at hand through wise, discreet, supportive supervising and delegating. The least successful Controllers are those who feel compelled to dictate and judge every detail of the lives of those around them. Ironically, the biggest challenge for Controllers is *self*-control.

Emotionality. Those with the Emotionality theme are born with an extraordinary capacity to deeply feel the highest of highs, the lowest of lows, and every shade of emotion in between. Their sensitivity is both a gift and a burden, and they need more than most of us to be mindful of the importance of balance in their lives.

Experiencer. Those who insist on trying any activity, indulgence, pursuit, or lifestyle that happens to catch their eye. They will move seamlessly from managing a retail store to joining an archeological dig in Egypt, to trying their hand at stand-up comedy, to attending rodeo clown school, not out of aimlessness, but because of a need to experience life as an active, varied series of participation events. Excessive self-indulgence to the point of irresponsibility is their greatest, most challenging hurdle.

Fallibility. Those with the Fallibility theme were born physically, mentally, or emotionally challenged. Only the most extraordinary spirits choose Fallibility as a theme, and when they find that choice discouraging, they need to remember what an inspiring example they're setting as they face and triumph over special hurdles the rest of us can only imagine.

Follower. Followers are, in their way, as essential to society as leaders, since without them there would *be* no Leaders. And offering strong, reliable support can be Followers' greatest and most generous contribution on this earth. What Followers have to be mindful of, though, is the importance of carefully selecting whom and what to follow.

Freedom. The anthem of this theme is "Don't Fence Me In." The Freedom theme is that of a gypsy, someone who likes to move often, go everywhere, and can't seem to stay in one place very long. Even if they find a permanent residence, they're always traveling and always on the go. They tend toward moodiness if they're kept in one place for too long, and they have trouble quieting their minds. Many of those who've been diagnosed with ADD or ADHD are actually trying to make peace with a Freedom theme.

Harmony. People with the Harmony theme make peace, calm, and balance not just their top priorities, but their *only* priorities, for they will go to any extremes to maintain those priorities. On the plus side, they're refreshingly cooperative and usually have a quieting effect in chaotic situations. On the minus side, they can find it very difficult to accept and adjust to the inevitable bumps, bruises, and stress life has to offer.

Healer. Healers are often drawn to the physical or mental healing professions, but are found in other areas as well. Their chosen theme of Healer can express itself in a variety of forms, all of them involving easing pain and improving general well-being. It's imperative that Healers protect themselves from empathizing too closely with those they're trying to heal and to pace themselves carefully to avoid an overload of the stress, pain, and illness their theme has drawn them to.

Humanitarian. Humanitarians are born to extend themselves to humankind. Instead of addressing life's inequities through sit-ins and protests, Humanitarians step past the protestors to directly feed the hungry, house the homeless, bandage the wounded, teach the uneducated, and generally tackle the world's ills head-on. They face a twofold challenge: knowing there's an infinite amount of work to be done, but also knowing when and how to keep themselves from burning out.

Infallibility. Those with the Infallibility theme are seemingly born with everything—looks, talent, intelligence, privilege, wit, grace, and so on. And believe it or not, theirs can be an unusually difficult theme. Their problems are rarely taken seriously. They're often re-sented for their advantages and can feel secretly unworthy for not having had to earn their privileged place in society. It's not unusual for them to be uniquely drawn to such excesses as obesity, promiscuity, or substance abuse, almost as if they are trying to balance the scales by creating difficulties they were not born with. Because many things have come easily to them, they can feel emotionally inept in situations that challenge their character.

Intellectuality. The best expression of this ultimate thirst-for-knowledge theme are people who study throughout their life and continuously use their wealth of education to inform, improve, nourish, and expand life on earth. The worst expression of this theme is found in the many versions of the "professional student" whose sole purpose is the self-directed goal of knowledge for the sake of knowledge, hoarded instead of shared, which is of no use to anyone but the one who possesses it.

Irritant. The constant, deliberate pessimists, the faultfinders, those who are never at a loss for something to complain about have chosen the Irritant theme. For such a difficult theme, it's amazing how many people seem to have chosen it. They're helpful in teaching us patience, tolerance, and nonengagement in negativity, while they struggle to overcome the very negativity their chosen theme demanded they embrace.

Justice. Those with the Justice theme are committed to an active, lifelong pursuit of fairness and equality. Some of our greatest presidents and activists are exquisite examples of the Justice theme at its finest. At its worst, when it is misguided and without God as its center, this passion for righting a wrong can result in riots, anarchy, and vigilantism.

Lawfulness. Law enforcement and the practice and teaching of law are among the professional expressions of the Lawfulness theme, which revolves around a driven concern with safeguarding that line between legality and illegality. Elevated, those with this theme are devoted public servants who fiercely help maintain order and balance in this world. Corrupt and abusive with their power, they're an insult to the theme they chose.

Leader. Oddly, people with a Leader theme might be gifted at their ability to lead, but they're almost never innovative, instead choosing to become Leaders in already established areas—for example, lawyers who gravitate toward highly publicized cases and thrive in the resulting spotlight, instead of devoting their expertise to making significant improvements in the judicial system. Perfecting this theme would involve changing their top priority from pursuing their own success to exploring new socially relevant frontiers.

Loner. Loners are often socially active and visible, but tend to choose careers and lifestyles that will allow them to be isolated. They're content alone and usually enjoy their own company, and they often struggle to overcome feeling drained and irritated when other people spend too much time in their space.

Loser. The Loser theme is essentially the Fallibility theme without the physical, mental, or emotional challenges. Those with the Loser theme have many advantages and good qualities, but because they're determined to feel sorry for themselves they insist on disregarding them. They seek attention through being martyrs, and if there's no melodrama in their lives, they will create it. Like Irritants, they can inspire us to be more positive and to dislike their behavior without judging them as people.

Manipulator. Manipulators approach their lives and the people in them like a one-sided chess game, controlling them to their advantage and often with remarkable talent. This is a powerful and not necessarily negative theme. When this theme is devoted to the highest, God-centered good, Manipulators can have an enormously positive impact on society. When the theme is abused, Manipulators are too self-absorbed to concern themselves with anyone's well-being but their own, at everyone else's expense.

Passivity. People with the Passivity theme are sometimes perceived as weak, when in fact they're more accurately described as uncommonly sensitive to emotional disruption. They have opinions, but express them most effectively in a nonconfrontational manner, and when they take a stand on issues, they're strictly nonviolent. It's difficult for those with a Passivity theme to cope with extremes, but a little tension can be a valuable tool for spurring them into their form of action.

Patience. One of the more challenging themes, Patience takes constant effort in a world in which impatience is almost considered an admirable coping skill. The choice of Patience over a less difficult theme indicates an eagerness to move more quickly on the spirit's journey toward perfection—in other words, Patience, in a way, indicates a spiritual *im*patience. Along with their ongoing battle against snapping at stress, those with a Patience theme frequently fight the guilt of occasional lapses in efforts toward their goal and of the anger they feel their theme demands they suppress. Recognizing how hard their choice of themes really is can help them be more forgiving of themselves.

Pawn. Pawns are those whose role is to be used as the fuse that ignites something of great magnitude, either positive or negative, to emerge; as such they are essential in the advancement of the universal spirit. Possibly the most classic historic example of a Pawn is Judas, whose paid betrayal of Christ was ultimately a critical element in the birth of Christianity. People who choose the theme of the Pawn, important in their way as they are, have to be vigilant in aligning themselves with only the worthiest, most loving causes.

Peacemaker. Peacemakers are those extremely dedicated to stopping war and violence. Unlike those with the themes of Passivity and Harmony, Peacemakers typically show a surprising amount of aggression and zeal in efforts for peace. Their allegiance to peace is far greater than their allegiance to any group or country, and they're not opposed to achieving a bit of celebrity as part of a noble, highly visible cause.

Perfectionist. The Perfectionist theme is exactly what it sounds like: those who need and expect perfection in every aspect of their lives—their work, their personal lives, their houses, their cars, their clothing, and their friends. Because they also expect perfection from themselves, they're most appreciated when they stop writing improvement memos to everyone else and direct those memos inward. They're very valuable in their ability to get things done and done well, but they also have to realize that nothing on earth is perfect and all things here are passing and transient.

Performance. Those with the Performance theme might pursue a career in the entertainment field, but are just as likely to be content with being the life of the local party, office, or classroom. They're nourished by the spotlight, however large or small it might be. Too often they form their opinions of themselves exclusively through the eyes of others, which they need to combat by reserving some of their considerable energy for introspection and learning to provide their own spiritual and emotional nourishment.

Persecution. Those with the Persecution theme are not only constantly braced for the worst possibility, but are actually convinced they've been singled out for special bad luck and negative attention. Happiness is literally frightening for them, because they're sure they'll have to pay too high a price for it or that it can simply be snatched away from them at any moment. Overcoming the Persecution theme takes enormous strength, but the reward for overcoming it is remarkable spiritual advancement.

Persecutor. Persecutors are typically aggressive, self-justifying sociopaths who will abuse and even kill without guilt or remorse and without the mitigating factor of mental or emotional illness. Obviously, it is almost impossible to understand the purpose of this theme in the span of a single lifetime, but they can inadvertently test, challenge, and inspire progress in our laws, our judicial systems, our forensics techniques, our moral boundaries, our social consciousness, and the unity of humankind.

Poverty. The challenge of the Poverty theme is obviously prevalent in third-world countries, but is almost more difficult in the midst of affluence, where privilege can look mocking and unfairly imbalanced by comparison. Even the advantaged can exhibit a Poverty theme, perpetually feeling that no matter how much they might have, it's not enough. Endurance, hope, and a perspective on the cosmic irrelevance of material possessions can provide brilliant spiritual growth for those who choose this uniquely demanding theme.

Psychic. You would think this would be my primary theme, but no. People who choose a Psychic theme often design strict childhood environments for themselves, where their ability to sense things beyond "normal" is met with severe disapproval. The challenge of the Psychic theme is to learn to accept the ability not as a burden, but as a gift and to put it to its highest, most unselfish, most spiritual use.

Rejection. Those with the Rejection theme usually experience alienation or abandonment in early childhood and proceed with those same patterns throughout their lives. Hard as it is, the challenge for those with this extraordinarily difficult theme is to recognize Rejection not as a burden beyond their control, but as a specific theme chosen so they can learn that when the spirit is whole and self-reliant for its identity, the acceptance or rejection of others is no longer relevant.

Rescuer. Rescuers gravitate toward Victims, wanting to help and save them, even if the Victims have obviously created their own crisis or don't particularly want to be saved. Rescuers are typically at their strongest in the presence of the weakest or most helpless, and they're highly empathetic, but they can easily be victimized if they don't maintain a safe emotional distance from those they're trying to rescue.

Responsibility. Those who choose a Responsibility theme embrace it not as an obligation, but as a form of emotional nourishment. Their joy is in active, hands-on accomplishment, and they feel guilty if they're aware of something that needs to be done and don't see that it's tended to. Their challenge is to become unselfish enough to remember that very often the people around them need the nourishment of assuming responsibility and accomplishing something too.

Spirituality. Those with the Spirituality theme spend a lifetime in a fervent search of their own spiritual center, if not as a profession, then certainly as a constant personal drive. The more they search, the more new territory they're compelled to explore, and at its highest level the Spirituality theme creates boundless inspiration, compassion, far-sightedness, and tolerance. At its lowest, it can manifest itself in narrow-mindedness, judgmentalism, and the dangerous isolation of fanaticism.

Survival. Yes, to a degree, we would all seem to have a Survival theme. But to those who have specified this theme, life is a relentless, ongoing struggle, something to be endured despite the fact that the odds are stacked against them. They usually excel in crisis situations, but they have trouble distinguishing between a true crisis and their grim view of common everyday challenges. They should all be given and take to heart a bumper sticker reading, "Lighten Up!"

Temperance. The Temperance theme is typically accompanied by an addiction to deal with and overcome. Even if the actual addiction never manifests itself, people who choose this theme have to fight a constant sense of vulnerability to potential addiction, whether it is to a substance, sex, a lifestyle, or another person. They also have to avoid the opposite extreme of becoming fanatically or psychotically repelled by what they perceive as something that may be a potential addiction. The key to the progress of the Temperance theme across the board is moderation.

Tolerance. You name it, those with a Tolerance theme feel compelled to find a way to tolerate even the intolerable. Obviously, this can become a pretty untenable burden, to the point where they will eventually focus all their energy on one area they feel they can universally tolerate most easily, while becoming either narrow-minded or oblivious to everything else around them. Their growth can be accomplished by recognizing the theme that is causing such an unrealistic and indiscriminate view of the world and learn that being magnanimous is only worthwhile when its target is worthy.

Victim. By definition, life's sacrificial lambs. Their purpose among us is to throw a spotlight on injustice and inspire us to take action and make changes for the better. Abused and murdered children, targets of hate crimes, and those who have been wrongly convicted of violent felonies and then subsequently proven innocent are among those whose Victim theme is devoted to the interest of the highest good.

Victimizer. Here to achieve absolute control over as many victims as possible, for the purpose of being surrounded at all times by visible proof of their own power. The will and feelings of their victims are meaningless until and unless they are in perfect agreement with those of Victimizers, and the only compassion they are capable of is toward their own hypersensitive, insatiable ego. On a small scale, they are the controlling lover or spouse, the stalker, the pathologically overzealous parent, and so on. On a larger scale, they are Jim Jones of the People's Temple, "Bo" and "Peep" orchestrating the Heaven's Gate mass suicide, David Koresh of the Branch Davidians—anyone who demands such slavish devotion that even children, who were given no options, were sacrificed not in the name of God, but in the name of the Victimizer.

Warrior. Our fearless risk takers, our soldiers, our pioneers, astronauts, firefighters, and countless other unsung heroes in countless other professions with the courage to step up to a physical, moral, or spiritual challenge. They work in every sphere, from the mundane landscape of everyday life; to the front lines of wars against crime, drugs, natural disasters, and homicidal tyrants; to the vast unconquered worlds in space. Without direction, Warriors' aggression can be destructive. But when focused, especially with a secondary

Humanitarian theme, those with a Warrior theme can make historic contributions of global significance.

Winner. The Winner theme differs from the Infallibility theme in that Winners have an active, pervasive compulsion to achieve and triumph. They are perpetual optimists, always believing that the next business deal, the next relationship, the next roll of the dice at the crap table, the next lottery ticket or sweepstakes entry, the next job or even the next marriage or child will be the one they have been waiting for, that will make all the difference. In its finest form, Winners' unfailing optimism and ability to pick themselves up from every failure and move on with confidence is inspiring and exhilarating. Without frequent reality checks, though, Winners can squander their money, their security, and their lives with too many impetuous, undisciplined, and uninformed decisions.

Mission Life Entities

Mission Life Entities are among the most advanced spirits among us on earth, which is why there are so few of them mentioned in this book.

Each and every one of us has our own God-devoted purpose, whether our conscious minds are aware of it or not. Every incarnation we live here and every moment we spend on the Other Side are stepping-stones toward fulfilling that purpose. It's essential to remember that no one purpose is more important than any other— every purpose toward God's greater good is indispensable and equally valuable. If you find yourself doubting that, try to imagine a world full of kings and presidents with no teachers, nurses, miners, charity workers, cooks, mechanics, homemakers, and all the other residents of this planet who contribute to our day-to-day lives, or an army filled with nothing but generals and not a single foot soldier. Whatever our purpose, it's ours to commit to, excel at to the very best of our ability, and know that, in God's eyes, the very best of our ability is all He asks.

Those who volunteer for the purpose of Mission Life Entity have essentially said, "Wherever on this earth you need me, God, I'll willingly go." They'll sacrifice their own needs and their own comfort for the mission they've signed on for: to compassionately, selflessly rescue, affirm, inspire, ignite, and celebrate the essential genetic connection to the divine in every one of God's children they encounter, no matter what it takes or where it takes them.

Mission Life Entities don't try to recruit or convert others or preach any specific dogma or religion. They're kind, generous, and tireless, never claiming superiority or some elevated closeness to God. They include and embrace humankind rather than trying to isolate or estrange anyone. And they can be found in all walks of life, with a variety of job titles and varying levels of social status. Their purpose isn't dependent on the amount of media exposure they can attract. It's expressed through quiet generosity, universal empathy, and their ability to enrich the spiritual well-being of humanity during their time on this earth, a profoundly satisfying, very advanced path often filled with hardship and turmoil, which is why it's a journey only a few rare souls choose to take.

Mystical Travelers

Mystical Travelers can most easily be described as Mission Life Entities with a broader range. What they have said to God about their soul's journey is, "Wherever in this universe you need me, I'll willingly go."

In other words, Mystical Travelers devote themselves to the same eternal purpose that Mission Life Entities do: strengthening the divine spiritual connection between us and God as a thriving, active force. But while Mission Life Entities limit their focus to earth, Mystical Travelers volunteer to incarnate and continue that purpose on any inhabited planet in any galaxy. Most Mystical Travelers have experienced many lifetimes on earth and are ready to "graduate" to more expansive horizons. It's as if their learning on earth earned them their Ph.D., and they're yearning to go elsewhere for their post-graduate work.

Mystical Travelers have all the transcendent qualities of Mission Life Entities—the peaceful acceptance of sacrifice and discomfort, the uncommon empathy, the generosity, the kindness, the unwill-ingness to sit idle if someone needs help. The only two I've met in my six-plus decades had the added bonus of seeming to have taken and excelled in every theological course ever conducted, coming away with none of the rhetoric and all of the joy of actively loving and being loved by God. Both of these Mystical Travelers made me feel like a beginner, and neither of them lived long enough to reach adulthood. They came, they gave us a glimpse of our spirits' greatest potential, and then they quickly left for their next assignment on the other side of the universe. You'll read about one of them in this book.

Orientation

Orientation is an essential part of our transition from life on earth to our joyful lives on the Other Side. It takes place in one of the countless satellite rooms in the Hall of Wisdom, after we've studied our most recent incarnation through the Scanning Machine. During Orientation we're debriefed on the lifetime we've just lived, with the help of our Spirit Guide, a team of trained Orientators, and any other spirits whose input can give us perspective.

For example, let's say there's someone your life deeply hurt, and watching your own cruelty through the Scanning Machine has left you devastated. The Orientators and your Spirit Guide can help you see if your actions might have resulted in some long-range unimagined progress in your soul's journey or in the journey of the person you hurt. You can even summon that person (if he or she is at Home) or that person's Spirit Guide to join the discussion. The point is to get an overview of the impact and inevitable ripple effect of your behavior, not so you can come away patting yourself on the back for what a great idea your cruelty turned out to be, but to give yourself enough perspective to make peace with the person you hurt and with yourself.

Another function of Orientation is to ease the transition to the Other Side for those spirits who were unprepared for the trip and are too confused or annoyed to be at peace when they first arrive, but don't need the more intensive "therapy" of cocooning. As we've discussed, and as you'll discover among Francine's celebrity comments, not everyone is instantaneously giddy about going Home, and the Orientators are impeccably trained to help. After unprepared spirits experience the Scanning Machine and the debriefing afterward, they're counseled by their Orientators to quiet their turmoil and resentment. They're then given as much time as they need doing activities that brought them comfort on earth—reading, hiking, golf, soccer, chess, movies and television, computer games (let's face it, there are those who wouldn't consider it heaven, if there weren't computer games), whatever will allow them to "decompress" at their own pace and renew their spirit's awareness that our *real* lives are those we live on the Other Side.

Quadrants

As we've established, all of the earth's continents exist on the Other Side, including the "lost" continents of Atlantis and Lemuria. And each of the continents at Home is divided into four quadrants. The division has nothing to do with government and politics, since there's no need for those on the Other Side. (It's sounding more like paradise by the moment, isn't it?) Instead, the quadrants are simply areas devoted to specific purposes corresponding to the chosen vocations of our lives there. One quadrant of each continent is dedicated to Orientation, for example, not only the "decompression" activities of those who need them, but also the training of aspiring Orientators. Another quadrant is specified to house all the sciences. Another is the center for the creative arts, and the fourth is where all the research of Home takes place.

There's complete freedom of movement among the quadrants, and as with all other areas of the Other Side nothing exists that's off-limits to anyone. A sentry is posted at the entrance to each quadrant, but only to keep track of the whereabouts of everyone who works there and direct their visitors or collaborators from other quadrants to their exact locations.

To make our lives there even more convenient, if you go to, let's say, the second quadrant of Asia to say hello to a friend, and the sentry tells you your friend left there to meditate in the Gardens of the Hall of Justice, as the "locals" love to do, you're not facing a long journey to catch up with your friend. Free of our bodies, with our skilled spirit minds sharp and clear, we enjoy the gift of astral travel, which is effortless, instantaneous, and taken for granted—we simply think ourselves from one destination to another and we're there.

The Scanning Machine

Once we've completed our overwhelming reunion in the meadow with all the beloved friends and animals who gather to welcome us Home, our Spirit Guide escorts us to an immense, sacred, private chamber in the Hall of Wisdom for our visit to the Scanning Machine. The Scanning Machine is a huge convex dome of blue glass, circled by curved white marble benches. And through that domed blue glass we watch every moment of the incarnation we've just completed replayed before our eyes, the ultimate home movie in three-dimensional hologram form. Because there's no time on the Other Side, the number of "years" it takes to review our lifetime in exhaustive detail is a nonissue.

Rather than simply being a nostalgic stroll down memory lane, our session at the Scanning Machine is essential to the journey of our spirit. We all slog along through our lives on earth with no conscious awareness of our charts—in fact, even if we astrally travel from earth to the Hall of Records and locate our current chart, we'll be staring at a blank parchment scroll, since our own charts are off-limits to us until we've done our best to live through them. But once we're Home again, we have total recall of our charts, and the Scanning Machine provides the means for us to literally see how our intentions stacked up against our actions.

I find it fascinating, and so logical, that it's not God who evaluates how well or how poorly we did. *We* evaluate how well or how poorly we did, stripped of the earthly devices of defensiveness and ego-driven self-justification. We come face-to-face with the unfiltered, unedited reality of a lifetime of actions, for better or worse, and it's ours to deal with, process, and learn from.

And by the way, next time you read about others' near-death experiences and they mention the fact that their whole life flashed before their eyes, you'll now know that they got as far as the Scanning Machine before they were resuscitated and came back to "life."

Soul Mates

The true definition of a soul mate, as opposed to the hyperromanticized definition that's become such an unfortunate myth, is simply this. Each of us is created with a spirit that has both male and female aspects. At the moment our spirit is created, an identical twin spirit is created right along with us. That identical twin spirit's male and female aspects are mirror images of our own. And that identical twin spirit is our soul mate.

While we're living our lives on the Other Side, we're more emotionally connected to our soul mate than we are to any of the other spirits we know, just as most identical twins are uniquely connected. But we also have separate and complete identities. Our soul mate is not the other half of us, nor are we the other half of our soul mate— none of us is half a person in need of completion. We and our soul mate at Home each have our own friendships, our own interests, and our own pursuits, while loving each other freely and unconditionally. Again, don't think romance, think identical twins, and you'll have a much healthier, more accurate idea of what a soul mate is.

Like all spirits on the Other Side, both we and our soul mates choose when, if, and how many times we feel it will benefit our growth to come to earth for another incarnation. Because we're separate, complete, and on our own unique journeys, we make the decision to incarnate independently and for intensely personal reasons to do intensely personal work on ourselves. Which makes the chances *very* slim that our soul mate would incarnate at exactly the same time we do, let alone that we would choose lifetimes on earth in which we're going to be together, since we see each other as often as we want on the Other Side. It frustrates me to no end when clients complain to me that they can't seem to meet their soul mate, when the truth is, it's highly probable that their soul mate is joyfully busy at Home and, when the time comes, will be the first to greet them when they emerge from the tunnel. So if you find yourself surprised or even disappointed by the scarcity of soul mates among the famous names in this book, now you'll understand.

Spirit Guides

Since my Spirit Guide, Francine, is the coauthor of this book, it only seems fair that I elaborate a little more on who Spirit Guides are and their role in our lives. As I said earlier, every one of us has a Spirit Guide, someone we literally trusted with the well-being of our soul on the Other Side, who agreed to be our constant, vigilant companion and helpmate when we decided to experience another incarnation on earth.

It's a requirement that Spirit Guides have experienced at least one lifetime here, so that the problems, mistakes, temptations, fears, and frailties inevitable in humans won't be completely foreign to them. In fact, most of us either have been or will be someone else's Spirit Guide during our soul's journey. But to clarify a point I'm frequently asked about, your relationship with your Spirit Guide was established between the two of you on the Other Side before you were born, so it's impossible for your Spirit Guide to be someone you've known in this lifetime.

Spirit Guides are responsible for encouraging, advising, and supporting us toward the goals we've set for ourselves here on earth. And they're equipped with plenty of information to help them live up to the astonishing challenge they've agreed to. They study us closely and objectively on the Other Side, once we've mutually signed on to this relationship, and they memorize and then continually refer to our charts every step of the way, while we lose conscious awareness of our charts the moment we're born.

Even when we think we wish they would, Spirit Guides never interfere with our charts or deprive us of our free will, no matter how far off track we seem to wander. At best, they'll steer us toward possible alternatives and give us warnings along the way. But our sacred pact with them is based on the fact that we've incarnated for the further education and growth of our souls, and those things can't be accomplished if our Spirit Guides are constantly shielding us from the exact lessons that we designed for ourselves in the first place. They're Spirit *Guides*, after all, not Spirit Bosses, Spirit Police, or Spirit Superheroes, doing precisely what God and we ask of them for our maximum benefit.

Spirit Guides communicate with us in several ways, so don't be discouraged if you don't have the advantages I do of clairaudience and the ability to channel. The vast majority of the time they express themselves telepathically and through infusion, directly from their spirit minds to ours. What you might habitually define as instinct, your conscience, or the ever popular "something told me" is really most likely to be your Spirit Guide sending you messages, and it's up to you to remain open-minded and alert enough to pay attention.

They're also the very last to say good-bye to us as we leave the Other Side to come here, and they're there when we return Home, among the crowd that welcomes us and the sure, steady hand that leads us to the Scanning Machine to start making sense of the lives we've just finished—in other words, our relationship with our Spirit Guide is one of the most unique, steadfast, and invaluable alliances we'll ever experience.

Spirits

Just to clarify something right up front, we're all spirits. The only difference between us and the celebrities in this book, not to mention our deceased loved ones, is that we're currently inhabiting a body and they're not. So in this discussion of spirits who've moved on from their bodies, when I use third-person pronouns like "they" and "them," please remember that not that long ago "they" were "us," and not long from now we'll be them again, just as we were before we incarnated.

The spirits we'll be talking about are those who've made it safely to the higher-frequency dimension of the Other Side, three feet above our own ground level. You know those countless descriptions you've heard of visiting spirits looking as if they're floating a few feet above the ground? They're not really floating at all; they're simply moving along on their own ground level, exactly three feet above ours.

Once spirits arrive Home and go through any Orientation or co-cooning processes they might need, they're living in a very real place of perfect bliss, where the atmosphere itself is charged with God's immediate presence, peace, and eternal, unconditional love. Living in that state of bliss, reunited with their memories of all their past lives on earth, and now at Home and back on the "time clock" of eternity again, they're literally incapable of the strictly human emotions of unhappiness, anger, resentment, pettiness, worry, fear, and negativity. Any emotional and physical burdens a spirit carried through an incarnation are resolved in the white light of the Holy Spirit on the Other Side. So if you ever encounter a being who seems sad, mean, or troubled in any way or who shows even a hint of wounds, disease, or other challenges, I promise you're dealing with an earthbound ghost, not a spirit. And if you ever find yourself worrying if deceased loved ones at Home are angry with you, if they've forgiven you, or if they are as ill or unhappy as they were during their lives, you can ease your mind. Needlepoint it on a pillow if you need to, because you can count on it: if they're Home, they're happy.

Unobstructed by our earthly limitations, spirits have any number of advantages over us on earth that we all have to look forward to:

- The natural ability to communicate with each other, and with us when they visit us, through the use of telepathy—that is, the instant transference of information from one entity to another without the use of the five physical senses. One of the most common observations you'll hear from people who've experienced spirit visits is that an entire conversation took place between them without either of them saying a word.

- The natural ability to bilocate—that is, literally be in two places at once. For example, deceased loved ones can easily visit two family members simultaneously who live hundreds of miles from each other, and each visit is unique and absolutely real.

- The ability to manipulate animate and inanimate objects on earth to get our attention. Spirits can easily communicate with our animals and cause them to respond to telepathic commands, so that, let's say, a conspicuous number of birds, butterflies, squirrels, or whatever will be impossible for the recipient of the visit to ignore, or a family pet will suddenly perform tricks it only used to perform for the visiting spirit. The variations in the use of inanimate objects as spirits' way of waving at us are literally countless. They'll move photographs or keepsakes, they'll rock their favorite rocking chair, they'll play a "broken" music box and make dormant toys spring to life, they'll hide keys and eyeglasses, they'll leave little clusters of coins in places that make no sense, they'll superimpose their own image on a painting or snapshot just long enough to be seen—anything it takes, sometimes obvious, sometimes subtle, for a spirit to try to express, "I'm here!" and be noticed.

- The ability to dramatically affect electrical devices. Spirits, after all, have to cross from the dimension of the Other Side into ours in order to visit us, and they often find it helpful to attach their energy to such readily available conductors as electricity and water (which is why the old movie cliché is true—the spirit world really does love a good thunderstorm). They can create utterly bizarre behavior in TVs (a popular favorite is changing the channels over and over and over again, as if someone's sitting on the remote control), appliances (particularly instances of doors of microwaves, refrigerators, and ovens swinging open and closed over and over again "on their own"), telephones (they don't call it "phantom ringing" for nothing, and if you've ever answered a ringing phone to nothing but blaring static, it's safe to assume you've been visited), and countless other electrical and electronic devices.

In almost all of Francine's comments you'll see that she mentions specific people on earth whom celebrities come to visit. It's my hope that those receiving visits—and all of you as well—pay attention and know what to watch and listen for. They're so eager to assure you that they really are alive, well, and with you, and I'd hate for you to miss them.

Visages

Through casual, completely unscientific polls among countless clients over the years, I've become familiar with the popularity of the myth that when we leave our bodies and rejoin the spirit world, we assume the form of wispy, shapeless blobs of fog. I guess a case can be made that with the gift of eternal life to be grateful for, it's petty to worry about what we look like at Home, but living eternally among an endless sea of floating fog blobs doesn't sound like a lot to look forward to either.

The truth is, we all have very distinctive individual identities on the Other Side that we return to when our lifetimes here are through. We have bodies of various shapes and sizes. We have faces with unique features, just as we have on earth, as well as a variety of hair colors, eye colors, and skin colors. We have eyes that blink, and mouths that smile. In fact, we even have hearts and other "human" organs, but their placement is a mirror image of our earthly bodies, so that everything is reversed from left to right. I once asked my Spirit Guide, Francine, why we have organs at Home when we no longer have to bother with annoying functions like digestion and waste elimination. She replied, "Because that's the way God made us." For the life of me, I couldn't think of a good follow-up question.

We get to choose our own visages on the Other Side, and we can change them whenever we like through simple thought projection, especially when we visit a loved one on earth and want to be sure they recognize us. The one exception to that choice is that we're actually bestowed with increasing physical beauty as our spiritual advancement increases—another of the major differences between here and Home, come to think of it. Sadly, we on earth usually come to learn sooner or later, whether we want to or not, that there's no reliable connection whatsoever between physical appearance and spiritual advancement.

The Waiting Room

It never fails—just when I think Francine and I have covered all there is to learn about the Other Side, I find out there's more, not because Francine's holding out on me, but because, as she tirelessly puts it, "If you don't ask the question, I can't give you the answer."

I knew that when we're about to descend into a new lifetime on earth, there's a long, beautifully designed process involved to guarantee that we haven't made the decision lightly, there's nothing haphazard about it, and we've taken every possible step to ensure that our brief trip away from Home will accomplish every goal we've set for ourselves. We've chosen our Spirit Guide. We've exhaustively designed our chart. The body we'll inhabit is taking form in the womb of the woman we've selected to be our biological mother. We lie down on a table in a sacred, soothing room in the Towers, with the sunset pastels of the sky filtering in through the blue glass façade. We're surrounded by comfort and support from those special, loving souls who are trained to keep us confident and unafraid.

I thought that was all there was, that the next step was our spirit entering the fetus in the blink of an eye, at the exact moment we choose. I was wrong.

One morning when she was six years old, my granddaughter Angelia told me about an astral trip she'd taken the night before. She routinely traveled to the Other Side while she slept, and she especially loved visiting the peaceful hush of the Towers. On that particular night she'd come across a room she hadn't noticed before, with a vast window covered by a veil. Like every other child confronted with something hidden, she was curious and wanted to know what was behind that veil, and she took a step toward the room. But Francine, who'd been watching her, stopped her and said, "I'm sorry, Angelia. You can't go in there." Angelia couldn't remember exactly what else Francine had told her, but by the end of the conversation she understood that behind the veil, inside that room, spirits about to leave Home to inhabit an infant body were actually diminishing in size, being transformed from their thirty-year-old physiques into babies themselves.

Honestly, I'd never given a moment's thought to that very last part of our trip to earth. I guess I assumed that one minute we're in our thirty-year-old body on the Other Side and the next minute, somehow, poof, we're occupying a fetus. I shared that assumption with Angelia. Who knew it would be one of the dumbest things she'd ever heard me say? She rolled her eyes, she shook her head at my hopelessness, and her hands went straight to her hips as she replied with utter exasperation, "They can't come in without getting *little*, Bagdah!"

With all the confidence of an older, wiser (and completely wrong) woman, I discussed with Francine this assertion that there's a place spirits go to "get little" before they come back to earth, and wasn't it typically adorable of Angelia to come up with such an imaginative dream? I should have seen this coming—it wasn't a dream at all; it was an astral trip, and Francine had indeed stopped Angelia from going into that place in the Towers called the Waiting Room. In fact, her exact words to me were, "Of *course* spirits physically diminish in size when they descend," and she sounded almost as exasperated with my ignorance as Angelia had been when she clarified that for me.

So, at the expense of my own pride, I can officially confirm that we're all thirty years old on the Other Side *until and unless we're about to reincarnate,* at which point we go to the Waiting Room in the Towers to essentially become babies again in preparation for entering the fetus we've chosen for our new lifetime on earth.

The Celebrities

Paul Newman

Paul Newman spent his most recent lifetime on earth as a prolific actor, director, navy pilot, philanthropist, entrepreneur, auto-racing champion, husband, and father. He was born in Shaker Heights, Ohio, on January 26, 1925. After getting his high-school diploma, he enrolled in the Ohio University Navy program, served in World War II, completed his college education at Yale with a degree in drama, studied at Lee Strasberg's renowned Actors Studio, and received his first official screen credit in a television series called *Tales of Tomorrow* in 1952.

His Broadway debut occurred in 1953, in the original production of William Inge's *Picnic,* and in 1954 he made his film debut in *The Silver Chalice.* The foreign press had the foresight to present him with a Golden Globe Award in 1957 as their "Most Promising Male Newcomer." Until his retirement from acting in 2007, Paul starred in more than sixty movies, television shows, documentaries, and plays; produced and/or directed a dozen more television and film projects; and earned an Academy Award as Best Actor (for the 1986 film *The Color of Money*), a Best Supporting Actor Emmy and Golden Globe Award (for the 2005 TV production of *Empire Falls*), a Golden Globe Award as Best Motion Picture Director (for 1968's *Rachel, Rachel*), almost fifty acting and directing nominations, and such prestigious honors as the Golden Globes' Cecil B. DeMille Award and the Screen Actors' Guild Lifetime Achievement Award.

He and his first wife, Jackie Witte, were married from 1949 until 1958 and had three children—a son, Scott, who died in 1978 from an accidental drug overdose, and two daughters, Susan and Stephanie. He married his second wife, accomplished actress Joanne Woodward, in 1958, a marriage that by all accounts continued happily, quietly, and devotedly for the rest of his life. They had three daughters—Elinor, Melissa, and Claire—and made their home in Westport, Connecticut, thousands of miles from the celebrity-driven glare of Hollywood.

Paul's passion for auto racing was ignited when he trained for the 1969 film *Winning*. He competed in and often won events sponsored by the Sports Car Club of America (SCCA) and other racing associations until 2005, was a race team owner, and, in honor of his integrity and dedication to the sport, was inducted into the SCCA Hall of Fame in 2009.

He was as intensely focused on his charitable work as he was on his acting career. The Scott Newman Foundation, founded in memory of his son's life and untimely death, combats drug abuse among young people. The Hole in the Wall Gang Camp is a residential summer camp for seriously ill children with locations throughout the world. Kenyon College in Gambion, Ohio, received a generous scholarship fund, and Catholic Relief Services donations toward its efforts to help Kosovo refugees. Through all these as well as his brilliantly successful, charity-devoted Newman's Own food company, Paul Newman saw to it that when he went Home on September 26, 2008, after a battle with lung cancer, he left this earth richer, better, and more compassionate than he found it.

From Francine

Paul's father was waiting for him at the end of the tunnel, silhouetted against the sacred white light, before Paul even reached Home. They emerged from the tunnel together, where Paul stepped into the ecstatic embrace of his son, Scott, before greeting the huge crowd of animals and friends from his forty-nine incarnations and from his stunningly productive eternal life here at Home. The Scanning Machine was both difficult and healing for him—he says that for all his blessings, he perpetually battled a deep sadness that he was aware of as far back as The Silver Chalice, *not caused by his wives and children at all, but rooted in what he calls "my own tendency to withhold, so that I wouldn't be destroyed if I felt I'd disappointed someone I loved, but of course by withholding I created the disappointment I was trying to avoid." He was relieved to watch himself overcoming that particular demon over the years and finally "becoming the husband and father my wife and children deserved," but he went immediately from the Scanning Machine to the Gardens of the Towers with Scott to ask his forgiveness for not "waking up sooner." They're often seen together now, loving and enjoying each other.*

Paul's chosen life themes of Aesthetic Pursuits and Humanitarian served him well. He says that while acting was never his passion, he enjoyed the process of it and appreciated it as a means to an end, with the end being the wealth and celebrity that allowed Newman's Own, the charity that was his passion, to be such a success and, as a result, help countless people and animals in need. He frequently wishes he'd chosen a less handsome face, to allow himself access to more "character roles," and he tells the story of how his face almost jeopardized his career in its early days. Paul was told not to get his hopes up for long-term success, because he looked too much like Marlon Brando.

Paul quickly, blissfully resumed his life on the Other Side. He's a popular lecturer on the subjects of philosophy and philanthropy, with a focus on the richness to be gained in giving rather than receiving, both finan-

cially and emotionally, and his seminars are virtually mandated for spirits who are preparing to reincarnate. He lives alone, quietly and modestly, in a small house with windows on only one side, so that he can look out on a thick forest of sequoias where wildlife thrives and visits him as if they're all his pets. He socializes with an interesting variety of friends, including James Dean, Harvey Milk, Walter Cronkite, and Spencer Tracy and Katharine Hepburn, and he's often seen at operas and plays, especially those continuing to be written by his frequent hiking companion Tennessee Williams. He occasionally performs "for the exercise," out of love for the material and the opportunity to play the rich character roles that were so elusive during his earthly career. While he continues to be attractive, his thirty-year-old visage at Home is more ordinary and therefore more within his comfort level.

He's also added a valuable new passion to his work on the Other Side since he returned. He and his son, Scott, are among the legions of spirits dedicated to welcoming suicide victims, from earth and from the Holding Place, and staying by their sides through any Orientation and cocooning they might need until they're able to resume their happy, peaceful, productive lives with their souls fully healed and God-centered again.

Paul believes that "usually those things that 'go without saying' are the exact things that most need to be said," so he makes a point of expressing that Joanne Woodward was his "rock" and his "anchor" and they're "too much a part of each other to be apart." He clearly remembers all four of their lifetimes together—two as husband and wife, one as brother and sister, and one as brothers—and he frequently visits her and hopes that she is aware of his loving presence. He has no intention of incarnating again, but promises he'll go right on making a contribution to life on earth "for as long as life on earth needs a helping hand."

Marilyn Monroe

Marilyn Monroe defined the terms "movie star" and "sex symbol" during her lifetime, and she continues to define them now, nearly five decades after her controversial death. She was shamelessly sensual but fragile, intelligent but helpless, ambitious but difficult, an icon of perfection but deeply flawed.

On June 1, 1926, in Los Angeles, California, Gladys Monroe Baker gave birth to a daughter she named Norma Jeane. Norma Jeane's paternity has never been authenticated, although Gladys's estranged husband, Edward Mortenson, is listed on the birth certificate. Whoever fathered Norma Jeane Baker, though, was definitely nowhere to be found, nor was Gladys on a regular basis. Mentally unstable and institutionalized from time to time, Gladys handed over most of the care of her daughter to a succession of orphanages, guardians, and foster homes, in some of which she was reportedly abused.

In June 1942, when she was sixteen, Norma Jeane married James Dougherty, a marriage arranged to keep her out of yet another foster home. Dougherty enlisted in the Merchant Marines in 1943 and during World War II left his young wife in the care of his mother. Norma Jeane was hired by a munitions factory, where she was photographed for an article in *Yank* magazine. As a result of that photograph, she was signed by the Blue Book Modeling Agency and, with its encouragement, transformed herself from a brunette to a blonde and became a successful model who began to dream of an acting career. Dougherty demanded, when he returned home, that she choose between their marriage and her career. She chose her career and divorced James Dougherty in 1946.

Norma Jeane quickly captured the attention of Ben Lyon, a Twentieth Century Fox executive, who signed her to a six-month contract and changed her name to Marilyn Monroe. After a couple of nonstellar film appearances in 1947, Marilyn was released from her obligations to Fox and returned to modeling until 1948, when she signed a six-month contract with Columbia Pictures.

It was her appearance in a Marx Brothers film called *Love Happy* in 1949 that attracted a successful agent named Johnny Hyde, who promptly signed her and was instrumental in landing critically acclaimed roles for her in John Huston's *The Asphalt Jungle* and Joseph Mankiewicz's *All About Eve*. Hyde is also credited with negotiating Marilyn's seven-year contract at Twentieth Century Fox in 1950.

Her film career was well on its way by the end of 1952 despite the stage fright that had begun to plague her, causing her to hide in her dressing room for hours while the rest of the cast and crew waited impatiently for her. She graced the cover of the first issue of *Playboy* in 1953, the same year in which she was suspended from her Fox contract for failing to appear for work and in which she met baseball superstar Joe DiMaggio, whom she married on January 14, 1954, a marriage that lasted less than a year.

Displeased with the quality of roles being offered to her by Fox and with the relatively small salary, Marilyn broke away from the studio and moved to New York, where she studied acting at the famed Lee Strasberg Actors Studio and began dating playwright Arthur Miller, whom she married on June 29, 1956. Her severe stage fright continued to plague her throughout her acting classes, but she was also recognized as a genuinely gifted standout. In the meantime, her film *The Seven Year Itch* was released to enormous success, and she re-signed with Twentieth Century Fox with a much more lucrative nonexclusive contract.

Under her new contract Marilyn starred in *Bus Stop* and *The Prince and the Showgirl* with critical acclaim and relatively few problems. She took a year off to focus on her marriage to Arthur Miller, but she sadly suffered a miscarriage in August 1957. She returned to Hollywood in 1958 to shoot Billy Wilder's *Some Like It Hot,* costarring Jack Lemmon and Tony Curtis, during which her compulsive tardiness, hostile refusal to take direction from Wilder, and general obstructive behavior contributed to her growing reputation for being difficult to work with. But the film was a huge box-office success, received five Academy Award nominations, and earned Marilyn the Golden Globe Best Actress Award.

By the late 1950s Marilyn's health was in a conspicuous decline, due largely to a growing dependence on prescription medication, particularly sleeping pills to battle her chronic insomnia, and the strains on her marriage were becoming more and more apparent.

Arthur Miller had written a screenplay called *The Misfits,* which began filming in July 1960 with Marilyn, Clark Gable, and Montgomery Clift, directed by John Huston. It was to become Marilyn Monroe's last completed film. She was often too ill and too anxious to perform, her fragile health further compromised by a steady stream of prescription medications and alcohol. A month after filming began she was hospitalized for ten days with an undisclosed illness, and when she returned to the set her open hostility toward her husband was a recurring obstacle. Clark Gable became ill while shooting *The Misfits* as well, and less than ten days after filming was completed, Marilyn Monroe and Arthur Miller officially separated and Clark Gable was dead from a heart attack.

Marilyn's addictions to alcohol and prescription drugs escalated following the lackluster box-office performance of *The Misfits,* and in February 1961, once her divorce from Arthur Miller was finalized, she checked into a psychiatric clinic. For the remainder of 1961 she battled a series of mental and physical health challenges, with her former husband and still loyal friend Joe DiMaggio by her side.

In 1962 she started filming *Something's Got to Give*, but her repeated failure to report to work forced Twentieth Century Fox to fire her and file a lawsuit against her. On May 19, 1962, she gave an unforgettably breathy, voluptuous, and somewhat slurred performance of "Happy Birthday" at the birthday celebration for President John Kennedy, with whom she was later reported to have had an affair. She launched into a busy series of interviews, photo shoots, and meetings about future projects. She and Fox resolved their dispute, and they renewed her contract. And *Something's Got to Give* was scheduled to resume filming in the early fall of 1962.

But at 4:25 A.M. on the morning of August 5, 1962, Marilyn's psychiatrist, Dr. Ralph Greenson, placed an emergency call to report that she'd been found dead in her small Brentwood, California, house. She was just thirty-six years old. Following an autopsy, the cause of death was listed as "acute barbiturate poisoning—probable suicide." Even now, nearly fifty years later, the circumstances surrounding her death continue to create any number of theories and allegations, including homicide. Marilyn Monroe was laid to rest on August 8, 1962, in the Corridor of Memories at Westwood Memorial Park, leaving behind a legacy of thirty films and an iconic standard of beauty and glamour at their most vulnerable that will never be duplicated.

From Sylvia

Several years after Marilyn's death I was asked by a nationally syndicated television show to visit her house with a film crew to see if she would communicate with me. A condition of filming on their part was that I wouldn't be allowed inside the house or even that close to it—just inside the gate was as far as we could go. A condition on my part was, "No promises." There are no spirits or ghosts who can be counted on to come when I call them, and I hadn't even established yet whether Marilyn had made it to the Other Side or if she was still earthbound. For all I knew we could end up with a lot of footage of me standing in front of a house staring mindlessly into the camera without a peep out of Marilyn.

I admit it, I'd done no research on her life before I arrived, so I didn't think much about being introduced to a lovely older gentleman named James Dougherty until I was told he was her first husband. He was quick to clarify that he'd never been married to Marilyn Monroe; he was married to the young (pre-Marilyn) Norma Jeane Baker. He spoke of her with deep affection, and her death had touched him deeply.

As soon as we'd arrived as close to the house as we were allowed to get, a brief Latin phrase came to me. I pronounced it as best I could, and when I saw him staring at me, I explained, "It's in the tiles above the entryway. It means something like 'Everyone is welcome here.'"

He asked how I knew about that, since I'd never been to the house before, and I told him. "Marilyn's telling me."

It was a nice surprise. She was definitely on the Other Side, she definitely had a lot to say, and she was ready to say it to me without preferring to talk through Francine. I can't judge or comment on its accuracy. I'll just report what she passed along and leave the rest to you.

She was adamant about the fact that she did not commit suicide. She described being alone in her bedroom that night, taking too many pills and making some blurry phone calls. But she had a clear memory of a man coming in and sticking a needle of what she believed to be Nembutol into her heart.

She never stopped loving Joe DiMaggio, and one of the sources of depression that plagued her in her later years was the fear that, because she confided so much in him about things she undoubtedly wasn't supposed to know, which she'd written in a red journal or diary, loving her might have brought him more pain and potential danger than joy. She visited him often from the Other Side, particularly when he slept, and she was already determined to be the first to greet him when he came Home.

Then she was gone. Even in that brief encounter, I was pleasantly surprised at how much I liked her and the depth of her sincerity.

From Francine

Marilyn was indeed the first to welcome Joe DiMaggio Home. They lead very quiet separate lives here, but they also spend a lot of time together walking on the beach. Marilyn is a voracious reader and can often be found studying the great literary classics in the Hall of Records.

Like everyone else on the Other Side, she looks back on her most recent lifetime with increasing clarity. She knows she was bipolar. She knows that she was at her most comfortable when she was acting—pretending to be someone else. She knows that if she'd lived a long life, she would never have been the icon she's become. She just wants those who try to emulate her not to fall into the same trap she did, the excess that comes with fame. People stop saying no to you. You stop saying no to yourself. And before long you've forgotten what a loving word "no" can be.

Cary Grant

Charismatic, debonair, and irresistibly handsome, Cary Grant epitomized the words "leading man" and "movie star" for three decades, more than earning his place among the American Film Institute's greatest male stars of all time.

He was an only child, born Archibald Alexander Leach on January 18, 1904, in Horfield, Bristol, England. His father, Elias Leach, barely made ends meet by pressing suits for a living, while his mother, Elsie, was a vague, unhappy presence until she disappeared when Cary was nine years old. Elias told his son that Elsie had gone away on a long holiday—somehow he decided that being abandoned by his mother would be easier on a child than the truth that she'd been institutionalized in a mental facility for a severe, crippling depression. (In fact, Cary continued to believe the abandonment story until he was in his thirties and found his mother in the asylum, where she'd been living for all those years. It was a less than joyful reunion. His mother had no interest in her wildly successful son or in getting to know him, and he never saw her again, although he paid for her care for the rest of her life.)

Cary was expelled from school in 1918 and joined the Bob Pender Stage Troupe, a comedy circus group that traveled throughout England, where he learned stilt walking, pantomime, pratfalls, and comedic timing. The troupe toured the United States in 1920, and when they were to return to Great Britain, their young star elected to stay in America and work his way toward a stage career. After some light comedies in St. Louis and finally on Broadway, Archibald Leach traveled to Hollywood in 1931 and evolved from Cary Lockwood to Cary Grant at the preference of Paramount Pictures, who eagerly put him under contract. He was quickly cast in 1932's *Blonde Venus* as Marlene Dietrich's leading man and was already headed for stardom when a force field named Mae West selected him as her leading man in two of her most successful films: *She Done Him Wrong,* which was nominated for a Best Picture Academy Award in 1933, and *I'm No Angel,* a huge box-office hit that rescued Paramount from bankruptcy. Paramount went on to cast Cary in a string of mediocre movies, and in 1936 he left the studio for a contract with Columbia Pictures, which promptly loaned him out to Hal Roach for his first real comedy showcase, *Topper.*

While Cary was sharing the screen in the 1930s and 1940s with some of Hollywood's greatest actresses, including Katharine Hepburn, Rosalind Russell, and Irene Dunne, he was devoting much of his off-screen time to the first three of his five wives. In 1934 he married actress Virginia Cherrill. She divorced him a year later, claiming that he hit her. In 1942 he married Barbara Hutton, the insanely wealthy socialite who was heiress to both the Woolworth and E. F. Hutton fortunes. Any accusations that Cary was only after her for her money (Hollywood cynics nicknamed them "Cash and Cary") were disproved when, after their divorce in 1945, it was revealed that he'd signed a prenuptial agreement waiving any claim to a single dime of her money. Cary and Barbara Hutton remained friends for the rest of their lives, and he continued to treat her son, Lance Reventlow, like a member of his own family. His next marriage was to actress Betsy Drake, on Christmas Day, 1949. That marriage didn't end until August 14, 1962, despite Cary's having fallen in love with Sophia Loren while filming *The Pride and the Passion* with her in 1957. Sophia was already very much in love with her future husband, Carlo Ponti, at the time of the filming of *The Pride and the Passion*.

These marriages took place, by the way, against persistent rumors that Cary was either bisexual or homosexual, particularly in light of his unapologetically being roommates with his great friend, actor Randolph Scott, off and on for twelve years. He was well aware of the rumors and was quoted as saying, "Look at it this way. I've always tried to dress well. I've had some success in life. I've enjoyed my success, and I include in that success some relationships with very special women. If someone wants to say I'm gay, what can I do? I think it's probably said about every man who's been known to do well with women. I don't let that sort of thing bother me. What matters to me is that I know who I am."

In the meantime, on the professional front, Cary Grant also teamed up for several films with director Alfred Hitchcock, who called Cary "the only actor I ever loved in my whole life." Their films together, which include *Suspicion* (1941), *Notorious* (1946), *To Catch a Thief* (1955), and *North by Northwest* (1959), are still considered classics, as are so many of the more than seventy movies Cary made in his lifetime.

He was smart enough, and rebellious enough, to be the first actor to form his own production company, Grantley Productions, in the mid-1950s. This allowed him to control all aspects of his career, and the films his company produced, distributed by Universal, included such successes as *Operation Petticoat* (1959), *That Touch of Mink* (1962), and *Charade* (1963; with the extraordinary Audrey Hepburn). His last movie, *Walk, Don't Run*, was shot in 1965. Thanks to Grantley Productions, Cary Grant received a share of the gross profits for these films, and his estate when he died was said to be worth approximately $60 million. It's theorized, though, that Cary's politically unpopular decision to turn his back on the well-established "studio system" and become an independent entity cost him the two Academy Awards for which he was nominated.

Cary's next marriage, at the end of his film career, was to actress Dyan Cannon. They eloped to Las Vegas in 1965, and to his profound joy, his only child, a daughter named Jennifer, was born on February 26, 1966. This troubled marriage ended in a bitter, widely publicized divorce in 1968 and an ongoing custody battle over Jennifer that continued well into the 1970s.

On April 11, 1981, Cary married his fifth and final wife, his longtime friend and companion Barbara Harris, a British hotel publicist who was forty-seven years younger than he. She traveled with him when, in the last years of his life, he began touring the United States in a one-man show called *A Conversation with Cary Grant*. On the afternoon of November 29, 1986, he was preparing for an appearance in Davenport, Iowa, when he suddenly seemed a bit confused and told his wife he needed to rest. When he headed off to his dressing room, she realized something was very wrong and called for an ambulance. He was pronounced dead at 11:22 P.M. in Davenport's St. Luke's Hospital of a massive stroke.

Cary's substantial fortune was divided between his wife, Barbara, and his cherished daughter, Jennifer, who, in August 2008, gave birth to her first child, a son she named Cary Benjamin Grant.

From Francine

Laughter spread through the large crowd that welcomed Cary to the Other Side, when he emerged from the tunnel and announced with his trademark droll wit, "Well, that was interesting." Alfred Hitchcock was among the first to embrace him, along with his soul mate, a woman named Rachel, who looks a great deal like Barbara Hutton, but with long braided black hair and a very tall, ample body. Cary was enormously introspective about his trip to the Scanning Machine, interested to find out that he was angrier about his lifetime while he lived it than he was aware of at the time. "I didn't much care what people thought or said about me, whether it was the studios or the fans. I knew exactly who I was and who I wasn't. What I did care about was the astonishing number of purported experts on me and my life who couldn't be bothered to take the simple truth for an answer. I had more than my share of faults, but lying wasn't among them." His life themes of Aesthetic Pursuits and Experiencer worked both for him and against him, he believes, making him a versatile, highly adventurous performer who had a marvelous career, but was "for the most part, an unfortunate choice for a husband."

He couldn't wait to return to his life on the Other Side, to which those same themes seem to apply. He changes homes frequently—at any given moment he might be living in a Greek Revival captain's house on what corresponds to your northern Atlantic coastline, a brownstone near the Towers where he goes to meditate, a simple tent in the midst of the jungle animals he adores, or a lavish castle carved into the rocky slopes of our Mount Everest. He delights in a very busy social life, never missing an opportunity to gather with everyone from actors and musicians to physicists and astronomers to former world leaders, all of whom comment after socializing with him about his charming eagerness to listen and learn, no matter what the subject. He continues to act, particularly in a brilliant stage interpretation of None but the Lonely Heart, which he performs with such "volunteers" as Grace Kelly, Ingrid Bergman, Rock Hudson, Lee J. Cobb, Anthony Quinn, and his great friends Katharine Hepburn and Spencer Tracy. He's also an avid golfer and is learning to play the cello, the sound of which he's always found soothing and "soul cleansing."

His great passion at Home, though, is his dedicated work with our many research teams determined to reverse global warming on earth and *infuse solutions to your diligent scientists, researchers, and environmentalists on earth. All of us are deeply concerned, but none more than Cary, who refuses to "stand by and do nothing while my innocent grandson grows up on an endangered planet."*

His visits to earth, by the way, are devoted entirely to his grandson, and he promises, "I'll be watching over that precious boy all his life."

—

George Carlin

Controversial comedian, actor, and author George Denis Patrick Carlin was born on May 12, 1937, in New York City. His mother, Mary, was a secretary and devout Catholic, and his father, Patrick, was a national advertising manager for the *New York Sun*. George was raised by his mother, who left his father when he was two months old. He attended parochial school and was an altar boy, to which he credited his avowed atheism by the time he reached adulthood. At fifteen he'd had quite enough of formal education and dropped out of school in the ninth grade. He also developed a pattern of running away from home on a regular basis, thanks to a very contentious relationship with his mother, and his enlisting in the U.S. Air Force in 1954, at the age of seventeen, seemed like a good idea at the time. He was stationed in Bossier City, Louisiana, trained as a radar technician, earned his high-school equivalency, and moonlighted as a disc jockey on KJOE radio in nearby Shreveport. On the downside, he also received three court-martials and several disciplinary punishments, was declared an "unproductive airman," and was discharged in 1957.

While working at KXOL Radio in Forth Worth, Texas, George met co-worker Jack Burns, and the two of them formed a comedy team, refining their act at a coffeehouse called the Cellar before moving to Los Angeles in February 1960. Calling themselves "The Wright Brothers," they hosted a morning show on KDAY Radio in Hollywood, performed at West Coast coffeehouses at night, and attracted the attention of the brilliant and highly controversial comedian Lenny Bruce, whose influence opened the door for a Burns and Carlin appearance on Jack Paar's *The Tonight Show*. Not incidentally, it was also in 1960 that George met Brenda Hosbrook while touring, and they were married in 1961. Their daughter, Kelly, was born in 1963.

Burns and Carlin went their separate ways, and George became a popular guest on variety shows, most famously *The Ed Sullivan Show* and *The Tonight Show*. In fact, between appearances as a guest and as a guest host, George was booked on *The Tonight Show* 130 times during both the Jack Paar years and the Johnny Carson decades. He sharpened his stand-up skills in Las Vegas as well, perfecting such classic routines as "Al Sleet, the Hippie-Dippie Weatherman" and "Stupid Disk Jockeys" and recording them in 1967 on his first album, *Take Offs and Put Ons*.

As his career progressed, his style and the subject matter of his routines became more and more unconventional. His short hair gave way to long hair. His clean-shaven face began sporting a beard. His conservative suits evolved into jeans and T-shirts. And on July 21, 1972, George was arrested at Milwaukee's Summerfest and charged with violating obscenity laws for his landmark comedy routine, "Seven Words You Can Never Say on Television." The case was ultimately dismissed. A similar Carlin routine broadcast on a New York City FM station in 1973 resulted in the station being fined for broadcasting "indecent but not obscene" material during the hours when children were most likely to be listening.

The controversy, combined with George's edgy, unconventional brilliance, made him even more popular, and he was a natural host for the first episode of the equally edgy and unconventional *Saturday Night Live* in October 1975. By then he'd already unapologetically declared himself a regular cocaine user, so it wasn't surprising when, after an unexpected five-year semihiatus from stand-up comedy during which he filmed the first few of what would be fourteen HBO specials between 1977 and 2008, he acknowledged that he'd suffered the first of three heart attacks.

George's acting career took hold in the 1980s, launching an impressive list of credits that included such feature films as *Outrageous Fortune*, *Bill and Ted's Excellent Adventure*, *Bill and Ted's Bogus Journey*, *The Prince of Tides*, *Dogma*, *Jersey Girl*, and *Cars* (a Disney/Pixar production in which Carlin is the voice of Fillmore, a psychedelic VW microbus). He also provided the voice for the children's television favorite *Thomas the Tank Engine and Friends* from 1991 until 1998 and appeared as "Mr. Conductor" on the PBS *Shining Time Station* from 1991 until 1993. And in 1993 he launched twenty-seven episodes of a Fox sitcom, *The George Carlin Show*.

Tragically, in 1997, Brenda Carlin, George's wife of thirty-eight years, died of liver cancer. In June 1998 George married Sally Wade, a marriage that lasted the rest of his life. (In fact, his death occurred two days before what would have been their tenth anniversary.)

George enjoyed long-standing status as a headliner in Las Vegas. But in 2005 he was fired by the MGM Grand after an ugly, profane exchange with his audience, and within a few weeks he checked himself into a rehab facility for addictions to alcohol and Vicodin. He announced to his audience at the Tachi Palace Casino in Lemoore, California, on February 1, 2006, that they were witnessing his "first show back" after being hospitalized for heart failure and pneumonia.

In mid-June 2008, George returned to his home in Los Angeles after a reunion with performing stand-up at the Orleans Hotel and Casino in Las Vegas. A week later, on June 22, he was admitted to St. John's Health Center in Santa Monica, complaining of chest pains. He died at 5:55 P.M. of heart failure that same day. At his request, his body was cremated and his ashes were scattered, with no memorial or religious services to mark his passing.

George was once asked what he was proudest of in his career. He answered that it was the number of books he'd sold, totaling nearly a million copies. Beginning in 1984, he wrote six books, the last two of which—*Watch My Language* and his autobiographical *Last Words*— were released posthumously.

From Francine

I wish you could have seen the look of shock on George's face when he emerged from the tunnel and rediscovered that there really is life after death after all. And when he found his first wife, Brenda, waiting to greet him, he was stunned into a long silence while he held her, after which I'm told he gaped at the hundreds of spirits and animals who gathered for the reunion and said, "I'll be damned." George is an excellent example of the fact that atheists are embraced on the Other Side as surely as the most devoutly religious, and with his humor, self-honesty, and misguided but honorable intentions, he tried to live a godly lifetime, no matter what words he used to define it.

Once he spent time at the Scanning Machine and in Orientation, all his memories came flooding back, not only of the life on the Other Side to which he'd just returned, but also of the life that preceded this most recent one—he was a black man in the mid-1800s, wrongly convicted of and executed for a murder he did not commit, the murder of a white woman, which, it was later learned, was actually committed by the presiding judge. It was understandable that George arrived angry and rebellious against "the system," and it was brilliant of him to have charted a sense of humor that would allow him to express his outrage through the power of laughter. He regrets that he found it difficult to distance himself from the penetrating anger that drove his comedy, so that he could genuinely relax and enjoy his success from time to time. He also recognizes that he was conflicted about his success, loving the comfort it afforded him, but also not wanting to get so comfortable that he'd lose his edge, and it was in pursuit of that edge that he allowed himself to indulge in his addiction to cocaine. He wants his daughter to know how much he adores her, wishes he'd been the father she deserved, and is intensely proud of her. He's also grateful to his second wife, who he says was more understanding and compassionate about the "baggage" he brought to their marriage than he could ever repay.

His life at Home is blissfully happy, in its own unique way. You need to remember that all of us maintain the same basic personality traits throughout the eternity of our spirits—the outgoing remain outgoing no matter how many times they incarnate and return to the Other Side, the introspective remain innately introspective, the humorless remain humorless, those with a sense of humor eternally have a sense of humor, and so on. George is no exception. He loves spending time in the Hall of Records, researching past and present charts of historically powerful men and women and entertaining at large gatherings with his singularly insightful perspective on those who experienced power on earth. He's also very devoted to study and meditation on the charts of his own lifetimes, intent on tracking the onset of his avowed atheism in an effort to learn how he grew to be so loudly, outspokenly wrong about the existence of God. He has no plans to incarnate again.

Rock Hudson

The personification of the words "tall, dark, and handsome," actor Rock Hudson was a Midwestern boy, born Roy Harold Scherer Jr. in Winnetka, Illinois, on November 17, 1925. His mother, Katherine, was a telephone operator. His father, Roy Harold Scherer Sr., an auto mechanic, abandoned his wife and son when Roy Jr. was eight years old, during the Great Depression. Katherine's second husband, Wallace Fitzgerald, formally adopted her young son and changed his name to Roy Fitzgerald.

Roy was a disinterested student at New Trier High School, much more intent on achieving a career as an actor than he was on his studies. After graduation he served as a naval aircraft mechanic in the Philippines during World War II and moved to Los Angeles when his tour of duty was over. His first effort at pursuing a serious acting career was an application to the University of Southern California drama program, but he was disqualified because of his lackluster grades. He drove a delivery truck to make ends meet and spent every possible nonworking hour distributing his "head shots" to every studio executive, filmmaker, and agent he could find.

His determination was rewarded when, in 1948, Henry Willson, an openly gay Hollywood talent scout, recognized Roy's potential as a true movie star, changed his name to the intensely masculine sounding Rock Hudson, and secured Rock's first job, a small part in the 1948 Warner Bros. film *Fighter Squadron*. He also began grooming his handsome new client for stardom, with lessons in acting, singing, dancing, horseback riding, and fencing as well as launching a publicity campaign that soon had movie magazines across the country featuring Rock Hudson's face on the cover. By the time he was twenty-nine, Rock was receiving some critical applause for his role in 1954's *Magnificent Obsession* with Jane Wyman, and his career was off and running.

In an effort to maintain Rock's masculine, heterosexual image at a time when show business wasn't embracing homosexuality, Henry Willson recruited his secretary, Phyllis Gates, to marry Rock Hudson in 1955, with widely publicized photos of the wedding and the happy couple at home. Although the marriage only lasted three years, it's widely believed that there was great affection and mutual respect between Rock and Phyllis for the duration of their relationship, and the public perception of Rock Hudson as a "straight" movie star was firmly established.

Rock's greatest career triumph to date followed shortly after his marriage, when he starred with James Dean and Elizabeth Taylor in *Giant* in 1956. Not only did Rock walk away with a truly prestigious film and his first Oscar nomination under his belt, but he also formed a close friendship with Elizabeth Taylor that would last for the rest of his life.

After several more moderately successful dramatic roles, Rock found a whole new niche in romantic comedies costarring another dear friend, Doris Day. Their charming chemistry resulted in three box-office hits—*Pillow Talk* (1958), *Lover Come Back* (1961), and *Send Me No Flowers* (1964).

Film roles became fewer and farther between as the 1960s progressed, and in 1971 Rock reluctantly waded into the television business with a movie of the week called *Once upon a Dead Man*, which evolved into the six-year detective series *McMillan and Wife*, with Susan Saint James, John Schuck, and Nancy Walker.

In 1982 Rock signed to star in a second series, *The Devlin Connection*, but filming was interrupted, and the show was ultimately cancelled, when Rock had a massive heart attack, his health compromised by many years of heavy smoking and scotch drinking. His quintuple bypass surgery was a success, but he never seemed to rebound completely. Although he was signed to play the recurring role of Linda Evans's character's love interest in the hit drama *Dynasty* in 1985, his increasing weight loss, unsteadiness, and apparent frailty forced the producers to write his character out of the series after fourteen episodes.

Rock went into seclusion for several months until July 1985, when he made his last public appearance to help his friend Doris Day launch her new talk show *Doris Day's Best Friends*. He was heartbreakingly gaunt, pale, and mumbling as he admitted the obvious to her and to the rest of the world—he was dying. Photographs of the ravaged star were broadcast around the world, and it wasn't long before Rock filled in the missing piece to the story and confirmed that it was AIDS that was taking his life.

On October 2, 1985, Rock Hudson died of AIDS-related complications. In the wake of his death, now having a once beautiful and beloved face to attach to the then relatively dismissed scourge of HIV-AIDS, the public, the medical establishment, and the Hollywood community began moving AIDS awareness and treatment to the top of their priority lists, with Elizabeth Taylor leading the march toward fund-raising, care, and compassion in the name of her dear fallen friend. Rock Hudson's legacy extends far beyond his more than seventy film and television roles—it's impossible to calculate the impact of his life and death on AIDS victims throughout the world from 1985 on.

From Francine

Like most AIDS victims, Rock was ecstatic to leave his body and come Home to fully restored health and vitality. His mother was the first to greet him, once she made it through a wildly enthusiastic herd of large dogs, led by an Irish setter he especially adored. They were promptly joined by Roddy McDowall, Marlon Brando, and a host of other Hollywood friends, including Montgomery Clift, with whom Rock had always felt a unique connection—Rock says he was among the first on the scene of the tragic car accident that nearly killed and, in the long run, devastated Clift's life, and it moved Rock to tears to see him thriving again.

He definitely returned Home with an agenda. It took all the patience he could muster to sit through the replay of his latest lifetime at the Scanning Machine, because he was so eager to begin training as an Orientator, to help other AIDS victims make as smooth and peaceful a transition as possible to the Other Side. He also volunteered himself for intensive study at one of our many medical research centers, where finding a cure for AIDS is a steadfast priority. Teams of brilliant minds at Home are vigilantly at work in search of treatments and cures, infusing any and all advances they discover.

Rock's home here is made entirely of windows, which overlook his vast hydroponic gardens. He's one of our most prolific and charming hosts, regularly entertaining the widest possible variety of friends, and during the course of a party he can always be counted on to sing one of his favorite songs, "Send in the Clowns," accompanied on piano by his frequent side-kick Martha Raye. (He wants those he left behind to know that he finally remembers all the words.) He never misses a concert of music from the 1950s and, a self-described "frustrated song and dance man" on earth, is excited to be in rehearsals for the title role in The Music Man.

About his most recent lifetime he says, "Of course I have regrets, especially about those times when I was completely irresponsible with the excuse that I was just having a good time. But for the most part, I loved my life, my career, and my dear, dear friends. I was blessed in so many ways, and whether or not I remembered to show it often enough, I was and am so grateful to God for every moment." His chosen life themes of Victim and Humanitarian became clear to him in his final months on earth, when he proved to the world what an equal-opportunity monster AIDS really is. When he was first diagnosed, he says, he didn't want anyone to know. But when his diagnosis and prognosis became undeniable, he took pride in the fact that he helped to "wake people up" and inspired global awareness, more informed prevention, and, above all, compassion.

He's often a tangible presence at AIDS clinics around the world and still stops by the courtyard of the home in the Hollywood Hills where he lived so many happy years. (It delights him that he's occasionally successful in setting off the motion detectors as he checks on what he continues to think of as "his house.") He was also the first to welcome Home his longtime partner, Tom Clark, who was by Rock's side for the last months of his lifetime.

Heath Ledger

Another star who left before the world was ready, actor Heath Ledger was born April 4, 1979, in Perth, Australia. His father, Kim Ledger, was both a race car driver and a mining engineer with the family company, the Ledger Engineering Foundry. Heath's mother, Sally Ledger, was a French teacher. Heath was an incredibly bright child, winning Western Australia's Junior Chess Championship when he was only 10. Inspired by his older sister, Kate, an actress and later his publicist, to whom he was very close throughout his life, he was cast, also around the age of ten, in the lead role in his elementary school's production of *Peter Pan*. Sadly, his parents' marriage fell apart at this same time, forcing Heath to spend the next few years moving back and forth between them. But his love of acting, which expanded into a love of dance and choreography as well, became his outlet, and his determination led to extra roles in a feature film called *Clowning Around* and the television series *Ship to Shore*.

He graduated from high school at the age of sixteen and promptly headed to Sydney, where he became even more serious about his career as an actor. He found television work almost immediately and made his first official appearance on the big screen in 1997's *Blackrock*, which was impressive enough to land him a starring role in the successful Australian series *Home and Away* and in a fantasy series called *Roar*. *Roar* was financed with American money, giving Hollywood its first exposure to Heath Ledger. His costar and girlfriend,

Liza Zane, convinced the nineteen-year-old actor to move with her to Los Angeles and find himself an agent.

Success came quickly after his arrival in the United States—in 1999 Heath costarred with Julia Stiles in the internationally successful movie *10 Things I Hate About You*, after which he was officially in demand. In 2000 he was cast by Mel Gibson in *The Patriot*. Next came Billy Bob Thornton's *Monster's Ball*, also in 2000, followed by *A Knight's Tale* in 2001. All the while, after a breakup with Liza Zane, the handsome young Australian rising star was having no trouble finding success in his personal life as well, and his reputation as a playboy was attracting the attention of the Hollywood social scene and the tabloids.

A string of smart, gifted performances in several independent films kept him busy and stimulated through the early 2000s. But then, in 2005, along came the glaring spotlight that accompanied the controversial "gay cowboy movie," *Brokeback Mountain*, in which he costarred with another rising star, Jake Gyllenhaal. The film was a triumph for Heath Ledger—he was nominated for a Golden Globe Award and an Oscar, and he won the 2005 Best Actor awards from the San Francisco and New York Film Critics Circles.

He also met actress Michelle Williams on the set of *Brokeback Mountain*. Their whirlwind romance produced a daughter, Matilda Rose, who was born in New York on October 28, 2005. By now Heath was relentlessly targeted by the paparazzi, and it was as a result of that exhaustive attention that he, Michelle Williams, and their baby daughter moved from their home in New South Wales to an apartment in Brooklyn, where they lived until 2007.

He followed *Brokeback Mountain* with an Australian film called *Candy*, in which he played a heroin addict whose effort to overcome his addiction is mentored by the brilliant Geoffrey Rush. He was rewarded with three nominations for *Candy* and won the Film Critics Circle of Australia Best Actor Award. Next came the award-winning

I'm Not There, a study of Bob Dylan with six actors portraying different aspects of his life, for which Ledger, the cast, director Todd Haynes, and the film's casting director won the 2007 Independent Spirit Robert Altman Award.

In the early fall of 2007 the relationship between Heath Ledger and Michelle Williams ended, at around the time he gave what was to be his last completed film performance, as the character of the Joker in a Batman sequel called *The Dark Knight*. During filming, as Heath described in a November 4, 2007, *New York Times* interview, he struggled with severe insomnia. "Last week," he said, "I probably slept an average of two hours a night. . . . I couldn't stop thinking . . ." He'd begun taking Ambien to help him sleep, and even two at a time did nothing more than leave him "in a stupor, only to wake up an hour later," with his mind still racing. Adding to his insomnia was a serious respiratory illness that struck in January 2008 while he was in London to shoot a Terry Gilliam film, *The Imaginarium of Doctor Parnassus*, a performance he would never complete.

On January 22, 2008, Heath was found unconscious in his bed at approximately 2:45 P.M. All efforts to resuscitate him failed, and he was pronounced dead in his apartment in Manhattan's SoHo neighborhood at 3:36 P.M. According to the autopsy performed the following day, he died of acute accidental intoxication from a combination of six prescription medications typically prescribed for insomnia, pain, depression, and respiratory congestion.

Tributes poured in from the film community and fans around the world, and after a private memorial ceremony in Los Angeles, Heath's body was taken home to Perth by his parents and sister for a second memorial attended by hundreds of mourners. Michelle Williams told the press that she was sure his spirit would live on through their daughter, Matilda, to whom Heath's family awarded her father's $16.3 million estate. In the aftermath of Heath Ledger's death at the age of twenty-eight, *The Dark Knight* broke several box office records, and for his role as the Joker he won both a Golden Globe and an Oscar as Best Supporting Actor.

From Francine

Heath was exhausted when he emerged from the tunnel and shocked to find himself here—he had every intention of waking up in his bed in his apartment a few hours after he settled in for a desperately needed nap. His spirit was safely Home before his unconscious body was found, and his first words when he realized where he was and what had happened were, "I want Matilda taken care of." After reunions he was too dazed to enjoy, he was taken to Orientation even before his trip to the Scanning Machine. He slept, "detoxed," received loving, reassuring therapy from his team of Orientators, and traveled frequently to the quadrant devoted to Orientation to meditate, take long, private canoe trips, read the works of Shakespeare (which he loves, I'm told), and listen to Mozart concertos (which I'm also told he loves).

His healing took nearly two years in your time, and he's thriving now, euphorically resuming his life on the Other Side. Heath appreciates the value of Orientation more than many, since he himself is a skilled Orientator. Since his latest incarnation he's begun specializing as a physical therapist for those who arrive with unintended prescription drug overdoses and addictions. He also returned with a passion for filmmaking, both in front of and behind the camera. "Loved the work, hated the fame," he often says. He exhaustively studies current films in production around the world, and, in anticipation of his next incarnation, which will begin in 2016, he's being trained as a film editor by the enormously gifted Verna Fields and honing his acting skills under the private tutelage of Spencer Tracy, whom he's always admired.

Heath says he never planned for this most recent incarnation to be a long one, after four previous lifetimes in which he suffered a great deal both physically and mentally in his later years. Although his prescription drug use wasn't recreationally motivated, he was painfully aware that it had developed into a serious problem that he would have to overcome if he were ever to be the involved, attentive father his daughter deserved. He wants Michelle and his family to know how deeply grateful he is to them for seeing to it that the entirety of his estate is being held in trust for her.

He also wants Michelle to promise their daughter that he will find his way to her when he comes back. She'll be eleven years old when he's born, and he'll reenter her life as an "oddly familiar stranger" when she's in her early thirties. He's looking forward to it already.

Grace Kelly

She carried herself like royalty and became a princess. Her name was Grace Patricia Kelly, and she came into the world on November 12, 1929, in Philadelphia, Pennsylvania, the third of four children born to Brendan "Jack" Kelly and his wife, Margaret. Grace's determination to decide what she wanted and go after it came from her hardworking, ambitious parents. Her mother was the first female head of the University of Pennsylvania physical education department, and her father was an Olympic gold medalist in sculling (rowing) who returned home to become a self-made millionaire as a contractor and owner of a brick business.

Grace knew from childhood that she wanted to be an actress. Her natural beauty made her a popular local child model and performer. After an education at the finest private schools in Philadelphia, she auditioned her way into the American Academy of Dramatic Arts in New York. She modeled to help support herself and finally won her first professional acting job, in a 1949 Broadway production of August Strindberg's *The Father*.

Television and Grace's career were in their prolific infancy at exactly the same time, and Grace was cast in almost sixty live television productions in New York before she happily gave in to the lure of Hollywood and headed west. Her first film role was a small part in 1951's *Fourteen Hours*, directed by the esteemed Henry Hathaway. It wasn't an important enough role to create any excitement on Grace's behalf, so she returned to theater and television work. She was performing a play in Colorado in 1951 when she was surprised by a telegram from producer Stanley Kramer, offering her a role in *High Noon*, starring Gary Cooper and Lloyd Bridges. *High Noon* was a success, and the career of Grace Kelly was on its way. Next came the offer of a seven-year contract with MGM and a part in its upcoming Clark Gable–Ava Gardner film *Mogambo*. It was a prestigious project and a hit for both MGM and Grace—she received her first Best Supporting Actress Oscar nomination for her work in *Mogambo* and won the 1953 Golden Globe Award in that same category.

Her talent and her virginal, pristine beauty caught the eye of director Alfred Hitchcock, and he cast her in his 1953 Ray Milland thriller *Dial M for Murder*, which elevated her to stardom and created a lasting professional relationship between Hitchcock and Grace. She'd finished her next film, *The Bridges of Toko-Ri* with William Holden, in 1954, when she received a telegram from Hitchcock confirming her appointment with Edith Head, Hollywood's most prestigious costume designer, to begin her wardrobe fittings for his next film, *Rear Window*. Despite the fact that Hitchcock had never formally offered her a role in the film, Grace promptly turned down a role opposite Marlon Brando in *On the Waterfront*, kept her appointment with Edith Head, and costarred with James Stewart in *Rear Window*, another critical and box-office success for Alfred Hitchcock and Grace Kelly.

Next came *The Country Girl*, in which she reunited with William Holden and added Bing Crosby to her list of costars and fans. Both Grace Kelly and Judy Garland were the talk of the town that year, Grace for her stunning performance in *The Country Girl* and Judy for her triumphant performance in *A Star Is Born*. They both won Golden Globes for their performances, and they were both nominated for Academy Awards, with Judy Garland being the odds-on favorite to win. After Grace won instead, Judy Garland was quoted as saying, "I didn't appreciate Grace Kelly taking off her makeup and walking away with my Oscar."

After a box-office failure called *Green Fire,* Grace was off to France for her third and final Hitchcock film, *To Catch a Thief,* with Cary Grant, with whom she developed a close friendship and probable attraction that lasted for the rest of their lives. When asked to name his favorite costar in all his decades of film work, he replied simply and immediately, "Grace Kelly."

Grace was delighted by the invitation to head the American delegation at the April 1955 Cannes Film Festival and travel to the Palace of Monaco for a photo session with Prince Rainier III, Monaco's ruling sovereign. She kept it to herself that, after she returned to the United States to shoot *The Swan* with Alec Guinness and *High Society* with Bing Crosby and Frank Sinatra, she and the prince began an active correspondence that continued until his arrival in America in December 1955.

It was widely rumored that Rainier had come to the United States in search of a wife, for the most unromantic reason: according to a decades-old treaty, if Prince Rainier failed to produce an heir, Monaco would become a part of France again. For her part, Grace was twenty-seven, with all the career success she could ever have hoped for and ready for marriage, if she could find a man who met with her parents' approval.

Shortly after his arrival in America, Prince Rainier III met with Grace and her parents. Three days later, Rainier proposed. The Kelly family provided the prince with the required $2 million dowry, and the world excitedly began to prepare for the "wedding of the century." On April 18, 1956, in the palace throne room of Monaco, in front of six hundred guests and thirty million television viewers throughout Europe, Grace Kelly became Her Serene Highness Princess Grace of Monaco in a real-life fairy tale.

Immediately following the wedding, Prince Rainier banned all

Grace Kelly films from the theaters in Monaco, and Grace never accepted another film role. Her first official act as Princess of Monaco was the founding of a nonprofit organization called AMADE Mondiale, dedicated to the well-being of children throughout the world. She also created the Princess Grace Foundation for the benefit of local artisans and held an annual Christmas party for local orphans. But her most important, highly publicized creations were her three children: Princess Caroline, born on January 23, 1957; Prince Albert II, born on March 15, 1958; and Princess Stephanie, born on February 1, 1965.

On September 13, 1982, Princess Grace was driving along a narrow mountain road, returning her daughter Stephanie to Monaco from their country home, when her car swerved off the road and careened down the rocky cliff. While Princess Stephanie survived the crash, Princess Grace died the following day at the age of fifty-two without ever regaining consciousness. A subsequent autopsy indicated that moments before Princess Grace lost control of the car, she suffered a catastrophic stroke, which was ruled to be the underlying cause of the accident.

Four hundred guests, including Cary Grant and Diana, Princess of Wales, attended the funeral, which was broadcast to an estimated hundred million viewers around the world. Princess Grace was buried in Monaco in the royal family vault, and Prince Rainier, who never remarried, was buried beside her when he died in 2005.

From Francine

Grace was too much in shock from the suddenness of her violent death to notice the large crowd that gathered to welcome her Home. She virtually fell into the arms of her father, who comforted her as best he could before he and her Spirit Guide, named Cordelia, gently took her to a cocooning chamber, while I'm told she repeatedly whispered, "Stephanie could have been killed. Stephanie could have been killed." She was reassured that her daughter Stephanie was going to be fine, but she was still so stunned and distraught that she was given the blessing of being cocooned for almost six years in your time. She emerged fully healed, radiant and eager to proceed to the Scanning Machine and then back to her thrilling life here.

She found her life themes of Infallibility and Winner to have been much more of a challenge than she'd anticipated when she chose them. But in the greatest possible overview of her last incarnation, which she insists really will be her last, she feels that the most important purpose she was on earth to fulfill was to bring her three children into the world—"not for my husband, not for the future of Monaco, but simply for the unique, extraordinary people they are." (She wants Albert to know, incidentally, that she always knew that he would ascend to the throne with dignity, and she's watching over him and his sisters "every moment of every day.")

Given a choice, she says she would absolutely have continued her film career after marrying Rainier. She missed it terribly—the stimulation, the challenge, the sense of accomplishment, and above all the dear friends "who kept on making wonderful movies while I watched from the palace." She quickly adds that her years as Princess Grace were painfully lonely, "but leaving would have meant losing my children, and that was unthinkable." But now she looks back from the perspective of Home and realizes that she had no one to blame but herself for her loneliness. "I was blessed with so much. I was privileged, right from the beginning. It was a thrilling whirlwind of a life for the most part. But—no excuses—I devoted virtually no time at all to nourishing myself spiritually. I'm not referring to my charitable work, which came from my heart and was deeply important to me. I'm talking about all those hours alone when I felt empty and kept looking outside of myself to fill the void rather than inside. I enjoyed other people's company far more than I enjoyed my own, and I found more depth in other people than I found in myself. The people I quietly envied were those who'd learned to be enough for themselves. It was an art I never took *the time and trouble to master, and it would have cured my loneliness. And that was no one else's responsibility but mine."*

Grace is making up for lost time on the Other Side. She's hardly cloistered, but she chooses to live alone in a Georgian style house that she says "feels like home." She studies both theology and spirituality and will begin training soon to become an Orientator. She's also resumed her research work, but has changed her focus from medicine to the forensic sciences, a new passion she neither explains nor discusses. She loves going to the theater with friends, but has no interest in performing, and she's an accomplished equestrienne.

She mentions in passing that she and Prince Rainier are perfectly pleasant on the rare occasions when they see each other, and she wants their children to know that they're both watching over them and cherishing them.

John Kennedy Jr.

His image is crystallized in the memory of a nation grieving the death of its president—an innocent three-year-old boy stepping away from his mother and his uncle to stand at attention and salute the American flag on his father's casket. At that moment John Fitzgerald Kennedy Jr., the first child born to a president-elect, became "our" child, beyond politics and conspiracy theories, just a baby who'd suffered a loss he couldn't possibly understand.

He was born on November 25, 1960, in Washington, D.C., sixteen days after his father, John F. Kennedy, was elected the thirty-fifth president of the United States. He was the second child of John and Jacqueline Kennedy—his sister, Caroline, was born three years earlier, and his younger brother, Patrick, born in 1963, died just two days after his birth.

After the assassination of President Kennedy on November 22, 1963, Jacqueline moved with Caroline and John to a Manhattan apartment on the Upper East Side in an effort to shield them from the glaring media spotlight destined to follow the two beautiful children of the idealized "Camelot" first family. Tragedy hit again, on June 6, 1968, when John's Uncle Bobby, Robert Kennedy, who'd become his father figure after the death of JFK, was assassinated as well, at the Ambassador Hotel in Los Angeles after winning the California primary in his bid for the presidency. Four months later John's mother,

Jacqueline, married Greek shipping tycoon Aristotle Onassis, a marriage that lasted until Onassis's death in 1975.

John, in the meantime, attended New York's Collegiate School, then graduated from Phillips Andover Academy. His curiosity and interest in his education intensified in his late teens, taking him to Brown University to study American history, to Guatemala to literally lend a hand after a devastating earthquake there, and to Africa, where he studied environmental issues and worked with a mining firm in Johannesburg. His extraordinary good looks inevitably led to a brief turn at acting in several Brown University plays, but his passions ultimately guided him elsewhere. After graduating from Brown with a bachelor's degree in history in 1982, he traveled to India and studied at the University of Delhi, then returned to the United States and devoted his time to such Kennedy family projects as the East Harlem School at Exodus House and his own creation, Reaching Up, a program to improve treatment for the disabled. He also worked for the New York City Office of Business Development and the 42nd Street Development Corporation before entering New York University Law School in 1986.

Rumors of John's potential entrance into the political arena spread like wildfire when, at the 1988 Democratic National Convention in Atlanta, his photogenic, charismatic, movingly articulate appearance to introduce his uncle, Senator Edward Kennedy of Massachusetts, became the talk of pundits across the country. Instead, he graduated from law school with a J.D. in 1989, passed the bar exam on his third try, and became an assistant prosecutor in the office of New York district attorney Robert Morgenthau, a position he successfully held for four years, winning all six of the cases he prosecuted.

In 1995 John took on the Herculean task of cofounding a new magazine, a glossy monthly called *George*, whose slogan promised "Not politics as usual." He wrote essays and editorials for the magazine himself, occasionally even targeting members of his own family.

While it wasn't a blazing success, *George* did hold on until 2001, two years after John's death.

His social life was a constant source of media fascination and every bit as active as expected for *People* magazine's 1988 "Sexiest Man Alive." He was romantically linked with Daryl Hannah, Julia Roberts, Madonna, Brooke Shields, and Sarah Jessica Parker, to name a few, before he finally proposed to publicist Carolyn Bessette. They were married on September 21, 1996, on Cumberland Island, Georgia, in a private ceremony that managed to elude the press and at which John's sister, Caroline, served as the matron of honor.

On July 16, 1999, John, his wife, Carolyn, and her sister, Lauren Bessette, were en route to Martha's Vineyard in a private single-engine plane with John as its pilot, ultimately headed to the wedding of John's cousin Rory in Hyannisport, Massachusetts. The plane failed to arrive as scheduled, massive search parties were dispatched, and finally, on July 21, the bodies of John F. Kennedy Jr., his wife, and his sister-in-law were recovered in the waters off Gay Head on Martha's Vineyard. Their ashes were scattered into the Atlantic from the USS *Briscoe*, and America mourned the loss of its handsome, magnetic prince of Camelot.

From Francine

John arrived Home in a heartbeat and immediately found himself in the arms of his mother; his grandparents, his Uncle Robert, and his father were waiting to greet him as well. It was all he could do to let go of his mother, from whose death on earth he had never fully recovered, to embrace the others, and there was almost a shyness about him as he and John Sr. met. "I was three years old when my father died," he says. "I never had a chance to know him. I was much closer to my uncles, who did a great job of taking over for him while I was growing up."

There was no sadness, confusion, or regret in him. Instead, John was exhilarated to find himself here and had no need for Orientation or cocooning, nor did his wife and sister-in-law. He left the Scanning Machine to resume his rich, busy life with Jackie—his soul mate—by his side. Please let go of the fallacy that soul mates, on the extremely rare occasions when they both incarnate at the same time, are limited on earth to romantic relationships. They can be family members. They can be good friends. They can have any connection they choose to construct for themselves, for their own purposes, during a shared incarnation. Jackie and John chose to be mother and son in their one shared incarnation, so that they could be there for each other through the uniquely difficult charts they designed for themselves. Now that they're Home again, they of course maintain their own highly distinctive identities and pursue their own interests, but they also live and work together.

Their house is built, decorated, and situated identically to the house on Martha's Vineyard, where they both felt safe and peaceful. "There was a gate at the road, at the entrance to our long driveway," John says. "Even if it had been all over the media that my mother or I was at the house, we could leave that gate open, and often did, and never worry about anyone bothering us. Everyone respected our privacy, and we respected theirs, and we loved it there." They continue to balance their love of privacy and social lives in which they each have their own friends with whom they prefer to spend time in small groups. Jackie loves gatherings at home with authors, artists, and classical musicians. John prefers hiking with historians, athletes, political leaders, and above all his uncles and his father—they're enjoying getting to know each other, and John Sr. has expressed his appreciation and respect for his son's decision not to become a politician, which John says he would never have pursued. His chosen life themes of Experiencer and Justice, he says, were incompatible with anything involving politics beyond studying and writing about them—as he puts it, he preferred getting things done to scheduling endless committee meetings to discuss getting things done.

John and Jackie work together with a vast research team focused on the prenatal detection, treatment, and cure of birth defects. The team actively infuses scientists and medical researchers in North America, Japan, and Brazil, and they anticipate the announcement of a collaborative global breakthrough in or around 2026 in your years. John is also part of a team of ecologists who are working toward solutions for restoring the earth's ozone layer.

He and Jackie were among what seemed like scores of family members who gathered to welcome John's Uncle Ted to the Other Side. Like the rest of the "Kennedy men," John will not be reincarnating.

Mattie Stepanek

The poet, the peacemaker, and the philosopher who played," Matthew Joseph Thaddeus Stepanek was born on July 17, 1990, in Rockville, Maryland. His mother, Jeni, with a Ph.D. in early childhood special education, had four children before she was diagnosed with the adult form of dysautonomic mitochondrial myopathy, a genetic disease that took the lives of her daughter, Katie, at the age of two, her son Stevie at the age of six months, and her son Jamie at the age of three. One of the miracles of Mattie was that he survived the same disease until he was thirteen and accomplished more in those years than many of us manage in a lifetime.

On one hand, Mattie led the life of a normal boy, loving trips to the beach, reading, and the Korean martial art hapkido, in which he earned a black belt at the age of eight before he became reliant on a wheelchair, his service dog Micah, and a ventilator. On the other hand, when he was three years old, he began writing poetry. His extraordinary gifts as a writer and poet led to six books of poetry and a collection of peace essays, all of which reached the *New York Times* bestseller list, and one of which, *Just Peace*, was awarded the Independent Publishing Gold Medal for "Peacemaker Book of the Year" in 2007, three years after Mattie's death.

His poetry and his charmingly transcendent presence attracted the attention of Oprah Winfrey and Larry King. His frequent appearances on their respective talk shows led to his appointment as the Muscular Dystrophy Association National Goodwill Ambassador in 2002, at the age of twelve.

Mattie's disease required that he be home-schooled, a situation that allowed his astonishing intellect to thrive. He was also hospitalized several times and had a near-death experience that only deepened his profound faith in God and led him to tell Larry King in a 2002 interview on *Larry King Live*, when asked if he was afraid of death, "I'm afraid of dying, but I'm not afraid of death."

On June 22, 2004, at the Washington, D.C., Children's National Medical Center, Mattie Stepanek left this earth and went Home. His funeral six days later was attended by more than a thousand people. Former president Jimmy Carter remembered in his eulogy Mattie's life philosophy: "Remember to play after every storm." Mattie's mother, Jeni, continues her beloved child's work as a motivational speaker, peace advocate, and inspiration.

From Francine

Mattie is a Mystical Traveler, such a rare, highly advanced spirit that he seems lit from within by his and God's complete sacred commitment to each other. The crowd of spirits and animals who gathered to celebrate his Homecoming went on for as far as the eye could see. Like most Mystical Travelers, he incarnated on earth once and only once, and he stayed just long enough to reignite the spark of faith in an incalculable number of people and inspire his mother to continue his work before briefly returning to the Other Side. Then, after a private audience with the Council, he left again, into the stars and on to another planet as desperately in need of him as earth was.

This is not to imply that he and his mother are ever separate for any length of time. He is with her at every appearance, large or small, and he sits beside her on her bed every night until she falls asleep, adoring her and thanking her for the blessed lifetime she gave him, exactly the lifetime he knew she would give him when he chose her to deliver him to earth and be his best friend, companion, and caretaker in the brief time he was there.

Walter Cronkite

The most trusted man in America," world-class journalist Walter Leland Cronkite Jr., was born on November 4, 1916, in St. Joseph, Missouri, the only child of dentist Dr. Walter Leland Cronkite and his wife, Helen. When Walter was ten years old, the family moved to Houston, Texas, pursuing his father's opportunity for a position at the University of Texas Dental School. Walter, a Boy Scout, credited his early interest in journalism to an article in *American Boy* about the lives of reporters on assignment in other parts of the world, and he became editor of the school newspaper and yearbook during his time at San Jacinto High School.

After two years studying political science and journalism at the University of Texas in Austin, Walter left college in 1935 to accept a part-time job as a news and sports reporter for the *Houston Post*. His first official broadcasting job was for the radio station WKY in Oklahoma City, and from there it was on to sports reporting for KCMO in Kansas City, where he met his future wife, Mary Elizabeth Maxwell, called Betsy throughout her life, in 1936. In 1937 he joined United Press International (UPI), and he became one of the premier American reporters covering the North African and European fronts during World War II. He was then appointed chief correspondent at the war crimes trials in Nuremburg and head of the UPI office in Moscow.

His long career at CBS News began in 1952, when he narrated a program called *You Are There*, which dramatized historical events.

He also anchored CBS coverage of the 1952 Democratic and Republican presidential conventions and established himself as an articulate, uniquely appealing television newsman.

In 1962 Walter made his debut as anchor and editor of the *CBS Evening News*, a position he held until, at the age of sixty-five, he stepped down on March 6, 1981. During his brilliant tenure there, he interviewed every president from Eisenhower to Reagan; was the first to break the news to America of the deaths of President Kennedy and President Johnson; traveled to Vietnam to report on the aftermath of the Tet Offensive; brought cohesive understanding and clarity as the long, complicated Watergate scandal unfolded; participated in the first live transatlantic news broadcast in 1962; and was the live on-air reporter for the most historic of the NASA space program's accomplishments, including the Apollo 11 moon landing on July 20, 1969.

By his side every step of the way was his wife, Betsy, to whom he was married for sixty-five years until her death in 2005. Their three children, Nancy, Kathy, and Walter III, ultimately presented the Cronkites with four grandchildren.

Walter's retirement from the *CBS Evening News* by no means indicated his retirement from broadcasting. To name just a handful of his post-1981 accomplishments, he did narration and voice-overs in an IMAX film about the Space Shuttle called *The Dream Is Alive*, special material for the film *Apollo 13*, Benjamin Franklin's voice in the educational cartoon series *Liberty's Kids*, a CBS documentary about Guglielmo Marconi called *WCC Chatham Radio*, and an eight-part television series for the Discovery Channel called *Cronkite Remembers*. He also chaired the Interfaith Alliance for the protection of American faith and freedom; supported the world hunger organization Heifer International; was a major fund-raiser for Citizens for Global Solutions; and was honored with the Presidential Medal of Freedom, NASA's Ambassador of Exploration Award, and four Peabody Excellence in Broadcasting awards. He was also inducted into the Academy of Television Arts and Sciences Hall of Fame.

On July 17, 2009, Walter Cronkite died of cerebrovascular disease in his New York home at the age of ninety-two after a long, fulfilling life of unparalleled integrity.

From Francine

Walter is as happy and gratified to be Home as anyone we've ever seen, not because he was eager for his lifetime to end, but because he feels he used every minute of it the best he could and, he says, "made plenty of mistakes, but never one I didn't learn from." He emerged from the tunnel to find his wife, Betsy, a very small woman I believe was his grandmother, and a joyful pair of Springer spaniels waiting for him. He was fascinated by his time at the Scanning Machine, cherishing the life he lived, but utterly enthralled by the historic events he covered throughout his career. While reviewing his lifetime he also enjoyed remembering that his trademark newscast-ending phrase, "And that's the way it is . . ." was his unconscious homage to a phrase used by his employer when he worked as a British newspaper editor in the mid-1800s—his employer ended every staff meeting with the words, "So there you have it," and Walter loved the memory and the paraphrase he'd brought over from a previous lifetime.

Orientation wasn't necessary. Walter virtually sprinted away from the Scanning Machine, out of the Hall of Wisdom, and quickly found John and Robert Kennedy, Martin Luther King Jr., and the seven crew members of the space shuttle Challenger, *all of whose deaths affected him even more deeply than the many others he reported. And then, as he describes it, he quietly returned to business as usual on the Other Side. He's great friends with several past presidents, particularly Jefferson, Lincoln, and Eisenhower, and they actively study current world events and infuse what solutions manage to penetrate the egos of those in positions of power. He and Carl Sagan have resumed their passionate research into the infinite secrets of the universe and their lectures on future NASA explorations to those who will reincarnate and initiate many of those explorations. But his two favorite recreational pursuits are sailing and playing tennis with his old pal from Home, Peter Jennings.*

He wants his children and grandchildren to know that he and their mother are still taking good care of each other and watching over them together and that he considers them his greatest accomplishments.

Abraham Lincoln

A braham Lincoln, the sixteenth president of the United States, was born in a log cabin near Hodgenville, Kentucky, on February 12, 1809. His father, Thomas, was a farmer. His mother, Nancy, had a total of three children—Sarah, the eldest, Abraham, and Thomas, who died as an infant. The family moved to southern Indiana when Abraham was seven, and he was nine years old when his mother died. A year later Thomas married Sarah Bush Johnston, who brought three children of her own into the family. Abraham's stepmother was a loving, positive influence in his life, encouraging him to read and study, which quickly became two of his passions, and he more than made up for the fact that he had no more than about a year of formal education.

By the time he reached adulthood, he was a stately figure at almost six foot four and 180 pounds, impressing the residents of his new home in New Salem, Illinois, with his integrity, honesty, and strength of character in a succession of jobs that ranged from surveying to managing a store to serving as the local postmaster, appointed by President Andrew Jackson.

Lincoln enlisted for service in the Black Hawk War in 1832, and after his brief military career he was elected to the Illinois legislature from 1834 to 1842. In the meantime, he studied law, and in 1836 he was admitted to the bar. In 1846 he served in the U.S. House of Representatives, where his opposition to slavery became widely known in Washington. His national recognition grew with a series of debates with Stephen Douglas in 1858, when the two men competed for a seat in the U.S. Senate. Douglas won that seat, but when they ran against each other for public office two years later, Lincoln defeated Douglas and, in 1860, was elected president of the United States.

Accompanying Abraham Lincoln to his new home in the White House were his wife, Mary Todd Lincoln, and their three surviving sons, Robert, William (Willie), and Thomas (Tad). (Their second son, Edward, died in 1850, at the age of four, from tuberculosis.) Mary Todd, who'd had a privileged upbringing in Lexington, Kentucky, was introduced to the rising legal and political star named Abraham Lincoln in 1839, and they were married on November 4, 1842. She tirelessly campaigned for her husband and was a loving, devoted mother to their children, but when she acquired the title of First Lady, she took it upon herself to refurbish the White House to her own extravagant tastes, lavishly ignoring the budget Congress allocated to her for the project.

On February 20, 1862, less than a year after Lincoln was sworn in as president, Willie Lincoln, age eleven, died of typhoid fever, a tragedy from which Mary Todd never fully recovered. Lincoln, also grief-stricken, was in the midst of a national crisis. Shortly after his election, eleven southern states seceded from the Union, rejecting Lincoln's and the Republicans' control over the government. Lincoln's determination to save the Union led to the four-year Civil War, the most costly conflict in American history. In the end, he successfully reunited the North and South and, with his famous Emancipation Proclamation in 1862, began the process of freeing the slaves as well.

He was reelected in 1864, continuing his record of historic accomplishments that have inspired many to consider him the greatest president in U.S. history. He passed the Homestead Act, which allowed impoverished Easterners to obtain land in the West, helping to populate the Great Plains. His legislation created the nation's first transcontinental railroad, protected American manufacturing, and initiated a network of national banks. And he gave some of the most brilliant speeches ever written, including the Gettysburg Address, dedicating that battlefield to the soldiers who died there, and his second inaugural address, which ended with the beautiful passage: "With malice toward none, with charity for all, with firmness in the right as God gives us to see the right, let us strive on to finish the work we are in, to bind up the nation's wounds, to care for him who shall have borne the battle and for his widow and his orphan, to do all which may achieve and cherish a just and lasting peace among ourselves and with all nations."

He accomplished all of this and much more against a backdrop of deep personal difficulties—the loss of two of his sons during their childhoods, the increasing instability of his wife, and his own pervasive, lifelong battle with what was then called "profound melancholy," but what would now be diagnosed as clinical depression, which manifested itself in occasional talk of suicide, weeping in public, and a need for solitude.

On April 14, 1865, Abraham and Mary Todd Lincoln went to Ford's Theater to see a play called *Our American Cousin*. During the play an actor named John Wilkes Booth, a racist and sympathizer with the Confederacy, made his way into the president's box and shot him in the back of the head. Lincoln died the next day at 7:22 A.M., the first U.S. president to be assassinated. The nation mourned a brilliant, courageous, compassionate leader as Lincoln's body was taken by train to be buried in the Oak Ridge Cemetery in Springfield, Illinois.

From Francine

Like so many Mission Life Entities whose lifetimes end abruptly, Abraham arrived Home deeply depressed and disoriented, a combination of the shock of death and an exquisitely sensitive spirit who felt personally responsible for elevating the integrity of a harsh world. His life themes of Justice and Rescuer were ideal for the profound work he charted for himself. But his empathetic spirit, the same spirit that made it impossible for him to walk away from those who needed him, never knew the comfort of being able to emotionally separate itself from the pain, oppression, and injustice being inflicted on innocents in a country he loved. He couldn't end his own suffering until he ended theirs, which only escalated both his resolve and his pervasive sadness. He also talks about a time in his life when he was given medication for a stomach or intestinal problem, and until he became alarmed enough to stop taking it, it dramatically exacerbated his emotional fragility, for reasons he never understood. "My poor wife was having enough difficulties of her own without my adding to them," he says. "I will always regret the tension I caused in our household for her and for our sons, and I'm eternally grateful for the loyalty they afforded me in spite of myself."

A throng that extended as far as the eye could see gathered to meet Abraham when he arrived, and it's worth adding that he was already on the Other Side before his body had even been carried from the theater. With the exception of his sons Edward and Willie (his mother had already reincarnated), the crowd was populated exclusively with loved ones from Home—this incarnation was Abraham's first, and it will be his last. His Spirit Guide, Kabir, took him from his sons' arms to the cocooning chambers, where he stayed to heal for nearly a decade in your years.

Abraham has always been one of our most brilliant scholars and orators, and he immediately resumed his quietly joyful work when he emerged, thriving and at peace, from the Hall of Wisdom. He's a constant presence in the Hall of Records, expanding his expertise in world history and politics, and his lectures on those subjects are treasured events through-out the Other Side. And he's returned to his seat on an esteemed panel of political, spiritual, environmental, and scientific experts who regularly confer with our Council on ways to achieve healing and future health on your planet and then infuse their insights to those on earth who are dedi-cated and open-minded enough to enact them. Your President Obama is a frequent recipient of the panel's suggestions, and of Abraham's personal wisdom as well—it's impossible to put into human words the awe with which Abraham viewed the inauguration of an African American president of the United States.

He lives alone, as he always has, but it's interesting that he's chosen a spot for his small lean-to that precisely corresponds to his birthplace on earth. He's a devout Christian who regularly attends a magnificent church whose massive stained-glass windows were designed by Leonardo da Vinci. And while he never socializes, it makes us all smile that he and his four sons have become avid, enthusiastic baseball fans and never miss a game in which Joe DiMaggio is playing.

George Harrison

George Harrison was the "quiet Beatle," a historically gifted musician, singer, and songwriter, the youngest member of the Liverpool band that became one of the most influential musical phenomena of the twentieth century. He was born in Liverpool, England, on February 24, 1943, the fourth and last child of bus conductor Harold Harrison and his shopkeeper wife, Louise. After an early education at Dovedale Primary School, he headed on to the Liverpool Institute, where he was a disinterested, introverted student. After his mother scraped together the money to buy her fourteen-year-old son the acoustic guitar he'd wanted for so long, he promptly formed a skiffle band (improvisational, with a heavy use of such homemade instruments as washboards, spoons, and comb-and-tissue-paper "harmonicas") and began exploring his natural talent on the guitar. Somewhere along the line he happened to meet a fellow Institute student and bus mate named Paul McCartney, who had a skiffle band called the Quarrymen with his friend John Lennon, and despite John's concern that he was too young to join the group, George became the Quarrymen's guitarist.

The Quarrymen evolved into the Beatles and headed to Hamburg, Germany, for a series of appearances at the Kaiserkeller in 1960, a trip that was abbreviated by George's deportation for being underage. And then, in November 1961, a record shop owner named Brian Epstein came to see the Beatles at the Cavern Club in Liverpool; he became their manager, and the magic of Beatlemania took root and lasted through the 1960s with a body of work that had an unprecedented impact on music and the youth of the world. George's contributions as a songwriter were often overshadowed by those of his fellow Beatles John and Paul, but such distinctively "George" songs as "Something" and "Here Comes the Sun" have become undeniable classics.

In the mid-1960s George was introduced to the sitar and one of its masters, Ravi Shankar. As George's passion for East Indian music and culture grew, so did his interest in Hinduism and transcendental meditation. His fellow Beatles accompanied him to India to study with the Maharishi Mahesh Yogi, and he and John Lennon returned in 1969 to explore the Hare Krishna tradition, a sect of Hinduism that George embraced and practiced for the rest of his life.

Beginning in 1970 with the breakup of the Beatles, George launched a string of albums whose success diminished as the 1970s progressed. Without a doubt one of his most notable accomplishments of that decade occurred in August 1971, when he became one of the musicians to organize a charity concert, the massively successful Concert for Bangladesh, at which George and fellow superstars Ravi Shankar, Bob Dylan, Eric Clapton, Billy Preston, Leon Russell, and Ringo Starr, among others, raised more than $15 million for UNICEF efforts in that country and around the world.

George was wonderfully creative and diverse throughout the 1980s and 1990s, once he recovered from the shock of losing John Lennon in 1980 and wrote "All Those Years Ago" in his memory. He recorded albums with his friends Bob Dylan, Tom Petty, Jeff Lynne, and Roy Orbison as an almost spontaneously formed group who called themselves the Traveling Wilburys. His film company, HandMade Films, produced twenty-three movies, including Monty Python's *Life of Brian*. He recorded with one of his idols, rockabilly pioneer Carl Perkins. He toured Japan with his old friend Eric

Clapton, whom George also referred to as his "husband-in-law"—George's first wife, Patti Boyd, to whom he was married from 1966 until 1977, was subsequently married to Eric Clapton from 1979 until 1988. He performed at charity concerts at Royal Albert Hall and Madison Square Garden. He appeared in Tom Petty's "I Won't Back Down" music video, was a guest musician on friends' albums, and continued producing albums of his own. And last but certainly not least among his post-Beatles accomplishments, he married Olivia Arias in 1978, a marriage that lasted until his death. Their son, Dhani, also born in 1978, is a successful musician today, with a look and a voice that are eerily reminiscent of those of his father.

In the late 1990s George began a series of battles with cancer, starting with throat cancer in 1997 and progressing to lung cancer, for which he underwent surgery at the Mayo Clinic in 2001. In the summer of that same year he began receiving radiation treatments for a brain tumor. He'd already curtailed public appearances at the end of 1999, after a crazed fan who believed George's spirit had possessed him broke into his home in England and attacked him, stabbing him seven times. By the time cancer overtook him, he was rarely seen outside his Hollywood Hills mansion, where he quietly passed away on November 29, 2001. According to Hindu tradition, his closest family members gathered for a private ceremony to scatter George's ashes in the sacred Ganges River.

From Francine

How appropriate that George's family followed Hindu tradition in his honor—he was a devout East Indian Hindu in the only other incarnation he lived on earth, which is why India, transcendental meditation, yogis, and the sitar struck such responsive, familiar chords in his soul. His previ-

ous life in India was a quiet, modest one, devoted to farming and raising his eight children with his wife, Marathi, whom he married again in this life in her current incarnation as Olivia Arias. He inherited his love of gardening and landscaping from that lifetime, giving thanks as he did every day in India to the generous earth, which provided nourishment to his family, and he's one of our most esteemed, creative horticulturists and teachers on that subject.

He was welcomed Home by a massive crowd of admirers, including a historic group of gurus, and it speaks volumes for our priorities here that, while George's music is widely known and appreciated, the word "Beatles" had nothing to do with the joy with which he was greeted, nor is it often mentioned. It's very much worth mentioning, though, that John Lennon was among the first to embrace him. They're frequently together, meditating in the Gardens of the Hall of Justice and taking long, quiet walks through what corresponds to your English countryside. But while John continues to compose and perform music, George plays the acoustic guitar, sitar, and mandolin only in the privacy of his secluded, windowless one-room cottage in the hills, a round adobe structure with a shrine centered inside. He still writes songs, but only to share with other Hindus at the temple where he practices his public worship.

He says he charted his part in the phenomenon of the Beatles, because he and the other three were kindred souls from Home, different from each other as they were, and made that contract for extraordinary success together before they incarnated. George knew they would create music together that would bring lasting joy to vast numbers of people and, in doing so, "help unify the world a little." He also knew it would provide him with a platform he would never have achieved on his own, not to loudly preach an agenda, but to quietly, by example, encourage the pursuit of individual spiritual growth.

George is a highly advanced soul, on the path to becoming a great guru in the tradition of his own treasured guru, the Maharishi Mahesh Yogi, who is now among us and is one of his most constant companions. George is as introverted, contemplative, and filled with light here as he was on earth. He says of his wife and son nothing more and nothing less than, "I am with them always." And to the world he left behind, but for which he continues to pray, he offers a peaceful "Namaste," which he roughly translates to mean, "The God in me greets the God in you."

Katharine Hepburn

Legendary actress Katharine Hepburn was born on May 12, 1907, in Hartford, Connecticut. Her father, Thomas, was a highly respected physician. Her mother, Katharine, was a suffragette whose outspoken rebellious liberalism was undoubtedly a model for young Katharine's insistence on marching to her own distinctive drummer throughout her life. She was one of six children, and her early years were marred by the tragedy of finding her older brother, Tom, to whom she was very close, hanging from the attic rafters. (Whether it was an accident or a suicide has never been clear.) Katharine, only fourteen at the time, sank into a depression that led to her being primarily home-schooled for the remainder of her high-school years.

She graduated from Bryn Mawr College determined to become an actress and was soon appearing in minor roles on Broadway, which ultimately led to her first film, *A Bill of Divorcement* with John Barrymore, in 1932. She was promptly put under contract by RKO, made five films in the next two years, and won her first Oscar as Best Actress in 1933 for her work in *Morning Glory*.

In 1928 she married a Philadelphia broker and socialite named Ludlow Ogden Smith, which seemed to solidify her antipathy toward the traditions of marriage and motherhood. By all accounts, including her own, she was too unconventional and independent to be a successful wife and too career-oriented to be a successful mother, and the couple divorced in 1934.

Neither Hollywood nor the moviegoing public could quite figure out whether they were attracted to or repelled by the aristocratic, athletic, unorthodox Katharine Hepburn. She was completely disinterested in giving interviews, attending the right parties, and following such other traditional studio rules as never being seen in slacks or without makeup. By 1938 audiences seemed to be steering away from her films, and she headed back to New York to star in a Broadway show called *The Philadelphia Story*. Not only was the play a success, but Katharine was shrewd enough to buy the film rights, forcing Hollywood to welcome her back and meet her demands in the process. Her eccentric, elegant, beautiful charm in the film version of *The Philadelphia Story*, surrounded by her personally selected costars James Stewart and Cary Grant, reformed her status from "box-office poison" to "bankable" and led to her third Oscar nomination.

Her life changed inalterably in 1942, when she starred in *Woman of the Year*. Her costar was the superbly gifted, iconic Spencer Tracy. The powerful chemistry between them kept them together onscreen for a total of nine films and offscreen for a romance that lasted until Spencer's death shortly after the making of their last film together, the classic *Guess Who's Coming to Dinner*, in 1967. Katharine's relationship with Spencer was as nontraditional as almost every other aspect of her life—as a Catholic, he would have betrayed his religion by divorcing his wife, so Tracy and Hepburn simply proceeded by their own rules without the "technicality" of a marriage license.

In the 1970s, with eleven Academy Award nominations and three Oscars to her credit, Katharine began to include TV movies in her long list of credits and won an Emmy in 1975 for her performance in *Love Among the Ruins* with Laurence Olivier. Her fourth Oscar followed in 1981 for *On Golden Pond*. She continued working until the mid-1990s, when her escalating battle with Parkinson's disease demanded her retirement from her career and public life. Katharine

Hepburn passed to the Other Side on June 29, 2003, in Old Say-brook, Connecticut, at the age of ninety-six.

From Francine

The look of joyful shock on Katharine's face when she emerged from the tunnel was touching enough, but finding her father, her brother Tom, and Spencer Tracy waiting to welcome her so overwhelmed her that she did nothing but silently hold them for a very, very long time. During a lifetime lived very much "in the moment," headstrong and practical, she wasted no energy wondering what was around the next corner or over the next hill, but instead focused intently on her immediate surroundings and what if anything needed to be tended to, so it was consistent with that approach that she believed, "When you're dead, you're dead." She referred to herself as an atheist or occasionally as an agnostic, but she also counted kindness, integrity, and lending a hand to those in need among her priorities, and in God's eyes how we live is far more significant than the rhetoric we use.

One of the most rare and interesting aspects of Katharine's most recent lifetime is that she and her soul mate charted themselves to incarnate together. Since soul mates spend an eternity together on the Other Side, they usually choose to incarnate separately for their brief trips to earth. But Katharine Hepburn and Spencer Tracy mutually agreed that they could help further each other's purposes if they spent part of their last lives on earth together as well, and with Katharine's unique life themes of Warrior and Loner, her charting of their unapologetic unconventional relationship, designed to include frequent separations, was inspired. She also, by the way, charted her brother from a past life as her father in this most recent life, and her son from a past life to be her brother Tom, which explains why his death was so especially devastating to her.

She and Spencer live together at the sea, as they always have and always will. Katharine works side by side with her father as a medical researcher, specializing in neurological disorders. (She is adamant, by the way, about the fact that, contrary to popular belief, the neurological problems she encountered later in life had nothing to do with Parkinson's disease.) They're currently developing a cure for epilepsy, which they plan to infuse to a research team in Sweden, who will announce a major breakthrough in 2019 by your years. She is also an avid golfer—Christopher Reeve is her favorite partner—and a master gardener. While we're able to create gardens here through simple thought projection, Katharine loves "the feeling of my hands in soil," and she's grown a blanket of fragrant ivory flowers that covers her and Spencer's beach home like a great cloak.

Her one regret about her most recent lifetime is the pain she caused by marrying despite the fact that she knew herself too well to make any such commitment. Professionally, she has no regrets about her insistence on ignoring the "studio system," which would have stripped her of her individuality "and therefore my very soul," and the role in which she took the greatest pride was her performance in Long Day's Journey into Night.

There is no one she visits on earth. She's learned that Spencer often visited her after he died, both when he was earthbound and after he'd transcended and become a spirit. "I kept hearing and seeing things and thought it was an intruder, and I'm not about to besiege my loved ones with that same annoyance," she explains. Nor, she adds with a radiant smile, is she any more sentimental in the bliss of Home than she was on earth, taking the position that "we'll all be together again soon enough." There is, however, a place there that she and Spencer occasionally visit together. She describes it as a very private courtyard, hidden in a square of brownstones in New York, where she and Spencer spent some of their most peaceful days together. He was ill and frail, confined to a wheelchair, and they would sit beneath a tree; she would read to him and feed him soup, and they would talk and quietly laugh, with no one around to disturb the intimacy of their treasured solitude. If any of you on earth know where that courtyard might be, watch for them there, listen for their whispered voices, and appreciate that you're being given a glimpse of your own immortality.

Brittany Murphy

An actress who seemed to pack a few lifetimes into her brief thirty-two years on earth this time around, Brittany Anne Murphy was born on November 10, 1977, in Atlanta. Her mother, Sharon Murphy, divorced her father, Angelo Bertolotti, when Brittany was two years old, and she was raised by her mother. Sharon and her baby daughter moved to Edison, New Jersey, where Brittany began performing at the age of two and starred in a regional production of the musical *Really Rosie* when she was nine years old. She was thirteen when her mother agreed to move to Los Angeles, so that Brittany could pursue her acting career in a more promising city, and the relocation immediately proved profitable when she landed her first television job on the sitcom *Blossom*. A supporting role on a short-lived Fox sitcom called *Drexell's Class* followed, as did a steady stream of other television appearances on such series as *Almost Home*, *Frasier*, *Party of Five*, and *Boy Meets World*. Through the course of her career she added TV movies to her resume, particularly *The Devil's Arithmetic*, *David and Lisa*, *Megafault*, and *Tribute*, and her talent as a voice actor won her the role of Luanne Platter on the long-running animated show *King of the Hill*.

She inevitably found her way to the big screen, where she starred in a variety of hit films, including *Clueless*, *Girl Interrupted*, and *Drop Dead Gorgeous*. She became a favorite of writer-director Edward

Burns, who cast her in *Sidewalks of New York* and *The Groomsmen*, and she costarred with her real-life boyfriend Ashton Kutcher in *Just Married* in 2003, a film whose success outlasted the tabloid-favored relationship, which ended shortly after the movie was released.

Her private life remained turbulent for a while, with two broken engagements in 2005 and 2006, but in 2007 she found happiness through her marriage to British writer Simon Monjack. In the meantime, her career continued to show great promise—she provided the voice for Gloria the penguin in the charming 2006 hit feature *Happy Feet*, gave an especially wonderful performance in 2008's comedy-drama *The Ramen Girl*, and completed the thriller *Abandoned* in 2009. But in late 2009, rumors of drug use and unprofessional behavior spread, and there was added concern over what appeared to be a sudden and shocking weight loss.

On December 20, 2009, she collapsed in the Los Angeles home she shared with her husband and her mother. Paramedics' efforts to resuscitate her failed, and at the age of thirty-two Brittany Murphy was pronounced dead on arrival at Cedars-Sinai Medical Center of an apparent cardiac arrest. According to the coroner who performed the autopsy, the cause of death was a combination of pneumonia, anemia, and both prescription and over-the-counter drugs. In her short life she completed an amazing thirty-seven films, six television movies, and, including her voice work on *King of the Hill*, almost three hundred TV series episodes, and loved ones and critics alike agree that she was just getting started.

From Francine

Brittany didn't chart a lengthy incarnation for herself this most recent time around, which is why she approached her personal and professional lives almost compulsively since childhood. Her chosen life themes of Experiencer and Catalyst were perfectly suited to her determination to telescope as much as possible into her abbreviated lifetime, and as with so many Experiencers, it felt natural to her to be occasionally undiscerning to the point of excess. As happens to all of us when we're Home again, she became fully conscious of her immortality and clearly remembered her two past lives— one in the late 1600s, when she was born prematurely and died in infancy from underdeveloped lungs, and a second from 1769 until 1852, in which she lived a long, harsh, cruel life as a slave in Virginia. It's not uncommon for those who've been confined in one incarnation to, let's say, overcompensate as Experiencers in their next lifetime and have trouble knowing when, where, and how to draw the line.

It's interesting too to notice how cell memory from her previous death in infancy affected her health in this most recent incarnation, as her body remembered those underdeveloped lungs and the resulting heart problems from oxygen deprivation (she talks of having had several severe heart murmurs) and recreated them so effectively that she was unable to successfully overcome pneumonia and the lethal combination of medications she believed were helping her.

Those who knew her well sometimes referred to her as a "young soul." In a way she was, but this is a commonly misunderstood term. All souls are eternal. We were all created by God an eternity ago, and we will all live eternally. Those souls you perceive as "young" are simply less experienced on earth than those "old" souls, who have incarnated many times. It's perfectly natural that Brittany, who was only on her third incarnation, often struck those around her as being oddly unworldly for someone who "on paper" seemed so experienced.

Brittany is a somewhat unique being here at Home in that she's stayed very much to herself since she arrived and continues to look rather thin and haggard at a time when most spirits have begun the process of healing. It seems that she's already made the decision to reincarnate and has been having preliminary audiences with the Council for its guidance in designing a chart that will act as what she refers to as "the hair of the dog that bit me"—she believes that her spirit will benefit most from a quick return to earth and a fresh start. All she seems certain of at the moment is that she will incarnate as a female, live in Portugal, and find peace in a life she describes as "exquisitely unremarkable."

James Dean

The brilliant, complex, and iconic actor James Dean, who managed to become a legend through a career that only lasted three short years, was born James Byron Dean on February 8, 1931, in Marion, Indiana. His father, Winton, was a dental technician. His mother, Mildred, was particularly close to her only child and yearned that he become a performer someday, seeing to it that he began learning tap dancing and the violin before he started kindergarten. Winton Dean moved with his wife and son to Santa Monica, California, when James was six years old. Three years later, in July 1940, Mildred died of cancer, and Winton, unable to care for James, sent him back to Indiana to live with his sister and brother-in-law, Ortense and Marcus Winslow, in Fairmount. James's years in the Winslows' Quaker household were fairly happy and unremarkable, filled with school, baseball, basketball, swimming, and drama classes.

He graduated from Fairmount High School on May 16, 1949, packed a bag and his beagle, Max, and moved back to California to live with his father and stepmother. After briefly focusing on prelaw at Santa Monica College, James followed his heart and transferred to UCLA to major in drama, signing up for additional classes at actor James Whitmore's esteemed acting workshops. He dropped out of UCLA in July 1951 to devote all his energy to the pursuit of his career. His first professional appearances included a Pepsi commercial, an Easter television special called *Hill Number One*, bit parts in the films *Fixed Bayonets* and *Has Anybody Seen My Gal?*, and a few lines of dialogue in the Dean Martin–Jerry Lewis comedy *Sailors Beware*. To help make ends meet, he was a parking lot attendant at CBS Studios.

With the encouragement of James Whitmore, James moved to New York in October 1951 and appeared in several television series until he was admitted to the most prestigious theater school of its time, the Actors Studio, where he studied method acting under the great Lee Strasberg. His career escalated, with more television appearances and theater work, leading to his role on Broadway in *The Immortalist* in 1954.

It was James's performance in *The Immortalist* that led director Elia Kazan to cast him as Cal Trask, the dark, emotionally troubled teenager in 1955's *East of Eden*. His on-set behavior included changing the interpretation of his character at any given moment and challenging his cast mates, but his performance was so mesmerizing that he received an Academy Award nomination for his first leading role in a motion picture.

He was immediately hired to play Jim Stark, a defiantly sensitive teenage misfit aching to belong in the 1955 film *Rebel Without a Cause*, costarring Sal Mineo, Dennis Hopper, and Natalie Wood. His brilliant interpretation of this complicated character raised him to heroic status among a young generation that related to Jim Stark's angry desperation to be understood and accepted. James won the Best Actor Academy Award for *Rebel Without a Cause*—the first posthumous Oscar in Academy Awards history, as it turned out. His next and final film was *Giant,* with Rock Hudson and Elizabeth Taylor. James completed the film, but died before it was edited, and he received another Best Actor Oscar nomination posthumously in 1956, the year the film was released.

Throughout the tragically brief course of his film career, James had begun buying himself a succession of cars with which to pursue his love of racing. He raced his Porsche 356 Speedster in Palm Springs, Bakersfield, and Santa Monica while filming *East of Eden*, then traded the Speedster for a Porsche 550 Spyder during *Rebel Without a Cause*. His *Giant* contract prohibited him from racing, but when his work on that film had wrapped, he was free to compete in races taking place in Salinas, California. Legend has it that on September 23, 1955, the distinguished British actor Alex Guinness told James that the Porsche Spyder looked "sinister" and warned him, "If you get in that car, you will be found dead in it by this time next week."

Seven days later, on September 30, 1955, James Dean, driving west on what is now state route 46 near Cholame, California, collided head-on with a 1950 Ford Custom Tudor coupe and was pronounced dead on arrival at Paso Robles War Memorial Hospital at 5:59 P.M., at the age of twenty-four. Contrary to decades of rumor, the officer on the scene noted that there was no indication that James was speeding at the time of the collision. He was buried in Fairmount, Indiana, after a funeral attended by three thousand people. To this day more than fifty thousand attend a festival in Fairmount dedicated to James Dean and held on the anniversary of his death, and *Forbes Magazine* estimates that his estate continues to earn approximately $5 million a year.

From Francine

James came Home at the exact instant of the collision and, he says, never felt a thing. He was greeted by a thrilled herd of animals, including his beloved Max, by his mother, and by a throng of friends from the Other Side. (Animals always are the first to arrive at reunions, by the way.) There were no friends from James's previous incarnations, for the interesting reason that James had no previous incarnations. His brief lifetime as James Dean was his first trip to earth, which explains why he didn't seem to live his life; he seemed to devour it. Because everything was new to him and he chose Experiencer as his primary theme (with a secondary theme of Loner), he had very few boundaries and tireless curiosity. In his words, "You name it, I wanted to try it. Acting? Great! Drugs? Great! Sex? Great! Racing? Great! I didn't intend to hang around for very long anyway, so saying no honestly just didn't occur to me."

He came away from the Scanning Machine shaking his head in amazement at his years on earth, the good and the bad. One of the many things he marveled at was that he had any career at all, not due to a lack of talent—he was pleased with his performances—but due to some of his behavior. He mentioned a television audition early in his career when he actually dozed off while meeting with the casting director. "She was such a nice woman that she assumed I was exhausted from bartending till all hours of the night. I didn't have the heart to break it to her that I was falling asleep because I was stoned." As for his sexuality, he never grasped the concept that his career could be compromised by it one way or the other. "If I wanted to have sex with someone and they wanted to have sex with me, I didn't see why it mattered." He also carefully studied his deep sensitivity, which he felt often manifested itself in moodiness and the occasional need to "shut everyone out," typical of the Loner theme. "I showed up with no calluses, from never having been there before," is his way of putting it. "I was easy to bruise, and I didn't always handle it well. I'll do better next time." In other words, he does intend to reincarnate, in 2017. He'll be an actor again, but next time he wants to "work hard, play it safe, have a wife and kids, and live till I'm ninety."

He had no need for Orientation or cocooning and instead immediately returned to his happy, busy life here, which he says will come as no surprise to anyone—he's a valued member of one of our teams of engine designers, developing motor vehicles fueled by something to do with common crops that will produce no pollutants and make farming a reliably successful vocation again. He's resumed the acting classes that prepared him for his incarnation as James Dean, taught by an actor named William Rowley, he's a voracious reader of historical biographies, and he loves horseback *riding on the trails near his Craftsman-style house in the mountains, where he lives alone.*

He was among the first to welcome Home his old friends Natalie Wood, Rock Hudson, and Sal Mineo, and he wants his friends in Indiana to know that he never misses the Fairmount festival.

Sammy Davis Jr.

Often called the "world's greatest entertainer," singer, actor, dancer, and impressionist Samuel George Davis Jr. was born in Harlem, New York, on December 8, 1925, to vaudeville dancers Elvera Sanchez and Sammy Davis Sr. His parents separated when he was three years old, and his father, not wanting to lose custody of him, made the tiny tap dancer a part of his act with vaudevillian Will Mastin and swept him away on tour. The child was such a hit with audiences that "Silent Sam, the Dancing Midget," as he was originally billed at the age of three, became a key part of the head-line act—"Will Mastin's Gang Featuring Little Sammy." In 1941 the Mastin Gang was the opening act for the Tommy Dorsey orchestra at the Michigan Theater in Detroit, where sixteen-year-old dancer Sammy Davis Jr. first met Dorsey's twenty-six-year-old vocalist Frank Sinatra, and a lifelong friendship took root.

In 1943 Sammy, accustomed to a life of applause and acceptance, joined the U.S. Army and encountered racial prejudice for the first time. Between his color and his small size, he endured regular harass-ment and fights with the white soldiers in his unit, until he became an entertainer with the integrated Special Services and discovered that the spotlight provided some protection from bigotry. Another bonus from his army years was the African American sergeant who finally taught him to read.

After he'd fulfilled his tour of duty, he rejoined his father and "Uncle" Will on the road; the group was renamed the Will Mastin Trio. By then Sammy had discovered his talent for impersonations, and with the act now including singing, dancing, and comedy, they enjoyed a whole new surge of popularity, headlining at such important venues as the Capitol Club in New York and Hollywood's legendary Ciro's. Sammy's old pal Frank Sinatra was there to help, inviting the trio to perform at the Copacabana, which had just become integrated. In 1954 Sammy signed a recording contract with Decca Records and released his first hit album, *Starring Sammy Davis Jr.*

That same year, on November 19, 1954, Sammy was returning from Las Vegas to Los Angeles when he was involved in a near-fatal car accident that cost him his left eye, which was replaced with a glass eye that he wore for the rest of his life. While he was hospitalized after the accident, one visitor was entertainer Eddie Cantor, who began talking to him at length about the similarities between Jewish and black cultures. Sammy began studying Judaism and converted a few years later. He emerged more popular than ever from his highly publicized brush with death and provided Decca with a string of hit singles that included such classics as "Something's Got to Give" and "That Old Black Magic."

His conversion to Judaism was only part of the controversy in Sammy's life. During the 1950s and 1960s Sammy had become a very popular ladies' man in Hollywood, and many of his relationships were interracial—a major taboo at that time. Among his girlfriends was the very blonde, very successful actress Kim Novak, who was under contract to Columbia Studios. Harry Cohn, head of Columbia, wasn't about to risk the reputation of his rising starlet or his studio by allowing the affair to continue, and, legend has it, he recruited his mobster friend Johnny Roselli to kidnap Sammy for a few hours to demonstrate that when Harry Cohn said, "Break up with Kim Novak or else," he meant it.

Sammy hit Broadway in 1956, starring in more than four hundred performances of the hit show *Mr. Wonderful,* and he returned to the big screen for a critically acclaimed role in *Porgy and Bess.* After a quick one-year marriage to singer Loray White in 1958, Sammy found himself entering an alliance that, in various configurations, would last him the rest of his life. In 1959 he became a member of what came to be known as the "Rat Pack," the small, elite group of fellow performers Frank Sinatra, Dean Martin, Peter Lawford, and Joey Bishop, who shared the stage as headliners in the most popular nightclubs around the country and went on to make three hit films together in the 1960s—*Ocean's Eleven, Sergeants Three,* and *Robin and the Seven Hoods.*

Sammy also continued his career as a solo act, becoming a superstar in Las Vegas in the late 1950s at a time when hotels were still segregated. Black performers were welcome onstage, but they had no dressing rooms, they were banned from the casinos and restaurants, and they were certainly not allowed to stay at the venues where they were headlining, usually being shipped off to boarding houses away from the Strip. Once Sammy had achieved true star status, he began refusing to perform at segregated establishments and was instrumental in integrating hotels, casinos, and nightclubs across the country.

He caused even more controversy when, in 1960, he married the Swedish actress May Britt, at a time when interracial marriages were illegal in thirty-one states; even while he was busy winning a Tony nomination for his brilliant performance in Broadway's *Golden Boy* in 1964, he was receiving hate mail for marrying a white woman. The couple had a daughter together and adopted two sons. In the meantime, Sammy's career was in full force. Between recording sessions, live performances from Miami to Las Vegas, shooting his own television specials, and appearing with the Rat Pack, by his own admission he was an absentee husband and father, and the marriage ended in divorce in 1968. Two years later he married dancer Altovise Gore, whom he met during the run of *Golden Boy*, and their marriage lasted for the rest of his life.

His film career continued to thrive in the 1960s, with *A Man Called Adam* and *Sweet Charity* rounding out his roles with the Rat Pack, and he enjoyed television success with *The Sammy Davis Jr. Show* and *The Swinging World of Sammy Davis Jr.* Sadly, both his physical and financial health were pushed to their limits by the seemingly nonstop drinking, partying, and heavy spending that defined the general Rat Pack lifestyle. By the early 1970s, despite earning more than $1 million a year, he was nearly bankrupt and began developing liver and kidney problems. He never slowed down, seemingly couldn't stand still, and continued his Las Vegas appearances, recording his surprise hit "Candy Man," guest-starring on a variety of TV series and specials, and returning to Broadway in 1978 to star in the musical *Stop the World—I Want to Get Off*. He took time out for reconstructive hip surgery in 1985 and managed to recover in time to costar with fellow dancer Gregory Hines in the film *Tap*.

Shortly after *Tap* was completed, Sammy announced that he had finally beaten long-rumored addictions to cocaine and alcohol, and he seemed reenergized when, in 1988, he launched a concert tour with Frank Sinatra and Dean Martin. When Dean fell ill and was unable to complete the tour, Liza Minnelli took Dean's place, and Sinatra, Davis, and Minnelli performed for sold-out crowds throughout the United States and Europe through the beginning of 1989.

In August 1989 doctors found a tumor in Sammy's throat. He immediately underwent a series of grueling treatments, and for a short time his prognosis was optimistic. By the end of the year, though, his cancer had returned, and on May 16, 1990, Sammy Davis Jr. died at the age of sixty-four, leaving behind a legendary career and a world that was less divided by race than it was when he entered it.

From Francine

Sammy's father, his "Uncle" Will, and a very thin older black woman named Ella were among the throngs that gathered to welcome Sammy when he returned to the Other Side, and he immediately swept Ella into his arms and danced with her, so elated to find himself free of the painful, debilitated body he describes as having "used up" during his latest incarnation. (Sammy's mother had already incarnated again by the time he came Home.) Ella and Sammy's Spirit Guide, Aaron, accompanied him to the doors of the Hall of Wisdom and then left him alone for his time at the Scanning Machine, from which he walked away disheartened—as proud as he was of his massive talent, his work ethic, the loyalty he showed to his closest friends, and above all the giant strides he made toward making the world as color-blind as he was, he was deeply disturbed by the self-indulgence with which he chose to live his life offstage. By his own description, "When you stay as busy as I did and party hard enough, you get to avoid thinking about consequences."

But as he watched his lifetime unfold, he saw exactly how inevitable the consequences were, whether he thought about them at the time or not, from his occasional deep depressions to his financial struggles to the abuse of his body and the toll it took. For many reasons, he's decided to incarnate again, in or around 2016 by your years. He wants to experience a lifetime in which he invests his energy in discipline, anonymity, and restraint. He intends to choose the same life themes he chose for this last incarnation—Caretaker and Catalyst—but he'll direct them toward the medical community next time, with a focus on pediatrics.

An interesting incident occurred when actor Richard Harris arrived on the Other Side. Sammy made a point of being among the first to greet him, and Richard seemed quite moved and relieved. From what I understand, it had something to do with a medallion of some kind that Sammy gave to Richard, but that Richard returned with a harsh note when the infamous photograph of Sammy embracing Richard Nixon was published.

Sammy, with no explanation, never spoke to Richard again. And Richard, who was drinking heavily at the time he returned the medallion, had no memory of having returned it and never understood why Sammy had stopped speaking to him. They're close friends here, and Sammy observed that the lesson is, "Communicate! If I'd simply told him he'd offended me, we could have talked it through and enjoyed all those years together, instead of wasting them in my silent resentment of what turned out to be just a foolish drunken impulse."

Sammy's life here is blissfully active. He continues to be as popular a performer as he was on earth, often appearing onstage with Michael Jackson, to whom he's very close, and with Dean Martin, who was his brother in two past incarnations and whom he joyfully greeted when Dean came Home. In anticipation of his next incarnation he's also a devoted researcher on the subjects of cystic fibrosis and childhood autism.

He visits his biological and adopted children, "making up for lost time," as he says, and he calls himself "a regular" in the clubs on Bourbon Street, particularly the Jazz Preservation Hall. And he can often be found in his favorite synagogue, offering silent prayers of thanks and celebration for all he's been given and all he has left to give.

Madalyn Murray O'Hair

Madalyn Murray O'Hair proudly wore and encouraged the title of the "most hated woman in America," and her death was, in many ways, as shocking as the life she lived. An avowed atheist, she was born Madalyn Mays on April 13, 1919, in Pittsburgh. Her Presbyterian parents, John and Lena Mays, had her baptized into their faith when she was an infant. After graduating from high school in Rossford, Ohio, where the financially struggling family had moved to live with Lena's brother, she married steelworker John Henry Roths in 1941, but they separated when they both enlisted to serve in World War II. He joined the Marine Corps, while she joined the Women's Army Corps and was assigned to a position in Italy, where, in 1945, she began an affair with William J. Murray Jr. Murray was an army officer. He was also a married Catholic, and although his religion prevented him from divorcing his wife, he and Madalyn conceived a child. She divorced John Roths, adopted the name Madalyn Murray, and gave birth to a son whom she named William J. Murray after his biological father.

After her military service ended, she returned to the United States with her child, graduated with a bachelor's degree from Ohio's Ashland University, and received a law degree from South Texas College of Law in 1952, but she failed the bar exam and never practiced law. Instead, she was hired by an airplane manufacturing plant, where she met and had an affair with Michael Fiorillo, a fellow employee, whom she never married, but their son, Jon Garth Murray, was born on November 16, 1954.

Madalyn joined the Socialist Labor Party in 1956, savoring her role as a relentlessly outspoken activist at marches and protests. This affiliation led her to take her two young sons to Europe with the intention of gaining citizenship in the Soviet Union. Her request was denied, and in 1960 she and her children returned to the United States, settling in Baltimore.

It was in 1960 that Madalyn Murray, now an avowed atheist, took great exception to the fact that her son Bill was being "subjected to" Bible readings at school, declaring it unconstitutional and filing suit against the Baltimore Public School System. After a long, complicated series of court rulings, Madalyn, armed with her considerable IQ and law degree and enjoying the spotlight at the top of her lungs, managed to propel her lawsuit all the way to the Supreme Court, which, in 1963, voted 8–1 in her favor, effectively ending prayer and Bible reading in American schools. The decision gained a lot of national media attention and outrage, and Madalyn's sons and other family members became flashpoints for that anger while she reveled in her newfound notoriety.

Her highly publicized success with the Supreme Court inspired her to participate in a variety of other "separation of church and state" causes, from an unsuccessful effort to challenge the tax-exempt status of churches to an equally unsuccessful lawsuit against NASA to declare it unconstitutional for American astronauts to broadcast prayers and Bible readings from space. Before long she managed to alienate not only much of the country, but also one of her own sons. Bill, a born-again Christian and preacher, eventually broke all ties with her and his half brother, Jon, who'd become one of her most ardent followers.

In 1965 Madalyn Murray married a Marine named Richard O'Hair, who presided over a pro–free thought, pro-atheist organization called the Society of Separationists. She took charge of the organization after his death in 1978. In the meantime, she founded the American Atheist Center and the American Atheist Press in Austin, Texas, both of which were created for the purpose of uniting practicing atheists and providing them with reliable information with which to support their beliefs. Before long her profane, controversial, combative persona was recognized by the entertainment media for, if nothing else, its guaranteed ability to draw attention and ratings, and she was soon giving interviews to *Playboy* magazine and appearing on national talk shows. She lectured at Dartmouth, Harvard, and UCLA and even became *Hustler* magazine founder Larry Flynt's "chief speechwriter" in his resoundingly unsuccessful presidential campaign in 1984. She also produced and hosted her own syndicated radio and television shows promoting atheism.

In 1986 Madalyn decided to retire and handed over the reins of the Society of Separationists and the multimillion-dollar American Atheists offices to her son Jon. Jon was not a popular leader, and many chapters began seceding from the Austin headquarters. Remaining local and state chapters were abandoned in 1991.

In the meantime, Madalyn had long since adopted her granddaughter Robin, William's daughter, and Madalyn, Jon, and Robin had become literally inseparable. They lived together, they worked together, they vacationed together, and, thanks to Madalyn's fiercely territorial control over Jon's and Robin's lives, neither of them ever dated or strayed far from Madalyn's side.

On August 27, 1995, the three of them suddenly and mysteriously vanished. A half-eaten meal was found on the dining table. Imperative medications were left throughout the house. The family's much adored dogs were abandoned with no arrangements made to care for them. A note was left on the locked office door of the American Atheists headquarters stating that the family had been called out of town on an emergency and had no idea how long they'd be gone. A handful of phone calls from Madalyn, Jon, and Robin over the next month only added to the mystery. They claimed that they were in San Antonio on business. Jon ordered $600,000 worth of gold coins from a San Antonio jeweler, but only collected $500,000 worth before disappearing again. Both Jon and Robin called various friends to claim that nothing was wrong, although they offered no explanation for their absence, and they reportedly sounded disturbed, stressed, and exhausted. The last communication from the Murray O'Hairs came on September 28, 1995.

An investigation finally focused on a convicted felon named David Waters, whom Madalyn had hired to work for American Atheists. In 1995 he pleaded guilty to the theft of $54,000 from the organization, and Madalyn wrote an article in her newsletter giving his lengthy rap sheet, which included a vicious assault on his own mother. The article reportedly enraged him, and law enforcement began pursuing a belief that Waters and an accomplice named Danny Fry had kidnapped, extorted money from, and then murdered Madalyn, Jon, and Robin.

That belief became fact when, in January 2001, David Waters, as a result of a plea deal, led police to a Texas ranch where the severed remains of the three Murray O'Hairs were buried. Waters was convicted of kidnapping, robbery, and murder and died in prison on January 27, 2003.

From Francine

The surprise is not that Madalyn went immediately through the Left Door and right back in utero again. The surprise is why. It has nothing to do with the fact that she was an atheist. Atheists who live lives of integrity, kindness, compassion, and sincerity are as welcome on the Other Side as the most devout Christians. What sent Madalyn through the Left Door was that her life was mean-spirited, cruel, dishonest, intensely narcissistic, and, it's important to add, devoid of any psychological or physiological challenges; and all of these traits were entirely her choice, calculated and deliberate. The fact that I can't see her chart means that this wasn't her first dark lifetime or her first trip through the Left Door. Whether it will be her last is completely up to her, although she's not off to an encouraging start.

In June 1996 Madalyn reincarnated. She returned as a male, born near the western mountains of the Ukraine. Her name is now Leon or Leonid. I don't know the last name, nor would I reveal it if I did. Her parents are fine, hardworking people who cannot understand why Leonid, the youngest of their four children, has grown up hateful, rebellious, dishonest, and already involved in criminal activity, while his siblings would make any parent proud.

With no chart, no Spirit Guide, no acceptance of input from the Other Side at all, it's impossible to forecast what lies ahead for this lifetime. But as with every dark entity that recycles through the Left Door again and again and again, we're vigilantly watching for an opportunity to reach out in mid-cycle and bring this soul Home into a Light so sacred and powerfully loving that no darkness can survive in its presence.

Bette Davis

The incomparable actress Bette Davis was born Ruth Elizabeth Davis on April 5, 1908, in Lowell, Massachusetts. Her parents divorced when she was ten years old, and from that point on she and her younger sister, Barbara, were raised by their mother, Ruth. In 1921 Ruth moved to New York City with her two daughters and became a portrait photographer, and it was there that Bette Davis's acting aspirations began taking shape. While attending Cushing Academy in Massachusetts, she saw a production of Henrik Ibsen's *The Wild Duck*, which she credited with solidifying her aspirations into a total, heartfelt commitment.

After graduating from Cushing Academy, Bette auditioned for and was promptly rejected by Eva Le Gallienne's Manhattan Civic Repertory—she was thought to be "insincere and frivolous." She moved on to John Murray Anderson's dramatic school, where she was a resounding success, and in 1929 she made her Broadway debut in *Broken Dishes*, followed by *Solid South*. It was in 1930 that Hollywood called, in the form of a contract with Universal Studios. The fact that her extraordinary eyes and highly distinctive looks didn't fit the Hollywood mold was demonstrated by the studio representative who was sent to meet her train from New York, but left without her, because he couldn't find any young woman among the disembarking passengers who looked like a movie star.

After nine months, six unsuccessful films, and mixed reactions to this unique newcomer (including a comment from one executive that she had "about as much sex appeal as Slim Summerville," a pleasant but notoriously homely actor), Bette was released from her Universal contract. Warner Bros. signed her to a five-year contract thanks to her critically acclaimed performance in *The Man Who Played God* in 1932, and she often credited its star, George Arliss, who'd chosen her as his female lead, with providing her with her first real break in Hollywood.

She won two Academy Awards in the 1930s—for *Dangerous* in 1935 and *Jezebel* in 1938—but she ultimately sued Warner Bros. for refusing to let her out of her contract, believing she wasn't being offered the quality roles she deserved. She lost the lawsuit, and the 1940s passed with a series of films that declined in success until her Warner Bros. contract finally ended in 1949. Her career jump-started again in 1950 with her brilliant Oscar-nominated performance in *All About Eve,* and that decade brought her a succession of films as well, but by 1961 the offers had tapered off to nothing. In response, she placed a "Situations Wanted" ad in the trade paper *Variety,* as a joke, she claimed, that read in part, "Thirty years experience as an actress in Motion Pictures. Mobile still and more affable than rumor would have it. Wants steady employment in Hollywood. (Has had Broadway.)."

Kidding or not, Bette enjoyed yet another comeback in the 1960s, and in the 1970s she added a TV miniseries to her volume of work, won an Emmy for her appearance in *Strangers: The Story of a Mother and Daughter,* and became the first woman to be presented with the American Film Institute's Lifetime Achievement Award.

More television projects followed until 1983, when she was diagnosed with breast cancer. Within two weeks of her mastectomy, she suffered a series of strokes that left her partially paralyzed, from which she recovered with the help of extensive physical therapy. She was able to resume her career on a limited basis through 1989, when she gave her final performance, in the title role of Larry Cohen's comedy film *Wicked Stepmother.*

She "retired" to a series of talk show appearances and was interviewed by everyone from Johnny Carson to David Letterman to Dick Cavett, and her career earned her such prestigious acknowledgments as the Kennedy Center Honor, the Film Society of Lincoln Center Lifetime Achievement Award, and France's Legion of Honor. It was while receiving the American Cinema Award in 1989 that she collapsed and subsequently learned that her cancer had returned. She managed a trip to Spain to be honored at the International Film Festival there, but her health declined so quickly and severely that she was only able to travel as far as the American Hospital in Neuilly-sur-Seine, France. She died there on October 6, 1989, at the age of eighty-one.

Her epitaph, "She did it the hard way," applied as much to her personal life as it did to her career. Her four marriages and affairs that included director William Wyler and Howard Hughes seemed to bring her very little security or happiness. She had a daughter, Barbara Davis Sherry, by her third husband, William Sherry; and she and her fourth husband, Gary Merrill, adopted two children, Margot and Michael. Tragically, Margot was severely brain damaged from an injury thought to have occurred during or shortly after her birth, and she was ultimately institutionalized. Bette's biological daughter, Barbara, in 1985, writing under her married name B. D. Hyman, published a very bitter memoir about the relationship between her and her mother called *My Mother's Keeper,* in which she portrayed Bette as an overbearing, abusive drunk. Following the release of the book, Bette disinherited her daughter and never spoke to her again.

In the end, with more than 120 film, television, and theater credits, two Oscars, ten Academy Award nominations, and dozens of other honors acknowledging her utterly unique style and talent—

flaws, abrasiveness, and all—Bette Davis more than earned her status as one of the American Film Institute's greatest female stars of all time.

From Francine

All who witnessed Bette's arrival described her emerging from the tunnel with a very apparent attitude of, "It's about time!" She was tired of fighting her illness, tired of fighting in general, and had been looking forward to returning Home since the strokes she now says she found far more demoralizing than her breast cancer. "I never looked the same. I never sounded the same. I was more painfully aware of those facts than anyone, and I hated it. My themes were Infallibility and Winner. How could I not have hated it? I was just too stubborn to hide in my room like a self-pitying coward."

She was greeted by an unusually large crowd of loving friends, many of them from her amazing fifty-six incarnations, and William Wyler and Howard Hughes in particular from what she calls "my best and my last lifetime." She was completely overwhelmed by her reunion with William Wyler, a kindred soul from five of those past lives and one of her fondest companions here at Home. His death years before hers had devastated her, and they held on to each other for a very long time before Bette's Spirit Guide, Remy, accompanied her to the Scanning Machine.

Reviewing her life left her satisfied for the most part—she was proud of refusing to be denied her great talent, "the finest gift I had to offer"— and she watched her performance in Dark Victory *twice and was most proud of that.*

Bette is extremely introverted and, as she always has, lives alone with her six cats, preferring to change homes often. She has an overstuffed red velvet chair that she loves, and she takes the position that as long as she has her chair, she's at home no matter where she is. She continues to express her passion for performing with an unending series of plays, particularly with her old friends Laurence Olivier and Carole Lombard, and she's also returned to another of her passions: she's one of our most admired Romance language teachers, specializing in classes for spirits preparing for new incarnations in which they've charted professorships on that subject.

She's currently taking great delight in mentoring a playwright named Keller or Kellogg. He's planning to incarnate in 2014 by your years, in northern Oregon, and will one day write and successfully publish a trilogy of plays called Houses of Glass, on which he and Bette are currently working.

There is no one Bette visits on earth, and she adds, "There will be no further incarnations, thank you. I think that world and I have had quite enough of each other."

Anna Nicole Smith

Anna Nicole Smith was born Vickie Lynn Hogan on November 28, 1967, in Harris County, Texas. Her parents divorced when she was still an infant, and she and her mother, Virgie, a Houston law enforcement officer, briefly lived with her Aunt Elaine until Virgie remarried in 1971. She attended school in Houston until the ninth grade, when she was sent to live with another aunt, Kay Beall, in Mexia, Texas.

After failing her freshman year at Mexia High School, she decided she'd had enough of formal education, dropped out in her sophomore year, and promptly found a waitressing job at a fried chicken restaurant. There she met and fell in love with the restaurant's cook; seventeen-year-old Vickie married sixteen-year-old Billy Wayne Smith on April 4, 1985. Their son, Daniel Wayne Smith, was born on January 22, 1986, and when the young couple separated in 1987, Anna Nicole moved back to Houston with her year-old son. The marriage legally ended in 1993.

She was performing as an exotic dancer in 1991, when she responded to a newspaper ad for upcoming *Playboy* auditions and was promptly chosen for the March 1992 cover of the magazine. It was also in 1991, at the strip club where she danced, that twenty-six-year-old Vickie Smith met eighty-nine-year-old billionaire J. Howard Marshall. They were married in 1994 amid a predictable swirl of accusations that she married him solely for his money, which she denied. He died thirteen months later, triggering a decade of court battles over his estate between Marshall's sons and her.

In the meantime, Anna Nicole's modeling career gained momentum. She was *Playboy*'s Playmate of the Year in 1993, having officially changed her name from Vickie Smith to Anna Nicole Smith by then, and that same year she signed a contract to model in print ads for both Guess Jeans and H & M Clothing.

Her very well endowed body attracted Hollywood attention, and she accepted the inevitable acting offers that came along, with no particular talent or success to show for them. By the late 1990s she'd reached that peculiar status of "famous for being famous," and between a conspicuous weight gain, ongoing litigation over her late husband's fortune, and increasingly bizarre behavior that often included slurred, almost incoherent speech in public, she became a tabloid staple. She ultimately attracted the attention of the E! cable network and, in 2002, *The Anna Nicole Show*, a "reality" series portraying her personal life in which her son, Daniel, was her constant companion and caretaker, enjoyed a dubious two-year run.

Her ongoing weight problem inspired an offer from a diet pill company called TrimSpa, and she became their spokesperson in 2003, reportedly losing sixty-nine pounds during her contract with them. By 2004 her behavior had become so alarmingly peculiar that rumors of drug problems were impossible to dismiss.

In the summer of 2006 Anna Nicole announced on her website that she was pregnant, and she was ecstatic at the birth of her daughter, Dannielynn, on September 7 at Doctors Hospital in the Bahamas. She'd been in a "secret relationship" with her attorney Howard K. Stern long enough that he believed he was the biological father and signed the birth certificate, although her former boyfriend, photographer Larry Birkhead, believed he was the father and sued to establish paternity.

Tragically, just three days after the birth of Dannielynn, Anna Nicole's beloved Daniel, who'd arrived to meet his new baby sister, died in his mother's hospital room of an apparent drug overdose at the age of twenty. The devastating death of Daniel, the paternity lawsuit over Dannielynn, and the ongoing rumors of addictions threw Anna Nicole into a relentless media spotlight, during which she tried to stabilize her emotional chaos by pledging her devotion to Howard K. Stern in a not legally binding commitment ceremony.

On February 8, 2007, Anna Nicole Smith was found unconscious in her room at the Seminole Hard Rock Hotel and Casino in Hollywood, Florida. Efforts to resuscitate her failed, and she died at the age of thirty-nine from what was ultimately ruled to be an accidental drug overdose involving nine different prescription medications, although no illegal drugs were found in her system.

The tabloid and legal frenzies over Anna Nicole Smith didn't end with her death, as the paternity and custody suit between Howard K. Stern and Larry Birkhead over Dannielynn proceeded in front of a national television audience. DNA tests finally established that the baby girl was the child of Larry Birkhead, and he was immediately granted custody of her.

In 2010, Howard K. Stern and one of Anna Nicole's doctors were found guilty of charges involving her use of prescription drugs. And the endless legal battle regarding the estate of Anna Nicole's husband J. Howard Marshall rages on, in the name of her daughter, Dannielynn Birkhead.

From Francine

Anna Nicole was only on her second incarnation, which explains why she was so oddly naïve throughout her life and had such a difficult time understanding whom to trust. As often happens when writing a chart in the perfect bliss of Home, she designed a lifetime of excesses, temptations, and chaos she was convinced she'd be strong enough and have faith enough to overcome. She compounded her upcoming challenges by choosing the two very difficult life themes of Rejection and Manipulator and charting herself to suffer from a bipolar disorder, which was never properly treated. *(Sylvia often compares the exaggerated bravado of writing our charts in an atmosphere of sacred perfection to shopping for groceries when you're very hungry.)* Anna Nicole's sincere but overzealous courage in preparation for her latest brief trip to earth was bolstered by the fact that she charted her father from her first incarnation to be by her side, in the form of her son, Daniel.

Daniel welcomed his mother Home before she even emerged from the tunnel, and he never left her side until she was safely cocooned. Only after she was healed and euphorically clear-headed again was she ready to proceed to the Scanning Machine, which she found as enlightening and cathartic as most spirits do. She understands exactly why, for example, she leapt at the Exit Point she chose, even though it was so soon after the birth of her daughter: not only was the thought of staying behind on earth without her son unimaginable, but she also felt her life had spiraled far enough out of control that she couldn't possibly be the stable, adoring, attentive parent her baby, Dannielynn, deserved. She knew with absolute certainty who her daughter's father was, she knew he would fight for custody of her and win, and she wants all concerned to know that she and Daniel were and will be present at every court hearing that involves the welfare of her child. As for the upcoming years of litigation not involving Dannielynn, she simply says, "I'm happy. I'm at peace. My daughter is where she belongs, and I'm grateful that my son and I are Home and healthy. The rest is between the litigants and God." She also sought out and had a sweet reunion with her husband J. Howard Marshall, for whom she cared deeply "and always will," all appearances and rumors to the contrary.

Her greatest regret is that she charted herself to be surrounded by any number of people she trusted to have her best interests at heart "and then *made it impossible for anyone who tried to protect me from myself." She would love to believe that someone, "even if it's only one person," will avoid that same trap after witnessing her decline on television and in the tabloids, and she adds, "What I never understood about being famous until it was too late is that it doesn't come with an 'off' button. Therefore, neither did I."*

Her life on the Other Side is a study in simplicity. She lives alone in a small yellow house by a river. (Daniel lives nearby, and although they're extremely close, he has a very active, very social life of his own.) Her visage is deliberately ordinary; she is short and round, with plain features and shoulder-length thin brown hair pulled straight back and tied at the nape of her neck. She's resumed her interest in Buddhism and is training to become a meditation teacher.

She frequently visits and reads to her daughter. She plans to reincarnate someday, but she's in no hurry, and next time she'll come without Daniel, an advanced soul who has no intention of leaving Home again.

John Belushi

Brilliant comedian, actor, and musician John Adam Belushi was born on January 24, 1949, in Chicago to Albanian immigrants Adam and Agnes Belushi. Adam managed a restaurant while Agnes worked as a cashier, and the Belushis raised their four children in the Albanian Orthodox Church. John knew from childhood that he wanted to be a performer, and in addition to being a popular class clown throughout his school years, he was also the captain of his high-school football team and played drums in a rock band. John and his future wife, Judy Jacklin, met as sophomores at Wheaton Central High School and were married from 1976 until his death in 1982.

He performed in summer stock between high-school graduation and starting college. He attended the University of Wisconsin and then the College of DuPage. After graduating in 1970, he successfully auditioned for Chicago's legendary Second City improvisational troupe, where he was an instant hit with his uncannily hilarious impersonations of Marlon Brando and Joe Cocker. Second City stardom led to a role in an off-Broadway production of *National Lampoon's Lemmings*. His rave reviews in that sketch-comedy show attracted the attention of Lorne Michaels, who hired John for a new late-night comedy series he'd created called *Saturday Night Live*.

John Belushi and the rest of the original *Saturday Night Live* cast made their first appearance on October 11, 1975, the show was a hit from the beginning, and John quickly became one of its most popular stars. Whether he was wielding a sword as an eyebrow-arching samurai, waddling around in a killer-bee costume, or doing impressions of everyone from Elizabeth Taylor to Truman Capote, he was magnetic and irresistibly talented. He and his friend and cast mate Dan Aykroyd developed a musical duo called the Blues Brothers during their years on *Saturday Night Live*, which resulted in an album (*Briefcase Full of Blues*) and a national tour with a backup band.

During a between-seasons hiatus from *SNL*, John made his first and possibly his best-known feature film, *Animal House*. Rumors of runaway drug use among some of the *SNL* cast were rampant by 1978 when *Animal House* came out, and the majority of the rumors centered on John and his reported love of cocaine.

His next films were disappointing despite their seeming potential—*Goin' South* was a western starring Jack Nicholson, and *Old Boyfriends* gave John an opportunity at a dramatic role opposite Talia Shire. John left *Saturday Night Live* in 1979 to focus exclusively on his film career, and he made three of his next four movies with his friend, former *SNL* cast mate, and fellow Blues Brother Dan Aykroyd—*1941*, directed by Steven Spielberg; *Neighbors;* and *The Blues Brothers*. Only 1981's *Continental Divide*, a romantic comedy, featured Belushi without Aykroyd.

By early 1982 John was working on several new projects, including a screenplay with former *SNL* cast mate Don Novello. He was also spinning farther and farther out of control when it came to his drug use. On March 5, 1982, he was in his room at the Chateau Marmont in Los Angeles with a small group of people that included, separately and briefly by most accounts, Robin Williams and Robert DeNiro. Finally, alone with a woman named Cathy Smith, he collapsed and died from a combined injection of cocaine and heroin known on the street as a "speedball." His death was initially ruled an accidental drug overdose, but Cathy Smith subsequently informed the *National Enquirer* that she'd personally administered the speedball that killed John Belushi. As a result of her *Enquirer* interview, she was ultimately convicted of involuntary manslaughter and served fifteen months in prison.

John Belushi died at the age of thirty-three, far sooner than his devoted wife, family, friends, and legions of fans were ready to say good-bye. He's buried near his house on Martha's Vineyard, Chilmark, Massachusetts.

From Francine

John was welcomed back to the Other Side by a huge crowd of friends from Home and from his fourteen past lives, but first to reach him were two black Labrador retrievers and a Jack Russell terrier, from whom he's been inseparable since he returned. We had all been watching him carefully, as we do with everyone who seems to be losing control, particularly when we learned from his Spirit Guide, Khalil, that the Council had advised John against reincarnating so soon after his previous life in France in the early twentieth century. It was a life of privilege and excess, and they were concerned that he needed more time to process his growth from that life. But John was eager to exercise the strength and discipline he was convinced he'd mastered, and he was intent on proving it by charting not only a steady exposure to drugs, but also the celebrity status that would make them even more accessible. Sadly, as so often happens, the euphoria of Home impelled him to create a chart for which he wasn't quite prepared. He does say, though, that three friends he declines to name were inspired enough by the shock of losing him so suddenly that they entered drug programs and became clean and sober, and he is gratified that something positive came from his self-destruction. He never believed he would live to be an old man, but had no conscious premonition that he would not leave his hotel room alive on the night his lifetime ended.

He is intensely proud of his body of work and his willingness to work hard throughout his life, he says, and he also gives himself credit, with a smile, for being smart enough to chart his marriage to Judy. Without elaborating, he wishes he'd listened to her. He still visits her often and wants her to "pay attention to the bookshelves."

He also loves visiting his house on Martha's Vineyard. He says there's an elevated gangway or passageway of some kind between the main house and the guest house, and he enjoys standing on that gangway watching storms come in over the Atlantic.

John is as popular and brilliantly funny here as he was on earth and is always surrounded by large groups of friends. (Contrary to what Sylvia tells me is a commonly held belief, most of us on the Other Side do have senses of humor and love to laugh.) He frequently entertains in his small A-frame cabin on what corresponds to your island of Cyprus, and he continues to perform comedy, to the delight of his parents, whom he was the first to welcome Home. He and his father are especially close companions, their mutual love of the sea expressed through their shared research in the fields of oceanography and marine biology, and through long peaceful journeys together on what John calls his "square rigger" sailing ship. He has no intention of returning to earth for another incarnation.

Bob Marley

Legendary singer, songwriter, and guitarist Bob Marley, the man who in his brief lifetime brought unprecedented worldwide attention to reggae music and the Rastafarian faith, was born Robert Nesta Marley on February 6, 1945, in the village of Nine Mile, St. Ann Parish, Jamaica. His father, Norval Marley, was a white British plantation overseer and officer in the Royal Marines, fifty years old when he conceived Bob with his black eighteen-year-old fiancé, Cedella Booker. Norval moved to Kingston before Bob was born and, although he financially supported his wife and son, was an absentee father until his death of a heart attack when Bob was ten. Bob's interracial heritage made him an object of ridicule during his childhood and remained an issue throughout his life, which he's quoted as addressing with his trademark Jamaican accent, "Me don't dip on the black man's side nor the white man's side. Me dip on God's side, the one who create me and cause me to come from black and white."

When Bob was fourteen, he left home and school for Kingston, where his music career began. After recording several obscure and not especially successful singles, he formed a quintet called the Wailers with fellow singers Peter Tosh, Bunny Livingstone, Junior Braithwaite, and Beverly Kelso. Their first single, "Simmer Down," was a major hit in Jamaica in 1964. But in 1965, when Braithwaite and Kelso left the group and the Wailers became a trio, not even their most popular singles received enough royalties to keep them solvent.

The Wailers went their separate ways—in Bob's case, to Newark, Delaware, his mother's home at the time, where he earned a living as a factory worker for almost a year before returning to Jamaica. In the meantime, he married his girlfriend, Rita Anderson, in 1966, and their first two children were born—Cedella in 1967 and David, nicknamed Ziggy, in 1968.

The Wailers reunited, made more fairly unsuccessful records, and, most significantly for the rest of Bob's life, became devout Rastafarians, largely due to Rita's influence and the continued teachings of Mortimer Planner, one of the faith's most highly regarded elders. Bob adopted and, through his music, began spreading such basic Rastafari tenets as peace and brotherhood, vegetarianism, and the spiritual use of cannabis.

The Wailers finally attracted the attention of Chris Blackwell, who signed them to his influential label, Island Records, in 1972, and their album *Catch a Fire* was their first to be marketed outside of Jamaica. Their second Island Records album, *Burnin'*, included a Bob Marley song called "I Shot the Sheriff," which was recorded by British superstar Eric Clapton and helped to elevate Bob's and the Wailers' notoriety, and in 1973 the Wailers set out on their first overseas tour.

By the end of 1973 Peter Tosh and Bunny Livingstone had left the Wailers to pursue solo careers, and Bob "regrouped," expanding his instrumental section and recruiting a female trio that included his wife, Rita, to form Bob Marley and the Wailers, who successfully toured Europe and the United States. By 1978 they'd achieved several hits in both England and the United States, and their albums *Rastaman Vibration* and *Exodus* soared into the top twenty on America's pop music charts.

Bob's popularity and influence back home in Jamaica had long since given him significant importance not only as a musician, but also as a spokesman on public issues. On December 3, 1976, he, his wife, and his manager, Don Taylor, were shot two days before Bob Marley and the Wailers were due to perform a free concert in support of the progressive Jamaican prime minister Michael Manley. All three survived what was generally believed to be a politically motivated assassination attempt, and Bob appeared at the concert as scheduled and then promptly left for England.

In mid-1977, shortly after the release of the *Exodus* album, Bob discovered that an unhealed wound on his toe was a malignant melanoma. Doctors urged him to have his toe amputated, but his religious beliefs impelled him to refuse. The *Exodus* promotion tour was abbreviated, but in 1978 the band was back in action, recording the album *Kaya* and performing in Jamaica's One Love Peace Concert; later that year Bob was presented with the United Nations' Peace Medal of the Third World.

In 1980, after producing several more albums and resuming tours of the United States and Europe, Bob fell ill during a New York City concert in early September and collapsed the next day while jogging through Central Park. He was rushed to the hospital, where doctors discovered that the cancer that started in his toe had spread to his liver, his stomach, and his brain. The prognosis was that he had less than a month to live.

He bravely and brilliantly performed a concert in Pittsburgh on September 22, but to his profound disappointment he was unable to continue the scheduled U.S. tour. He traveled to Miami and was formally baptized at the Ethiopian Orthodox Church, and from there he and Rita flew to a treatment center in Germany in an effort to prove the New York doctors wrong.

When it became apparent that the controversial German therapy wasn't working, Bob and Rita set out for Jamaica, attempting to honor Bob's wish to die at home. They got no farther than Miami, where Bob was rushed from the airport to Cedars of Lebanon Hospital. He died there on May 11, 1981, at the age of thirty-six.

Bob Marley was honored with a state funeral in Jamaica attended by the Jamaican prime minister along with hundreds of thousands of mourners. He was laid to rest in a chapel mausoleum in his hometown of Nine Miles. Among his many posthumous honors are his induction into the Rock and Roll Hall of Fame, a Grammy Lifetime Achievement Award, the BBC's "Song of the Millennium" award for his classic "One Love," and *Time* magazine's "Album of the Century" award for *Exodus*.

From Francine

Bob, one of our most highly advanced spirits, began making regular trips Home while he was still in Germany. I'm sure there are those who would confirm that he was having conversations with many of his friends here months before he finally left his body once and for all, which actually happened during his flight to Florida. There were throngs of friends from Home and from his forty-four past lives waiting to greet him, including his father. The two of them have an interesting relationship—they shared a previous incarnation as half brothers in Kenya who lived in separate homes and were never particularly close. Bob grew up more advantaged than Norval and supported him from a distance throughout his life out of respect for their familial connection. The two of them charted a very similar dynamic for themselves in this most recent lifetime. Norval repaid his karmic debt to Bob while still keeping his distance—like some kindred souls, Bob and Norval are very good at fulfilling specific, important purposes in each other's lives, but they bring out the worst in each other when they spend too much time together. It's interesting that Bob's remarkable influence on your world was partially a result of the strength he gained from growing up without his father and refusing to define that fact of his life as a disadvantage. He entered his final incarnation with great clarity about his life themes of Harmony and Justice, which gave him an unusual insight and sense of direction about obstacles that would have discouraged less focused spirits.

Bob arrived Home with that same clarity, joyfully looking forward to resuming his full life here. He lives communally with a large, fluid group of friends on what corresponds to your island of Tasmania, where he continues composing beautiful songs of peace and unity and infusing them to a young Rastafari musician named Muata, who lives in western Ethiopia. Bob is also one of our most popular performers, joining a wide variety of other musicians from Jim Croce and Jimi Hendrix to Louis Armstrong and Andrés Segovia for brilliant concerts throughout the Other Side. It might interest you on earth to know that Bob's song "One Love" is as familiar and beloved at Home as it is here. He's an avid soccer and lacrosse player and, always a passionate master craftsman, has begun creating his own bass guitars to give to his many music students.

Bob quickly resumed his position as an esteemed member of our network of peace councils—never believe there aren't constant efforts on the Other Side to find realistic solutions to your world's problems. His other great passion here is his work with and on behalf of animals, researching cures for common and often fatal viral diseases among the earth's animals and also exploring the vast potential of stem cells in the treatment of a variety of orthopedic challenges.

He was so eager to see his mother, Cedella, when she left her body that he actually traveled through the tunnel to hold her hand and personally bring her Home, and she now lives with him in his island commune. He closely follows his wife's work with her foundation, and he thanks his son, Ziggy, for his ongoing efforts with the documentary about his life and urges him not to get discouraged by the "inevitable frustrations." He was disappointed that he didn't live long enough to fulfill his intention of writing his autobiography, and he's hard at work on it now—when he's satisfied with it he'll be infusing it to a woman he says his son has met, but doesn't know well yet, who will make herself apparent to Ziggy at the appropriate time, and the two of them will see it through to fruition.

John Ritter

Wonderfully gifted actor and comedian John Southworth Ritter was born on September 17, 1948, in Burbank, California. His performing talent came naturally from his mother, actress Dorothy Fay, and his father, legendary country singer and actor Tex Ritter. John's older brother, Tom, was diagnosed as a child with cerebral palsy, triumphed over it, and grew up to become a lawyer.

John was student body president at Hollywood High School and, after a very brief diversion appearing as a contestant on *The Dating Game* and winning a vacation two hundred miles from home, headed on to the University of Southern California, where he majored in psychology and minored in architecture. At the end of his sophomore year, curiosity drew him to an acting class taught by actress Nina Foch. He knew he'd found his niche and changed his major to theater arts. Between studies, in 1968 and 1969, he gained valuable acting experience by performing in a series of plays throughout Europe, and he graduated in 1971 with a bachelor's degree in drama.

His first TV guest spots read like a history of television in the 1970s—*Hawaii Five-O*, *The Waltons*, *M*A*S*H*, *The Bob Newhart Show*, *The Streets of San Francisco*, *Kojak*, and *The Mary Tyler Moore Show*, to name a few. While working on *The Waltons*, on January 2, 1974, he received the devastating news that his father had died suddenly of a heart attack in Nashville.

In 1975 ABC-TV bought the rights to the Americanized version of a British comedy series called *Man About the House*. John was the first to be cast in the new sitcom. Joyce DeWitt joined the cast after a poorly received first pilot was shot. Suzanne Somers was hired after a poorly received second pilot was shot. And finally the right combination of characters and chemistry came together for the hit show *Three's Company*, which ran for a very respectable eight seasons with John as the culinary student and ladies' man Jack Tripper, who pretended to be gay to keep the landlords from objecting to his living with two attractive female roommates. During those eight years he began building his film career, with appearances in such moderate hits as *Hero at Large*, *Americathon*, *Wholly Moses!*, and *They All Laughed*. He also emceed the 1977 United Cerebral Palsy Telethon with his brother, Tom, which became one of his treasured annual traditions, raising many millions of dollars for a cause that was understandably close to his heart.

When *Three's Company* had run its course and John had done his best in the inevitable short-lived spin-off *Three's a Crowd*, he had no problem making the transition right back to film again, with roles in almost thirty films between 1986 and 2006. In those same years his television appearances, including guest spots, specials, TV movies, and series, numbered almost sixty, making him one of the busiest, most versatile, and most sought-after actors in Hollywood for nearly three decades. He was rewarded with a Best Actor Emmy out of six nominations and a Best Actor Golden Globe Award out of five nominations.

John's personal life was refreshingly quiet and scandal-free. He married his first wife, actress Nancy Morgan, in 1977. They had three children—Jason, Tyler, and Carly—with whom John remained very close after he and Nancy divorced in 1996. John and his second wife, Amy Yasbeck, originally met in 1990 when they costarred in an episode of *The Cosby Show*. They officially began dating in the late

1990s, shortly before costarring in the hilariously tongue-in-cheek 1998 TV movie *Dead Husbands*. They were married in 1999, a few months after the birth of their daughter, Stella.

In 2002 John began shooting a new television series, *Eight Simple Rules for Dating My Teenage Daughter*, which won the 2002 People's Choice Award for Best New Comedy. On September 11, 2003, he was rehearsing with his close longtime friend Henry Winkler, who was guest-starring on that week's episode, when he suddenly fell ill. He was rushed to nearby Providence St. Joseph Medical Center, where he died at 10:45 that same night. The cause of death proved to be an aortic dissection, a tear in the wall of the aorta caused by a previously undiagnosed congenital heart defect. He was buried at Forest Lawn, Hollywood Hills Cemetery, after a private service at which John's family and close friends said a reluctant good-bye to one of the industry's most endearing, prolific, and highly respected actors.

From Francine

John is every bit as beloved, kind, and hilarious here as he was on earth, and although the suddenness of his Homecoming was a surprise, a huge crowd, led by his father, quickly gathered to welcome him. He was understandably a little disoriented, but a long embrace from his father and the sight of so many treasured friends calmed him into a quiet, joyful acceptance of what had happened and where he was, and there was no need for Orientation or cocooning. He worried about the grief his wife and children were going through and quickly began visiting them to reassure and comfort them and to let them know how blessed he felt to have lived such a wonderful lifetime and then to have had the luxury of being in the midst of doing what he loved, with Henry by his side, when he began his trip Home. While death was never a subject that preoccupied him, he says that, when he did think about it, he hoped he would go quickly, as his father did, and it fascinated him that both he and his father went Home so close to their respective birthdays. [Tex Ritter died ten days before his sixty-ninth birthday, John six days before his fifty-fifth.]

It's also very much worth mentioning that John and Lucille Ball, kindred souls on earth and on the Other Side, had an ecstatic reunion when John emerged from his time at the Scanning Machine to resume his busy life. They often socialize and perform together, and it hasn't escaped their notice that the causes of their respective deaths were very similar: John's was a tear in his aortic wall, Lucy's was a ruptured aorta. As a result, the two of them have begun taking courses in cardiovascular ge-netic disorders and imaging toward the goal of becoming part of our vast network of coronary researchers. John sends the message, "Please thank everyone involved in publishing the rules," and adds, "They'll know who and what I mean." [From Sylvia: My staff checked the Internet and found "Ritter Rules," which are described as "life-saving reminders to recognize, treat and prevent thoracic aortic dissection." You can find a discussion of Ritter Rules at http://cbs2.com/local/john.ritter .heart.2.1565915.html.]

John has also returned to his work as an Orientator in the oxygen chambers, where he's treasured for his unique blend of faith, comfort, and humor among the new arrivals who need Orientation care. He and his father live in a modest house near their old friends Jesse and Patrick Swayze, the four of them sharing the idyllic, fenceless horse ranch they've always loved.

He doesn't plan to reincarnate, believing that from now on he can ac-complish more on the Other Side and be of greater service than he ever could on earth. And, he adds, "With the exception of being here, I could never ask for more than I was blessed with that last time around."

Farrah Fawcett

One of the true iconic "poster girls" of the baby boom generation, actress Farrah Leni Fawcett was born in Corpus Christi, Texas, on February 2, 1947, to oil-field contractor James Fawcett and his wife, Pauline, a homemaker. She was educated in Catholic school, at W. B. Ray High School, and then at the University of Texas at Austin, where her photograph as one of the school's "Ten Most Beautiful Coeds" caught the attention of a Hollywood publicist. He encouraged her to move to Los Angeles to pursue a modeling career, and after some initial hesitation, her parents accompanied her to the West Coast at the end of her junior year. Within two weeks she was under contract as a model and in overwhelming demand for commercials and print ads.

She also caught the eye of a handsome young actor named Lee Majors, who was starring in a series called *The Big Valley*, and they had their first date on July 28, 1968. They celebrated the five-year anniversary of their first date by getting married, on July 28, 1973, in a garden wedding at the elegant Bel Air Hotel. Farrah made several appearances on her husband's subsequent series *The Six Million Dollar Man*, and the "supercouple" was a staple of the tabloids through the 1970s and early 1980s, where their separation in 1979 and divorce in 1982 often got as much press attention as their respective careers.

After a number of guest spots on a variety of television series starting in 1969, Farrah costarred in the ABC Movie of the Week

Charlie's Angels in 1976, which became a series that same year. It was also in 1976 that the classic poster featuring Farrah, with her signature mane of blonde hair, wearing a relatively conservative red one-piece bathing suit, hit the market and became one of the bestselling posters of all time, with sales figures reaching well over ten million copies.

Thanks to *Charlie's Angels*, Farrah Fawcett was a fan sensation by the end of 1976 and was named Favorite Performer in a New TV Program at the People's Choice Awards. She left the show after its first season, was sued by Aaron Spelling for breach of contract, and eventually settled out of court by agreeing to make six guest appearances in upcoming seasons. She promptly turned her professional attention to feature films and television miniseries, and in 1979 she turned her personal attention to actor Ryan O'Neal. While they were never married, they were together until 1997 and again, off and on, from 2001 until her death. Their son, Redmond, was born in 1985.

Farrah's next professional success came in 1983, when she replaced Susan Sarandon as an intended rape victim who takes revenge on her attacker in an off-Broadway production of the play *Extremities*. She received equal praise from the critics, not to mention an Emmy nomination, for her portrayal of an abused wife in the highest rated television movie of 1984, *The Burning Bed*. And her 1986 appearance in the film version of *Extremities* earned her a Best Actress Golden Globe nomination. Two more Golden Globe nominations followed as well as another Emmy nomination in 1989 for the disturbing fact-based miniseries *Small Sacrifices*. Her career as a respected dramatic actress continued until 2004 with a variety of film and television roles and a third Emmy nomination.

Life seemed to imitate art during Farrah's relationship in 1997 with producer-director James Orr. After playing several noteworthy, highly acclaimed roles as an abused, battered, or victimized woman, she herself experienced an incidence of domestic abuse by Orr when she told him she wanted to end their relationship. He was convicted of assault and sentenced to three years' probation.

Despite her turbulent personal life and rumors of a drug problem after her peculiar behavior during a 1997 *David Letterman Show* interview, Farrah's beauty hadn't diminished by the mid-1990s, and her *Playboy* photo spreads were prominent features of the magazine's two bestselling issues of the decade.

In 2006, less than a year after the devastating death of her mother, Farrah was diagnosed with anal cancer. She began a long, aggressive, highly publicized fight against her illness, with Ryan O'Neal by her side. She filmed even the most difficult moments of her battle for what would become a two-hour documentary called *Farrah's Story*, which she coproduced with her friend Alana Stewart. The documentary aired on May 15, 2009, was watched by approximately nine million viewers on its network debut, and was presented with an Emmy for Outstanding Nonfiction Special.

On June 25, 2009, less than three months before her Emmy victory was announced to a worldwide audience, Farrah Fawcett died in St. John's Health Center in Santa Monica, California. Ryan O'Neal and Alana Stewart were with her when she took her last breath, and her troubled son, Redmond, who was convicted in 2009 of felony drug possession and was serving time in a detention center when his mother died, was allowed to attend her funeral.

From Francine

Sadly, Farrah arrived Home depressed and disappointed. Although she'd grown very weary of fighting her battle against cancer and her spirit knew her chosen Exit Point had arrived, her strong-willed conscious mind was clinging until the end to the hope that she would win that war, provide a happy ending to her documentary, and inspire others not to give up, no matter what challenge they might be facing. Her mother, grandparents, and countless friends from her nineteen past lives were there to embrace and comfort her the instant she emerged from the tunnel. But not until she was cocooned was she able to experience the sacred bliss of the Other Side and appreciate that her fierce, courageous battle alone was inspiring enough, and the death of her body was to be celebrated rather than mourned.

Like so many who return Home as the result of earthly diseases with high mortality rates, Farrah emerged from cocooning ready and eager to participate with medical researchers who are hard at work on a cure. She and all other cancer victims are invaluable to the process of someday eradicating the disease entirely, as they're studied and tested before God's promised healing takes place, and she has dedicated herself to classes in biomedical sciences so that she can become a core member of a cancer biology research team.

Otherwise, Farrah's life is very much as it was before her latest brief incarnation. She prefers living alone, surrounded by what we've always referred to as "her cats," a beautiful pride of lions who adore her and, like all of our jungle cats, are as gentle and playful as kittens. She's a gifted, prolific impressionistic artist, and her gallery showings are among the few social events she attends. She's considering another incarnation in which she says she would aspire "to be famous for something that matters" and not repeat her most recent life themes of Follower and Temperance, which she feels she handled poorly.

Patrick Swayze

Gifted, charismatic actor and dancer Patrick Wayne Swayze was born in Houston, Texas, on August 18, 1952. His mother, Patsy, was a choreographer, dance instructor, and the director of the Houston Jazz Ballet Company, and dance was a part of Patrick's life virtually since he took his first baby steps. His father, Jesse, who died in 1982, was a champion rodeo rider and an engineering draftsman. Patrick, his two sisters, and his two brothers were raised in the Houston suburb of Oak Forest, and from elementary school through high school he put his exceptional skills to a wide variety of uses, excelling in everything from ballet and gymnastics to football, swimming, and ice skating to performing in school plays.

After two years at Houston's San Jacinto College, Patrick was hired as a dancer and ice skater, playing Prince Charming on a national tour of "Disney on Parade." When the tour ended and he returned to Houston, he met Lisa Niemi, a sixteen-year-old student in his mother's dance classes. He moved to New York in 1972 to pursue his dance career, and Lisa joined him there when she graduated from high school. They were married in 1975, a marriage that lasted for the rest of his life.

Complications from knee surgery forced Patrick to shift his focus from a promising ballet career to acting, and in 1976 he debuted on Broadway in a production of *Goodtime Charley*, followed by a revival of the classic *West Side Story*. But it was his starring role in *Grease* in 1978 that attracted the attention of Hollywood.

His television and film work on the West Coast was steady since its beginning in 1979's *Skatetown U.S.A.*, including a prestigious nod from Francis Ford Coppola for a film called *The Outsiders*. There's no question, though, that it was in 1987 that he officially became a star thanks to his versatile, multitextured performance in *Dirty Dancing*. His confident physicality made him an obvious choice for the action films that followed, but his next real "star" vehicle came in 1990 with the paranormal love story *Ghost*. Both *Dirty Dancing* and *Ghost* earned Patrick lead actor Golden Globe nominations.

People magazine's 1991 "Sexiest Man Alive" had been battling an alcohol problem since the death of his father in 1982, and in 1994, after his sister's suicide, he voluntarily checked into a rehab clinic and then recuperated with his wife, Lisa, out of the spotlight, at the two ranches where they bred Arabian horses. He returned to the screen in 1995 as a drag queen in *To Wong Foo, Thanks for Everything, Julie Newmar* and was rewarded with his third Golden Globe nomination.

The next few years brought a combination of film work and physical injuries, including a broken leg from a horseback-riding accident and carbon monoxide exposure while flying his private plane. But it was in January 2008 that real tragedy struck—Patrick Swayze was diagnosed with stage IV (inoperable) pancreatic cancer. He immediately began treatment at the Stanford University Medical Center, while the tabloids began offering an endless barrage of photographs and updates, only some of which were accurate, but which made his battle intensely public whether he wanted it to be or not. His appearance on a rare network simulcast of the television special *Stand Up to Cancer* in September 2008 helped raise money and awareness on behalf of cancer patients around the world.

The finale of Patrick's career was the lead in an A&E Network series called *The Beast*. It premiered in January 2009, the same month in which he was hospitalized with pneumonia and in which he revealed during a Barbara Walters interview that doctors had found a "tiny little mass" in his liver. His deteriorating health made it impossible for him to promote *The Beast*, and it was cancelled in June 2009, while the tabloids continued to feature photos of him, painfully and increasingly gaunt, with his wife, Lisa, by his side, as she'd been for almost forty years. On September 14, 2009, Patrick Swayze lost his battle with pancreatic cancer at the age of fifty-seven. His ashes were scattered at his beloved horse ranch in New Mexico.

From Francine

Like countless others preparing for their trip Home, Patrick began visiting and receiving visits from the spirit world long before his body died. Many of your well-intentioned health-care professionals dismiss the ensuing conversations as illness-related delirium, but I assure you, those visits are very real, sacred, and helpful for a peaceful transition from your dimension to ours. By the time Patrick had taken his last breath, he was joyfully prepared for the euphoric reunion that awaited him the instant he emerged from the tunnel. Thrilling herds of horses and dogs immediately surrounded him, led by a black Arabian stallion, until finally Patrick's father and sister were able to make their way through the menagerie and embrace him. (Jesse Swayze was one of the most frequent visitors to Patrick's hospital bedside, by the way, filling him in on the details of the horse ranch they'd be sharing on the Other Side.)

Patrick was deeply moved by his trip to the Scanning Machine, in awe of the love that surrounded him all of his life, particularly from his wife and best friend, Lisa, "the strongest, most courageous person I've ever met." He says he also "sat at the table watching her in the kitchen."

He experienced a fairly rare "relapse" of deep sorrow after leaving the Scanning Machine, and he's currently cocooned at his own request to help him through it. He was a private person on earth, with the difficult life themes of Rescuer and Loner. While he faced his battles with alcoholism and cancer head-on and with great courage, it was never his intention that those battles be fought in the spotlight. The moment they became public knowledge, he took on the typical Rescuer responsibility of overcoming his illnesses not only for himself, but also for everyone else who might look to him as someone who "beat the odds." He fulfilled that responsibility with his triumph over alcoholism, and he had every intention along the way of being a cancer survivor on so many others' behalf. He's being cocooned until he heals from the mistaken heartbreak of thinking that his death represents a failure and recognizes the inspiration he provided for so many with the dignity, generosity, and determination of his long, brave fight.

When he emerges from the cocooning chamber he'll rejoin his father on the magnificent horse ranch they share with John and Tex Ritter. Although all horses are welcome on those vast unfenced acres, the ranch seems to especially attract Arabians and Friesians. Patrick and Jesse delight in giving riding lessons, and many newly arrived spirits in Orientation have received enormous peace and healing from the beautiful, spirited, gentle creatures at the Swayze-Ritter ranch. Patrick will also return to his status as a highly valued dance instructor and acting coach, although he's said he has no desire to continue performing here. Spirits are unable to visit anyone on earth while they're cocooned, and Patrick wants Lisa and his brother Don in particular to know that he'll be with them again very soon.

Clark Gable

Clark Gable was called the "king of Hollywood," a title earned by his status as the biggest money-making male star in the film industry during the 1930s. He was virile, charming, a rogue, and the man you wanted on your side in a fight. He was born February 1, 1901, to William "Bill" Gable, an oil-well driller, and his wife, Adeline, in Cadiz, Ohio. His mother died of a brain tumor when Clark was ten months old, and Bill married Jennie Dunlap in 1903. Jennie taught her tall, shy stepson to play the piano and to be well-dressed, and she also encouraged his love of the written word, including Shakespeare's sonnets, while Bill appreciated Clark's more "manly" talents as a mechanic.

After graduating from high school, Clark began his acting career, touring in stock companies between work in the oil fields with his father, and finally found his way to Portland, Oregon, where he met acting coach Josephine Dillon. She recognized his physical, professional, and romantic potential, transforming everything from his posture, teeth, and high-pitched voice to his hairstyle, diction, and underweight body, and in 1924 she took her new and improved Clark Gable to Hollywood, became his manager, and married him, despite being seventeen years his senior.

He found some extra work and a few very minor jobs, but with no significant roles coming his way, he went back to the stage, expanding his range in a variety of parts and ending up on Broadway, where his portrayal of the intensely desperate Killer Mears in *The Last Mile* finally springboarded him back to Hollywood and a contract with MGM in 1930. That same year he and Josephine Dillon were divorced, and he immediately married a Texas socialite with the imposing name of Ria Franklin Prentiss Lucas Langham.

The "studio system" was firmly in place when Clark signed with MGM, with its breathless attention to its stars' images both onscreen and off, and Clark's popularity began to soar as his virile, he-man persona took shape. The studio wisely cast him with such established female stars as Joan Crawford, Norma Shearer, Greta Garbo, and Jean Harlow. He was loaned to Columbia Pictures for *It Happened One Night*, won the 1934 Best Actor Oscar for his performance, and returned to MGM even more successful than before. He earned his next Academy Award nomination in 1935 for his portrayal of Fletcher Christian in *Mutiny on the Bounty*.

His second marriage withered and died in the 1930s, leaving him available in 1939 to marry the undisputed love of his life, the beautiful, high-spirited, outspoken actress Carole Lombard. Legend has it that it was Carole Lombard who first suggested the idea of Clark Gable for the role of Rhett Butler in *Gone With the Wind*, the breathtaking classic with which he's always been most closely and fondly associated. His astonishing performance and the chemistry between him and his costar, Vivien Leigh, seemed enough all by themselves to cinch the 1939 Best Picture Academy Award, and Clark appropriately credited *Gone With the Wind* with the sought-after leading man status he enjoyed for the rest of his life.

The marriage of Gable and Lombard was, by his description, the happiest time of his personal life. Carole had a successful career in her own right, she was a great hunting and fishing companion for Clark and his friends, and she even understood him enough to put up with his infidelities (which reportedly included an on-and-off ten-year affair with Joan Crawford). The couple bought a ranch in

Encino, California, and hoped to become parents, but Carole's only pregnancy ended in a miscarriage.

It was January 16, 1942, three years into this marriage of kindred souls. Carole Lombard had just finished her film *To Be or Not to Be* and boarded TWA Flight 3, returning to the Burbank, California, airport from Indianapolis, where she'd been on tour selling war bonds. After an unscheduled stop in Las Vegas, the airliner crashed into a mountain, killing everyone on board. Clark flew to the crash site and tried to join the search party, but the raging fire ignited by the burning plane made it apparent that the cause was hopeless—the love of his life was dead.

A month after Carole's death Clark managed to return to work, in *Somewhere I'll Find You* with Lana Turner. He managed to give a professional performance, but his devastation was apparent to all who knew him well, and there was some concern about how heavily he began to drink in an effort to numb the pain of his grief. He lived out his life on the Encino ranch where he and the wife he adored had been so happy.

In 1942, as Carole had suggested, Clark enlisted in the U.S. Army Air Force as part of the World War II effort. He was trained and served as a tail gunner, rising to the rank of major, and by the time he was discharged and returned to Hollywood, he was an even bigger star than ever for his heroism on behalf of his country.

He made several more films for MGM in the 1940s, but was increasingly unhappy with the quality of roles he was given, and in 1953 he left the studio and began to work independently. In the meantime, he caught Hollywood by surprise when he briefly married Lady Sylvia Ashley, a British actress and socialite, on December 20, 1949. They were divorced on April 21, 1952. He then married Kay Spreckels, a former model and actress, in 1955, and she gave birth to Clark's only "legitimate" child, John Clark Gable, on March 20, 1961, four months after Clark's death. Clark's first child, a daughter born in 1935, was the result of his affair with actress Loretta Young. An elaborate scheme was devised to hide the pregnancy, including Loretta Young's pretending to adopt her own child nineteen months after her birth. The deception became more and more apparent as the little girl grew to look exactly like a combination of Loretta Young and Clark Gable, but neither of them ever publicly acknowledged the parentage of their daughter.

Clark's films in the 1950s were occasionally successful and sometimes disastrous flops, but in 1960 he gave what many still consider to be the finest performance of his career in *The Misfits*, which proved to be his last film and the last film of his costar Marilyn Monroe. He was in poor health when the film started, a heavy smoker and drinker with a weakened heart, and a few short days after finishing work on *The Misfits*, on November 16, 1960, Clark Gable died of a heart attack at his home in Los Angeles. His body is interred in the Great Mausoleum at Forest Lawn in Glendale, California, at rest beside the body of Carole Lombard, where he'd yearned to be for so many years.

From Francine

The first face Clark saw when he arrived Home was that of Carole, his beloved, joyfully alive kindred soul. The second was that of his soul mate, who, it may surprise you to know, was his mother, Adeline. By their mutual agreement here on the Other Side before he was born, she stayed on earth just long enough to ensure that he would be a strong, healthy baby; then she "got out of the way," so that Clark would have a father and stepmother who would give him the wide array of skills he would need to fully satisfy his chart. Clark was relieved to have left his tired, debilitated body, grateful that he'd found enough strength to complete The Misfits, *but more aware than anyone else that, if his life had continued, there would be* no more films and nothing but continued decline to look forward to. He's said more than once that, with no disrespect intended to those he worked with and cared for, his life essentially ended the day Carole's did, and the rest was just "going through the hazy, stumbling motions."

The Scanning Machine left him dazed and a bit incredulous at the dizzying ride he designed for his final incarnation. He loved his work, he loved his many friends, he loved the lifestyle his success afforded him, and he loved how blessed he was in so many ways. But for the first time he saw an irony to his life that left him a bit shaken. He'd prided himself in being a "man's man, always leading with my testosterone and flexing my virility every chance I got. But really, compromising my marriage to the love of my life to stroke my own ego with other women? And denying my own child? Does it get any weaker than that?"

Clark, Carole, and Adeline live communally in a modest compound of small stone bungalows with an ever changing group of actors, writers, and artists that has included everyone from John Barrymore, Truman Capote, Pablo Picasso, and Marilyn Monroe to Spencer Tracy and Katharine Hepburn. They're a stimulating, very social crowd, actively performing as well as never missing their many friends' performances, lectures, and exhibits. Clark is intensely devoted to his Orientation work with new arrivals who struggled with alcohol addiction, and he invests a great deal of his energy in visiting patients at earthly alcohol rehabilitation facilities, "where I belonged but, for all my false pride and lame excuses, was simply too much of a coward to check myself in." He and Adeline have also become devout Christians and are enthralled by the sermons and Bible study they regularly attend at a magnificent open-air church among a circle of palm trees on what corresponds to your island of Kauai.

He's never far from his daughter and his son, although he doesn't believe they sense his presence. "They never knew me on earth. What right do I have to expect them to feel me with them now?" But he beams with joy at his certainty that his two grandchildren were well aware of his singing lullabies to them when they were very young—from time to time, he

says, his granddaughter in particular began singing along with him, and
he wonders if these lyrics might still sound familiar to her:

> *I, my loved one,*
> *Watch am keeping,*
> *All through the night.*

Johnny Carson

The incomparable "king of late-night television" was born John William Carson on October 23, 1925, in Corning, Iowa, to Ruth and Homer Lee Carson, who worked for the Iowa Service Company. He was eight years old when his parents moved with their three children—Johnny, his older sister, Catherine, and his younger brother, Richard—to Norfolk, Nebraska, where Homer took a job with the Iowa-Nebraska Light and Power Company. Johnny's entertainment career began in Norfolk when, at the age of fourteen, he began performing magic as "The Great Carsini" at local venues. After receiving V-12 officer training at Millsaps College in Jackson, Mississippi, he joined the navy on June 8, 1943. He was commissioned as an ensign and served on the USS *Pennsylvania*, stationed in the Pacific, after which he became a communications officer, decoding encrypted messages.

He returned to Nebraska when his navy days ended and attended the University of Nebraska in Lincoln. He graduated in 1949 with a B.A. in radio and speech and a minor in physics. In 1950, he went to work for radio and television station WOW in Omaha as a writer and host of a morning show called *The Squirrel's Nest*. From there he headed to Los Angeles for a staff announcing job at KNXT-TV, where he hosted *Carson's Cellar*, a sketch-comedy show, from 1951 until 1953. In that year Johnny's sense of humor caught the eye of a regular viewer, comedian Red Skelton, who recruited him to join his weekly television variety series *The Red Skelton Show* as a writer. His absence from on-camera performing was short-lived. One night, minutes before airtime, Red Skelton collided with a breakaway door and was knocked unconscious. Johnny went onstage in his place and, on a moment's notice, delivered Skelton's monologue to a live national audience.

From the writers' room of *The Red Skelton Show* he headed back in front of the camera again, first as host of a game show called *Earn Your Vacation* in 1954 and then with his own variety hour, *The Johnny Carson Show*, in the 1955–56 season. Next came two concurrent game shows—he hosted *Who Do You Trust?*, where he met and worked with his future right-hand man, Ed McMahon, from 1957 until 1962, and during those same years he was a panelist on the classic *To Tell the Truth*.

In 1962 Jack Paar left his five-year run on NBC's *The Tonight Show*, citing the fact that the pressure of putting on an hour of television five nights a week had become more than he could handle. On October 1, 1962, Johnny Carson made his debut as host of *The Tonight Show*, with Ed McMahon by his side. From that night until his retirement on May 22, 1992, he ruled late-night TV, won six Emmy awards, and wove his way into the fabric of the American culture. Across the country, everywhere from college campuses to retirement homes, the question, "Did you see the monologue last night?" might have been answered, "No," but it was never answered, "What monologue?" On his first night he interviewed the legendary Groucho Marx. On his last night he was serenaded by superstar Bette Midler, in a historically classic television event. In between he interviewed everyone from politicians to musicians, dramatic actors, and comedians, securing some careers and compromising others, all the while keeping his own political views to himself—he believed his job was to be an entertainer, not a commentator. He could say more with one look into the camera than most television personalities can say in a long-winded paragraph, and no one appreciated talent more than he did.

No one was more frank and sometimes chagrined than Johnny about his multiple marriages, some of which ended very expensively. The first of his wives, and the mother of his three sons, was Joan Wolcott. Theirs was apparently a mutually unhappy marriage that lasted from 1949 until 1963. Next came Joanne Copeland, whom he married shortly after his "quickie" divorce from Joan Wolcott in 1963 and divorced in 1972, for which she received cash and artwork worth about half a million dollars and an annual $100,000 in alimony for the rest of her life. Wife number three was former model Joanna Holland. She and Johnny were married on September 30, 1972, just over a month after his divorce from Joanne Copeland was finalized. Joanna Holland filed for divorce from Johnny on March 8, 1983, and, thanks to California's community property laws, walked away from the marriage with $20 million in cash and property. Last but not least came Alexis Maas, who was thirty-five when she married sixty-one-year-old Johnny Carson on June 20, 1987. They never divorced.

Without a doubt the greatest tragedy of his life was the death of his son Richard, who was killed on June 21, 1991, at the age of thirty-nine, when his car plunged down a steep embankment off of Highway 1 near San Luis Obispo, California. Johnny devoted the final segment of his first *Tonight Show* following the accident to a touching, deeply personal tribute to his son.

Johnny's retirement as host of *The Tonight Show* in 1992 wasn't necessarily intended to be his permanent retirement from show business. He strongly hinted at first that he might return to television if a new project excited or inspired him enough. But except for a handful of appearances on *The Late Show with David Letterman* and a 1993 NBC tribute to Bob Hope, his retirement turned out to be a permanent one after all. The notoriously private, semireclusive king of late-night spent the last years of his life quietly enjoying his home in Malibu. He was sleeping there on March 19, 1999, when he was awakened by severe chest pains. He was rushed to Santa Monica Hospital and underwent emergency quadruple-bypass surgery, from which he recovered.

But on January 23, 2005, at 6:50 A.M., Johnny Carson died of respiratory arrest at Cedars-Sinai Medical Center in Los Angeles after struggling for years with emphysema. He was seventy-nine. Out of respect for the wishes of his family, his body was cremated, and no public service was held.

From Francine

Johnny emerged from the tunnel into the waiting arms of his parents, an aunt, and his son Richard. As ecstatic as he was to be free of his perpetually struggling body, he found it almost jarring to be in an atmosphere of such peaceful, sacred bliss. He's commented many times that he never realized how depressed he was throughout his most recent lifetime until he came Home and rediscovered happiness. His depression came from the difficult series of conflicts he charted for himself for what he quickly announced will be his last incarnation, compounded by the mutually challenging themes of Controller and Loner. He became legendary for being an unparalleled host to a wide variety of people, but off-camera there were very few people whose company he enjoyed or with whom he felt comfortable—in fact, left to his own devices he much preferred socializing as little as possible. He enjoyed the power he came to wield over countless careers, but it made him even more guarded and untrusting, knowing he was often "liked" for the doors he could open. He was fiercely loyal, but quick to sever a relationship over a perceived slight. He loved being loved but was, in his words, "a disaster" when it came to intimacy. Because of all those conflicts that he watched himself act out at the Scanning Machine and the depression he'd struggled with for so long, he devoted many months, in your time, to

Orientation before he was ready to resume and fully appreciate his life on the Other Side.

His chosen passion here is astronomy, which he teaches and researches. He also enjoys sailing, tennis, and singing, at which he always wished he were more gifted on earth. Here at Home he has a beautiful baritone voice and loves performing with Rock Hudson, who was also a frustrated singer on earth, but who excels at it in his life here. He lives alone in a house he says is a precise duplicate of his house in Malibu.

One of his great regrets from his last incarnation was his "completely unfair, utterly inexcusable" temporary estrangement from his son Richard, for which he takes full responsibility, and he's deeply grateful for the friendship they now enjoy.

Sharon Tate

One of the most beautiful, and by all accounts sweetest, rising stars in Hollywood in the 1960s, Sharon Tate was born in Dallas, Texas, on January 24, 1943. She and her two younger sisters, Patti and Debra, were army brats, the daughters of officer Paul Tate and his wife, Doris. Frequent army moves (six different cities in seven years) affected Sharon in two profound ways: she learned to form friendships quickly and to maintain those friendships long after the Tates had relocated again, and she developed a strong bond with her family that lasted throughout her life.

Her beauty came naturally—she won her first title, "Miss Tiny Tot of Dallas," at the age of six months. Although her early intention was to become a psychiatrist rather than an actress, she found success in her teens as a beauty pageant contestant and model, and the lure of Hollywood began tempting her. Her first official onscreen appearance happened serendipitously. Eighteen-year-old Sharon was walking down the street, when a choreographer for an upcoming Pat Boone special approached her and asked if she'd be willing to make a brief appearance on the show. She was thrilled, and her parents gave their permission, on the condition that a guard be posted all night outside the door of the hotel room where she'd be staying. The condition was met, and Pat Boone serenaded the young, spectacular Sharon Tate on national television in 1961.

Another promotion and reassignment sent Colonel Tate and his family to Italy in 1962. The film of Ernest Hemingway's *Adventures of a Young Man,* starring Paul Newman and Richard Beymer, happened to be shooting near the Tates' new home in Verona, and Sharon and some friends went to visit the set. Sharon quickly caught Richard Beymer's eye, and in the course of the casual dates that resulted, he gave her the business card of his agent, the powerful Hal Gefsky, and encouraged her to get her inevitable show business career off the ground.

The Tate family returned to America, Sharon headed to Hollywood, and Hal Gefsky eagerly signed her, joining forces in carefully developing her skills and grooming her for stardom with Filmways chairman Marty Ransohoff. Finally Gefsky and Ransohoff decided that Sharon was ready for her official debut and cast her for a major role in the 1965 film *Eye of the Devil,* starring David Niven, Deborah Kerr, and David Hemmings. Sharon had begun a relationship with hairdresser-to-the-stars Jay Sebring in 1964, and the two of them traveled together to England and France, where the film was being shot.

In 1966 Ransohoff was casting and coproducing a film called *The Fearless Vampire Killers* with Polish director Roman Polanski. Polanski had his heart set on hiring up-and-coming actress Jill St. John for the female lead, but Ransohoff convinced him to hire Sharon instead. Polanski and Sharon were less than enchanted with each other when they first met, but as filming in Italy progressed, their relationship evolved into a serious romance.

Next for Sharon came a mediocre beach comedy called *Don't Make Waves* with Tony Curtis, in which her wardrobe consisted primarily of a bikini. She was mortified by the film and began referring to herself sarcastically as "sexy little me." Compounding her unhappiness was the fact that she was away from Polanski, who was still in Italy doing postproduction work on *The Fearless Vampire Killers.* But she did appreciate and continue to treasure the one positive aspect of her work on *Don't Make Waves*—she and Tony Curtis maintained a close friendship for the rest of her life.

Don't Make Waves was followed by yet another movie that valued her beauty more than her acting ability, a script based on one of the bestselling books of all time, which she considered "trashy"— Jacqueline Susann's *Valley of the Dolls*. Sharon rose to the occasion, gave it her best, and managed to stay out of the war zone the set of the film became. Morale had seriously deteriorated as the cast went from believing they were working on an important, prestigious film to feeling as if they were trapped in a doomed, unsalvageable embarrassment.

The good news and bad news turned out to be that the eagerly anticipated drama known as *Valley of the Dolls* was greeted as an unintentional laugh riot when it debuted on November 14, 1967. It became a cult classic, and it's probably the film for which Sharon Tate will always be most remembered. She was featured in *Esquire*, *Playboy*, and countless movie magazines around the world, and *Playboy* officially declared 1967 as "the year Sharon Tate happens."

While Sharon was filming *Valley of the Dolls*, Polanski was busy shooting his greatest commercial success, *Rosemary's Baby*. They reunited in London when their respective films were finished, and on January 20, 1968, the couple the world press had proclaimed as the epitome of "rich hippies" were married, Sharon in a white minidress and Polanski in what was described as "Edwardian finery." Sharon's "big hang-up," as Polanski called it, was his refusal to promise monogamy, but she was utterly devoted to him and was quoted as saying, "We have a good arrangement. Roman lies to me, and I pretend to believe him."

Back in Los Angeles, Mr. and Mrs. Roman Polanski were celebrated and embraced by a crowd that was diverse, dazzling, and without a doubt the cream of the crop in Hollywood. Sharon in particular loved that their leased house in Beverly Hills was invariably filled with friends, and friends of friends, and everyone felt comfortable, casual, and welcome there.

She went back to work in the summer of 1968 on a Dean Martin film called *The Wrecking Crew*, was nominated for a Golden Globe Best Newcomer Award, and was deeply appreciative that her career finally seemed to be on the rise. In late 1968 she was ecstatic to learn that she was pregnant, as a result of which, on February 15, 1969, she and Polanski moved into a home Sharon called her "love house," a place she admired every time she visited her friends Terry Melcher and Candice Bergen there—a private gated property above Beverly Hills in Benedict Canyon at 10050 Cielo Drive.

In March 1969, despite Polanski's concerns about Sharon traveling during her pregnancy, she left for Italy to film a comedy with the legendary Orson Welles called *The Thirteen Chairs*, while Polanski headed to London to direct *The Day of the Dolphin*. In their absence, friends Wojciech Frykowski and Abigail Folger house-sat on Cielo Drive. Sharon visited Polanski in London when she finished work on *The Thirteen Chairs*, but returned to Los Angeles alone on July 20, 1969. Polanski promised to come home on August 12, in time for the birth of their baby, and asked Frykowski and Folger to stay at the Cielo Drive house with Sharon until then.

On the evening of August 8, 1969, Sharon Tate, Jay Sebring, Abigail Folger, and Wojciech Frykowski went to dinner at the popular El Coyote Restaurant, arriving home at around 10:30 P.M. Their bodies were discovered the next morning by Sharon's housekeeper, all of them slaughtered in what would become one of the most notorious and horrific crimes of the twentieth century. Charles Manson and his "family" were ultimately tried and convicted of the insanely senseless murders and sentenced to spend the rest of their lives in prison. And to add to the long list of resulting tragedies, the crimes and those who committed them were so sensational and endlessly publicized that the exquisite Sharon Tate became more famous for the way she died than for the kind, sweet, generous, and gifted way she lived. She was buried on August 13 at the Holy Cross Cemetery near Los Angeles, holding her infant son in her arms.

From Francine

Sharon was met on the Other Side by a very short older woman with gray-blonde hair, who I believe is her grandmother, and by throngs from Home and from her twelve past lives. She is as cherished here as she was on earth for being an especially gifted, thoughtful friend, and there was widespread relief at how much at peace Sharon was despite such an obscene end to what she says will be her last incarnation. Her Spirit Guide, Amelia, escorted her to the Scanning Machine, from which she walked away filled with light and understanding about her life and death.

She charted herself to be beautiful and talented enough to acquire fame and the respect of her peers, and to be a substantial enough person to make friends easily and make a strong impact on those who knew her, which served her intended purpose—Sharon Tate is an excellent example of a spirit who never intended to live a long life and who knew that her death would somehow serve a greater good. If she had been less famous and less adored, her death would have been far less widely publicized, determination to solve the murders would not have been so intense, and dozens more lives would have been needlessly taken by the Manson family if Sharon hadn't been among the victims.

She's adamant about the fact that if her lifetime had continued, she would have left Roman Polanski. Her prolonged times away from him made her realize that, because she couldn't trust him as a husband, she could never rely on him to be the kind of father she believed every baby should have. She also realized that as a result of her having been slightly in awe of him, she tended to feel inferior when she was with him, and she was a stronger, healthier, happier woman when they were apart.

Sharon lives with a small group of friends in a green two-story house surrounded by a stand of tall pines. She spends most of her time in the Waiting Room in the Towers, caring for the babies who are about to enter a fetus on earth. She has a calming, reassuring way with them and would have been a wonderful mother. She visits a friend in your dimension named Shirley or Sheila as well as her sister Debbie, and she wants Debbie to know how proud she is of her for carrying on their mother's work as a victim's advocate.

She was the first to greet her parents and her sister Patti when they came Home, and the four of them are rarely seen apart, as devoted to each other here as they were during their lifetimes.

Natalie Wood

Natalie Wood's movie career began at the age of four and ended too soon in an accidental drowning when she was forty-three. Her birth name was Natalia Zakharenko, and she was born in San Francisco on July 20, 1938, to Russian immigrants Nikolai Zakharenko, an architect, and his wife, Maria, a ballet dancer. (Natalie's sister, Svetlana, was born eight years later, in 1946, and became known as Lana Wood, an actress and producer.) Nikolai and Maria changed their surname to Gurdin while Natalie was an infant. The family soon moved north to Santa Rosa, where Maria, determined to make her beautiful four-year-old daughter a star, took Natalie to an audition for "extra" work on a Don Ameche film called *Happy Land*, which was shooting locally. "Natasha Gurdin" (Natasha is the diminutive of Natalia) was cast in the uncredited role of a little girl who drops her ice cream, which was all the encouragement Maria needed to insist that the family move to Hollywood to pursue her child's destiny as an actress.

Maria happened to be right. Warner Bros. quickly changed Natasha Gurdin to Natalie Wood and cast the seven-year-old as a German orphan in *Tomorrow Is Forever* with Orson Welles and Claudette Colbert, which was immediately followed by *The Ghost and Mrs. Muir*, starring Rex Harrison and directed by the esteemed Joseph Mankiewicz. Next came the classic *Miracle on 34th Street*, in which she played the little girl who doubted Santa Claus, securing her reputation as the favorite new child star in Hollywood. By the age of sixteen she'd appeared in twenty films, working with some of the biggest names in the business.

Natalie Wood was one of the few child stars who made a graceful transition into the teen years, and at the age of sixteen she was cast in a role that brought her her first Academy Award nomination for Best Supporting Actress: costarring with up-and-coming superstars James Dean and Sal Mineo in 1955's *Rebel Without a Cause*. Eager to reach adulthood offscreen as well, she dated the film's director, Nicholas Ray, twenty-five years older than she, moving on from him to actor Scott Marlowe and from Marlowe to a rising rock-and-roll star named Elvis Presley. And then along came Robert Wagner.

Natalie told the story that when she was ten years old, she saw the handsome eighteen-year-old actor walking down a hallway at Twentieth Century Fox; she turned to her mother and announced, "I'm going to marry him." On her eighteenth birthday she went on her first date with Robert Wagner, who was twenty-six by then, and they were married on December 28, 1957. They separated in 1961 and were divorced in 1962, but that was far from the end of their story.

Natalie was then cast in *The Searchers*, a John Ford western starring John Wayne. Natalie still found time to graduate from Van Nuys High School in 1956, which paled in comparison to the Golden Globe Award she won in 1957 that proclaimed her "New Star of the Year (Actress)." After a role in 1958's *Marjorie Morningstar* opposite Gene Kelly, Natalie starred in one of her most memorable films, Elia Kazan's *Splendor in the Grass*, with the wildly popular Warren Beatty, which earned her a second Academy Award nomination. She established herself as a versatile talent in 1961's film version of Leonard Bernstein's *West Side Story* and a year later in *Gypsy*. Her third Oscar nomination came in 1963 for *Love with the Proper Stranger* opposite heartthrob Steve McQueen.

Her professional life was clearly thriving in the early 1960s, but she was losing her struggle to successfully balance marriage and a career. The strain became worse when her marriage went through a rocky patch, and Natalie filed for divorce. She then found herself in a string of box-office failures and, during the summer of 1966, after slipping into a deep depression, she overdosed on sleeping pills in what she admitted was a failed suicide attempt.

By the time 1969 rolled around she'd not only recovered, but was beginning to thrive again. She starred in the highly acclaimed *Bob and Carol and Ted and Alice* with Robert Culp, Elliot Gould, and Dyan Cannon, and she married Richard Gregson, a successful British producer and agent, whom she'd dated for two years. Their daughter, Natasha, was born on September 29, 1970, and Natalie seemed to have found the stable family life she'd been looking for since childhood. Sadly, in 1971, she reportedly overheard an inappropriate and unmistakably intimate phone conversation between her husband and her secretary. Feeling doubly betrayed, she fired her secretary and filed for divorce.

Several months later, in early 1972, she ran into her ex-husband, Robert Wagner, at a party, and they resumed their relationship. Three months after her divorce from Richard Gregson was final, Natalie Wood remarried Robert Wagner in Malibu on July 16, 1972. Their daughter, Courtney, was born on March 9, 1974, and their marriage lasted until the premature end of Natalie's life. Not wanting to repeat the experience of stressfully juggling marriage and career, Natalie focused the majority of her attention on her husband and daughter and only accepted the television version of *Cat on a Hot Tin Roof* with Laurence Olivier in 1976 when her husband was signed to star right along with her.

In 1979 she won a Best Actress Golden Globe Award for the miniseries *From Here to Eternity*, but her next two feature films were unsuccessful both critically and financially. Eager to get her career back on track, Natalie had high hopes for her next film commitment, a science fiction thriller called *Brainstorm*.

Location work in Raleigh, North Carolina, on *Brainstorm* finished at the end of October 1981, and the cast and crew returned to Los Angeles in November to film interior scenes. On November 28, Natalie, Robert Wagner, and Natalie's *Brainstorm* costar Christopher Walken sailed to Catalina Island aboard the Wagners' yacht *Splendor*. Late on the night of November 29, Natalie disappeared from the yacht. Frantic and distraught, Wagner alerted the Coast Guard, who, after an all-night search, found the body of Natalie Wood two hundred yards offshore, still wrapped in the down-filled coat and wool sweater she'd been wearing when she was last seen onboard.

Hollywood and the tabloids shifted into high gear, breathlessly sharing every possible sensational story that could be dreamed up about a sudden death, a yacht in the dark of night, and three Hollywood stars. But after the autopsy and a police investigation, the sad conclusion was a simple one: Natalie, after several glasses of wine, had gone to the yacht's dinghy, either to board it or to secure it more tightly to the side of the boat; intoxicated, she slipped overboard. She was a poor swimmer with a lifelong terror of dark water, so she panicked, tried unsuccessfully to climb into the dinghy with her heavy, wet coat and sweater pulling her down, drifted too far away from the yacht for her cries to be heard, and drowned in the Pacific near the Catalina coast.

In the aftermath of Natalie Wood's shockingly premature death at the age of forty-three, *Brainstorm* was finished with a revised ending, a stand-in, and some sleight-of-hand with camera angles. It was released in 1983 and was neither a critical nor a commercial success, but it's still valued as the last work of one of Hollywood's favorite, most memorable stars. She was laid to rest in the Westwood Village Memorial Park Cemetery.

From Francine

Natalie made the transition from earth to the Other Side instantaneously, but she was understandably stunned to find herself emerging from the tunnel after such a sudden death. She was welcomed Home by her old friend and costar Steve McQueen (a new arrival himself) and by a tiny woman who, as all spirits do here, greeted her as she'd appeared on earth to make sure Natalie would recognize her: long steel-gray hair pulled tightly up into a topknot, large deep-set eyes, a rather prominent nose and thin lips. (Natalie says her family will know immediately who the woman is from this description.) As emotionally sensitive as Natalie was during her last lifetime, she was watched carefully during her time at the Scanning Machine, but she made a quick, peaceful adjustment to being Home and was so eager to resume her life on the Other Side that cocooning wasn't necessary.

While no one on earth is allowed to see the chart they wrote for any given lifetime until they've returned from that lifetime, there are those who are uniquely able to remember fragments of their charts without being aware that that's what they're doing. Natalie was one of those people. She knew at the age of ten, on seeing Robert Wagner for the first time, that he was the man she'd charted herself to marry—not once, but twice. And her lifelong fear of dark water was a memory of having written an Exit Point into her chart involving dark water. In fact, if you talk to those who were closest to her, you'll find that she was often extraordinarily intuitive. It was part of her strength and part of her fragility.

She wants her daughters to know that not a day goes by when she doesn't visit them, especially when they're "alone" in their cars. She says they taught her about love and priorities, and nothing in this world meant more to her than being their mother. She also wants to assure them that she's at peace about the night she died and that "everyone who matters knows everything they need to know about what happened." Beyond that, there's nothing more to say, and she's very happy that they were able to move on and grow into such successful, beautiful, interesting women.

Her life at Home is, of course, blissfully busy. She loves to socialize with her many cherished friends from her most recent lifetime—Steve McQueen, James Dean, Elvis Presley, Sal Mineo, Bette Davis, and a British woman named Judy Fox, to whom she seems especially close—as well as loved ones from her twenty-three past incarnations. She both performs and teaches ballet, and she's also training to work in the cocooning chambers. She has no intention of incarnating again, but she does intend to become a Spirit Guide for an acquaintance on the Other Side who's preparing for another lifetime and has chosen life themes identical to those Natalie just experienced, Rejection and Aesthetic Pursuits.

Elvis Presley

On January 8, 1935, in a two-room house in Tupelo, Mississippi, built by Vernon Elvis Presley, his wife, Gladys Smith Presley, gave birth to identical twin boys. The first, Jessie Garon, was stillborn. Thirty-five minutes after Jessie's sad arrival, the second twin, Elvis Aron, was born, healthy, thriving, and, as the saying goes, "ready to rock and roll." The Presleys were a close-knit family, surrounded by aunts, uncles, grandparents, and cousins in Tupelo, and Vernon worked odd jobs to keep his wife and son above the poverty line as best he could. But when he was incarcerated for eight months for check fraud, Gladys lost their house, and she and Elvis moved in with relatives. Elvis was first exposed to gospel music at the Assembly of God Church he attended with relatives, and it resonated in him throughout his life, as did his family's favorite country music radio station and the blues sung on the porches and street corners of the predominantly black neighborhood where the Presleys briefly lived.

Elvis was ten years old when he gave his first professional performance. Standing on a chair so that he could reach the microphone, he sang a song called "Old Shep" for a talent contest at the Mississippi-Alabama Fair and Dairy Show and won the $5 fifth-place prize. On his eleventh birthday he was disappointed to learn that instead of the bicycle he was hoping for, his parents presented him with a more affordable $12.95 guitar. His pastor and two of his uncles gave him his first guitar lessons, and the somewhat shy loner found a good, reliable friend in the guitar he began bringing to school to practice with during lunch and recess.

In November 1948 Vernon and Gladys and their son moved to Memphis, Tennessee, hoping for better job opportunities. They settled into low-income housing, and all three of them worked where they could while Elvis attended L. C. Humes High School. He was rarely seen without his guitar and began spending as much time as possible on Beale Street, the heart of blues music in Memphis. He loved the music and the clothing, just as he continued to love all the gospel and country performers he sought out. Not only was his musical style taking shape, but his personal style was evolving as well, with flashy clothing, sideburns, and long slicked-back hair that set him apart from his high-school classmates and offered a glimpse into the singular legend he would become.

In August 1953, two months after getting his high-school diploma, Elvis walked into Sun Records in Memphis, wanting to buy enough studio time to record two songs: "My Happiness" and "That's When Your Heartaches Begin." Sam Phillips, who owned Sun Records, made a note after the session that read, "Elvis Presley. Good ballad singer. Hold."

From there, after some rejections, failed auditions, a truck-driving job, assurances that he'd never make it as a singer, and accusations of being a "danger to the security of the United States" because of the way he kept time to the music with his hips when he performed, by the end of 1956 Elvis Presley had a manager (music promoter "Colonel" Tom Parker), a contract with RCA Records, his first number-one hit record ("Heartbreak Hotel"), and a string of national television appearances that culminated in three triumphant appearances on *The Ed Sullivan Show*. At the end of his third appearance, Ed Sullivan informed his audience and the country that Elvis was "a real decent, fine boy," giving his coveted blessing for the superstardom that was well on its way.

In 1957 Elvis bought Graceland, a gated mansion on 13.8 acres of land in Memphis, and proudly moved there with his parents. Graceland continued to be his home for the rest of his life, and it was at Graceland in 1958, while Elvis was serving in the army, that his beloved mother, Gladys, died.

It was also while serving in the army, stationed in Germany from 1958 until March 1960, that Elvis was introduced to karate, amphetamines, and a beautiful fourteen-year-old girl named Priscilla Beaulieu, whom he brought home to Graceland when his army service ended in 1960 and married in Las Vegas on May 1, 1967. Exactly nine months later Priscilla gave birth to their only child, a daughter named Lisa Marie. The marriage ended in divorce on August 18, 1972, with Elvis and Priscilla agreeing to share custody of Lisa Marie.

Contrary to Elvis's fears, his popularity hadn't diminished during his absence in the military, and he recorded some of his greatest hits in the early 1960s. Unfortunately, a barrage of ill-conceived, thrown-together movies that Elvis found embarrassing—twenty-seven of them between 1961 and 1970—compromised his credibility and his popularity. But in 1968 Elvis starred in what came to be called his "Comeback Special," a brilliantly conceived and executed TV hour featuring his first "live" appearance since 1961. It was NBC's highest-rated show of the season, it was magic, Elvis Presley never looked or sounded better, and it triggered an unprecedented career resurrection as requests for live performances poured in from around the world.

By the early 1970s, despite spectacularly successful tours and recording sessions, Elvis's health began to decline as he battled both a weight problem and dangerous prescription drug addictions. His performances became increasingly unreliable, sometimes bordering on incoherent, and he often seemed nervous and self-conscious, aware of his ballooning weight and in visible emotional pain. When he wasn't onstage, he would isolate himself in his room with a hand-ful of insiders, where he was paranoid, germophobic, and obsessive.

On June 26, 1977, Elvis Presley gave what was to be his final performance at the Market Square Arena in Indianapolis. He was scheduled to leave Memphis again to begin another tour on the night of August 16. But that afternoon, his fiancée, Ginger Alden, found him unresponsive on the floor of his Graceland bathroom. He was pronounced dead at 3:30 P.M. at Baptist Memorial Hospital. While a sanitized autopsy listed the cause of death as cardiac arrhythmia, it was later established during a criminal investigation of Elvis's pri-mary physician, Dr. Nichopoulos, a.k.a. Dr. Nick, that, even though Dr. Nick was ultimately exonerated for criminal liability in Elvis's death, "in the first eight months of 1977 alone he had prescribed more than 10,000 doses of sedatives, amphetamines and narcotics, all in Elvis's name." Dr. Nichopoulos's license was permanently revoked during the 1990s.

Elvis Presley and his cherished mother, Gladys, are buried side by side at Graceland's Meditation Garden, and today the only house in America visited by more tourists per year than Graceland is the White House.

From Sylvia

You could have knocked me over with a feather when, less than twenty-four hours after Elvis Presley died, the *San Francisco Chroni-cle* called to ask if Francine could possibly contact his spirit and give them the results of her interview with him. I was hardly the only psychic interviewed by the press on the subject of Elvis that day, but I wasn't particularly famous in 1977, and I certainly wasn't a renowned Elvis Presley fan. In fact, all I really knew about him was that he was a rock-and-roll singer, he had a beautiful voice when he sang ballads, and he was drop-dead gorgeous in his prime. But if the *San Francisco Chronicle* wanted comments from Francine about him, I was happy to oblige if she was. As it turned out, she was so cooperative that we made the front page of the *Chronicle*, which announced that a psychic named Sylvia Brown (I hadn't added the *e* yet) "through her spiritual guide, an Aztec-Inca spirit named Francine," had contacted him less than twenty-four hours after his death.

I was "absent," of course, during the trance with Francine, but I'm happy to pass along the information I heard on the tapes of that interview. It's worth adding, by the way, that he was able to go into this much detail precisely because she was talking to him so soon after he'd arrived back on the Other Side, when his memories of his just-ended lifetime on earth were so fresh. It's not surprising that the more settled we get again into our blissful lives at Home, the less we think about all but the most essential parts of the lives we left behind.

Elvis died in a very, very small room, he told Francine, and he was immediately aware that he'd passed over. He'd had a headache earlier that day, and his back hurt, and he went into this small room with a book. He'd had problems with his lower intestine for the previous two and a half years, problems he'd mentioned to a few friends, particularly a "John" and a "Charlie," and he was on medication and steroids. His death, though, was unintentional and accidental, and he had a quick, easy trip Home, which was no surprise to him thanks to his devout lifelong faith in God.

He was met on the Other Side by his mother, Gladys, whom he affectionately nicknamed "Gladiola" here on earth, his twin brother, Jesse, and a friend named Chuck. His life at Home was filled with music. His voice was even richer than it was on earth, and he and countless other transcended musicians loved giving grand, celebrated concerts. He said that although he was best known as a rock-and-roll singer, his real musical passion and inspiration was gospel music, but his favorite of all the songs he ever recorded was "Heartbreak Hotel."

He regretted that he wasn't as skilled at loving individual people as he was at loving large anonymous groups of them, although the greatest pride, joy, and accomplishment in his lifetime was his daughter, Lisa Marie. As much as he loved Priscilla, and he did, he felt their marriage was doomed, because his lifestyle didn't allow them to spend enough private, "normal" time together.

Because he was aware of sixteen separate attempts on his life, he spent many years feeling paranoid and fearful. Relaxation and sleep seemed impossible without medication. He said he had a premonition of his death six months before it happened, and he thought of his last performances of "My Way" as his way of saying farewell to his fans.

He passed along a few personal messages to his father, Vernon. One was the name "Ruta May." Another was a game they played when Elvis was a child, in which one of them would start a nursery rhyme and the other one would finish it.

I don't mind telling you that I couldn't have been more flattered when, a few weeks after the *Chronicle* article appeared, both Vernon Presley and Elvis's friend Charlie Hodge called to validate the information Francine passed along.

In preparation for this book, I asked Francine about one more piece of information she shared in that article, that she said Elvis had already planned his next incarnation. He was going to be a singer again, this time with light hair and light eyes, and he would be born in 2004. What follows is her 2010 update.

From Francine

Elvis began his new incarnation in late November 2004. His hair is blond, although it will darken as he gets older, and his eyes are blue, as he chose them to be. *He was born in France and lives on a vineyard there with his parents and his two brothers. The family travels to Italy a few times a year to visit relatives there.*

He will grow up to have a very beautiful singing voice, but he will not be a famous singer or recording artist again. He will devote his voice and his talent as a composer to his devout Catholicism, writing hymns and performing them solely for church services and special events. He feels that he sacrificed depth and introspection for fame and wealth in his last life, and in this new life he intends to contribute to this world in quiet, thoughtful, charitable anonymity by becoming a monk and working with the poor throughout the French countryside.

Dean Martin

The singer and actor nicknamed the "king of cool" was born Dino Paul Crocetti on June 7, 1917, in Steubenville, Ohio. His parents, Gaetano and Angela, were Italian immigrants, and neither Dean nor his older brother, Bill, spoke a word of anything but Italian before they started school. School didn't hold much interest for Dean, and he dropped out of Steubenville High School in the tenth grade. A whirlwind of jobs followed immediately; he was a bootleg liquor deliverer, a shoe-shine boy, a blackjack dealer, a steel mill worker, even briefly a fifteen-year-old boxer called "Kid Crochet." He also became a skilled croupier in illegal casinos, where he was exposed to a variety of entertainers and began thinking he might have what it took to be one of them. One night in August 1934 some friends convinced him to go onstage and sing, and from then on a lot of local Steubenville bands found themselves accompanying the young, talented crooner "Dino Martini." In 1938, while singing at the State Restaurant in Columbus, Ohio, he was "discovered" and hired as a featured vocalist by Cleveland bandleader Sammy Watkins, who convinced Dino Martini to change his name to Dean Martin.

Dean married Betty McDonald in 1941, an unhappy marriage that lasted until 1949 and produced four children (Stephen, Claudia, Barbara, and Deana), of whom Dean was awarded custody after the divorce. That same year he began a twenty-three-year marriage to

Jeanne Biegger, which resulted in three more children: Dean Paul, Ricci, and Gina.

Dean's career continued to gain momentum in the 1940s. In 1943 he signed a contract to sing exclusively at New York's Riobamba Room, following its previous entertainer, another young singer named Frank Sinatra; in 1944 he began broadcasting a fifteen-minute radio program called *Songs by Dean Martin;* and in 1946 he was given a recording contract with Diamond Records. His one-year stint in the army in 1944, during which he was stationed near home in Akron, Ohio, caused very little disruption in his growing popularity.

One night in 1946, at the Glass Hat Club in New York, Dean Martin met an up-and-coming comic named Jerry Lewis, who was also performing there. They began participating in each other's acts, and a comedy team was born, with Dean as the smooth, low-key crooner and straight man and Jerry as the manic, disruptive, unpredictable clown. They were a hit, given their own radio show in 1949, and signed by Paramount Pictures producer Hal Wallis for his film *My Friend Irma*. Next thing they knew, they had a major-league agent, Abby Greshler; a very lucrative contract that included complete control over their club and recording material and their radio and television appearances; new homes in Los Angeles, which Dean loved; and a shared income of millions of dollars. The team of Martin and Lewis made a total of sixteen films, including *Sailor Beware*, *You're Never Too Young*, and *Hollywood or Bust*. But Dean finally became disillusioned with his role as straight man, which consistently led critics to praise Jerry Lewis as the real talent in the team, and in 1956 he ended the partnership and became a solo act again.

First on his career agenda was to become a legitimate actor. His first effort, *Ten Thousand Bedrooms*, was a failure, but in 1957 he took a huge salary cut for the opportunity to costar in *The Young Lions* with Marlon Brando and Montgomery Clift. It proved to be a smart move and the beginning of Dean's comeback. Next came *Some Came*

Running in 1958 with his old Riobamba counterpart Frank Sinatra, which was also a success, and Dean Martin's acting career was on its way again with no need at all for a zany partner.

His recording career was thriving as well by the late 1950s. In his lifetime he recorded more than a hundred albums, and he even succeeded in knocking the Beatles' hit "A Hard Day's Night" out of first place on American charts with his signature song, "Everybody Loves Somebody Sometime." He also became one of the most popular headliners in Las Vegas, soon to be joined on the stage by a small group of famous friends whom the public would come to call the "Rat Pack" (Dean, Frank Sinatra, Sammy Davis Jr., Joey Bishop, and Peter Lawford). The Rat Pack also made four movies together between 1960 and 1964—*Ocean's Eleven, Sergeants Three, Four for Texas,* and *Robin and the Seven Hoods.*

In 1965 Dean launched his successful NBC variety series *The Dean Martin Show,* filled with singing, comedy, and cream-of-the-crop celebrity guests; Dean, invariably in a tuxedo, was the laid-back, alcohol-buzzed, suave, and sometimes silly host. Despite plenty of rumors to the contrary, Dean enjoyed drinking, but he was invariably disciplined about it and was never an alcoholic. In fact, he was a notorious homebody, preferring a round of golf and an evening of watching westerns on TV to the night life more typical of the rest of his Rat Pack cronies. The 1960s also ushered in a series of four Matt Helm movies, with Dean in the title role as the comedic superspy.

In the early 1970s, when his television series was still thriving and his recording career was still rolling along nicely, Dean suffered what many considered to be a mid-life crisis. He suddenly divorced Jeanne, his wife of twenty-three years, and dissolved his partnership with the Riviera Hotel in Las Vegas, signing instead with the MGM Grand and securing a three-picture deal with MGM Studios. He quickly married a hair-salon receptionist named Catherine Hawn in 1973, a marriage that lasted less than three years. He and Jeanne ultimately reconciled, although they never remarried. *The Dean Martin Show* was cancelled at the end of the 1974 season, but it did evolve into a series of specials called the *Dean Martin Celebrity Roast,* which lasted through 1984.

By 1976 Dean's old partner Jerry Lewis, from whom he'd remained estranged, was hosting an annual Labor Day telethon for the Muscular Dystrophy Association. In one of the most talked-about television events of the decade, Frank Sinatra, to the shock of Jerry Lewis and his vast television audience, walked onstage with Dean. Martin and Lewis embraced, the personal reconciliation took hold, and they remained friends until Dean's death.

On March 21, 1987, Dean's son Dean Paul was killed in a jet fighter crash while flying with the California Air National Guard. The loss shattered Dean, and he never recovered. He made a few more appearances with the Rat Pack, ending in 1989 at Bally's in Las Vegas, and celebrated Frank Sinatra's seventy-fifth birthday onstage in December 1990, but he never performed again.

By September 1993 Dean had been diagnosed with both emphysema and lung cancer. On Christmas morning, 1995, with his former wife Jeanne at his side, Dean Martin died of respiratory failure at the age of seventy-eight. Las Vegas most certainly still remembered him and honored him by dimming the lights along the fabled Strip, where he entertained so many for so long, at the news of his passing.

From Francine

As often happens when the darkness of grief overwhelms the spirit, Dean's grief over the death of his son Dean Paul separated him from his faith and all the love around him. And when his body died, his grief kept him lost and earthbound, wandering from his house to his favorite restaurants in search of solace and only wondering in passing why no one seemed to even acknowledge him anymore. We all watched over him and rejoiced when, in an act of pure eternal grace, Dean Paul reached out from the Other Side to embrace his father and bring him Home. He stayed with him at the Scanning Machine and through Orientation, and Dean emerged replenished, his faith deeper and stronger than ever, his extraordinary capacity to love and be loved fully intact. It was then that Dean was reunited with his father and mother, his Uncle Leonard, Sammy Davis Jr., and a host of lifelong friends, particularly a Joe or Joey from "the neighborhood."

His experience at the Scanning Machine made Dean especially eager to apologize to Sammy for moments when he was unkind and made jokes at Sammy's expense, betraying the genuine love he felt for him for the sake of what he referred to as "a cheap laugh." I have no idea what Dean was referring to, but his apology was heartfelt, Sammy accepted it with enormous compassion, and their friendship remains strong. One of the countless joys of Home is that there is no anger here, no resentment or ill will toward anyone here or on earth, and while no apologies are ever necessary, they provide great opportunities for further growth and cleansing of the soul.

Dean still enjoys performing here, and he's enormously popular for his voice, his charm, and a sense of humor that far surpasses what you experienced on earth. He also loves entertaining in his home overlooking a cliffside golf course that corresponds to your northern California coastline. He much prefers small crowds to large ones and cherishes time to himself, which he most typically spends horseback riding. He devoutly attends Mass at his favorite church—not one of our magnificent cathedrals, but an intimate outdoor altar hidden in the Gardens of the Towers. He continues to study acting and often appears in classic musicals, and he takes joy in giving vocal lessons to the many aspiring singers on the Other Side.

Dean occasionally visits his wife Jeanne and his children. To this day he and his friend Peter Lawford return to what Dean laughingly refers to as their favorite "haunt," a restaurant called the Hamburger Hamlet in Hollywood, where they've likely been fleetingly spotted by a *few waiters and more than a few patrons, but dismissed as products of overactive imaginations.*

Rarely does anyone return to the Other Side and their time at the Scanning Machine without regrets. Dean says his biggest were his tendency to abruptly leave situations when he began to get a self-imposed feeling of being nonessential and easily replaced—particularly his breakup with Jerry Lewis and his divorce from Jeanne, whom he still loved—and the fact that he never sought help in recovering from his grief over the death of his son, which caused him to, as he puts it, "check out on so many people who loved me." His chosen life themes were Performance and Passivity, the areas in which he found his highest highs and his most crushing personal disappointments, a statement he's certain those who knew him best will understand.

Richard Pryor

On December 1, 1940, comedian, actor, and writer Richard Franklin Lennox Thomas Pryor III was born in Peoria, Illinois. His mother, Gertrude, a prostitute, worked in his grandmother's brothel, and his father was said to be a boxer and bartender to whom his mother was briefly married when Richard was three years old. Richard was raised in the brothel and abused throughout his childhood—beaten by his violent grandmother for even the slightest disobedience, raped by a teenage neighbor when he was six years old, and molested by a priest. He found his emotional escape and inspiration in the darkened movie theater near his chaotic, cruel home.

He was first "discovered" at the age of twelve by Juliette Whittaker, who supervised a public recreational facility. Recognizing his natural comedic performing ability, she cast him in a local production of *Rumpelstiltskin* and arranged talent shows specifically for the purpose of shining a spotlight on this hilarious, edgy little boy. She remained an important influence on Richard until the end of his career.

His formal education ended with expulsion when he was fourteen, launching him into a succession of professions: strip-club janitor, shoe-shine boy, drummer, meat packer, truck driver, billiard hall attendant, and occasional juvenile offender. His military career was limited to two years in the army from 1958 to 1960, most of which he spent in an army prison for an assault charge while he was briefly stationed in Germany.

After his discharge from the military, he spent just enough time at a cabaret in Peoria to discover that his talents did not lie in the areas of singing and accompanying himself on the piano, and he quickly switched to professional stand-up comedy in clubs throughout the Midwest. It was also in 1960 that he married Patricia Price, the mother of his first child, Richard Jr., who was born in 1961. The marriage ended in divorce a year later.

Richard moved to New York in 1963, drawn there by one of his great inspirations, Bill Cosby, and quickly rose through the ranks of club comedians until he found himself appearing with such seminal performers as Bob Dylan, Richie Havens, and Woody Allen. Television came calling in 1966, and he gained national exposure thanks to, among others, *The Ed Sullivan Show* and *The Tonight Show* with Johnny Carson. And from there it was off to Las Vegas, where he was the opening act for Bobby Darin at the Flamingo Hotel. But before long, performing in relatively middle-of-the-road Las Vegas became too confining for his more outrageous sensibilities, and in September 1969 he walked out on his scheduled performance at the Aladdin Hotel with a rhetorical, "What the f*** am I doing here?" Before leaving Las Vegas he recorded his first album, *Richard Pryor*, in 1968; he broke into film with small roles in *The Busy Body* (1967) and *Wild in the Streets* (1968); and he became a father again, twice— he had his second child, Elizabeth, with his girlfriend Maxine Anderson in 1967, and his two-year marriage to Shelly Bonus produced his third child, his daughter Rain, in 1969.

Richard headed from Las Vegas to Berkeley, California, where he took a hiatus from comedy and sharpened his wit, his edge, and his perspective in the free-spirited, outspoken counterculture atmosphere of Berkeley in the late 1960s. He recorded his second album, *Craps (After Hours)*, in 1971 and began writing for television, including *Sanford and Son*, *The Flip Wilson Show*, and a Lily Tomlin special for which he shared a Best Writing Emmy. He also won critical acclaim for his role in 1972's *Lady Sings the Blues* with Diana Ross.

His career was thriving by 1974, when he cowrote the Mel Brooks film *Blazing Saddles* and released his hilarious Grammy Award–winning album *That Nigger's Crazy*. Eager to break into more mainstream television appearances, he was a guest host on the first season of the groundbreaking series *Saturday Night Live* in 1975 and starred in *The Richard Pryor Show*, an NBC variety series that lasted for only four episodes in 1977 before it was cancelled. But for the most part, his popularity in both television and film never faltered from the 1970s through the 1990s, with some fifty movies, guest appearances, and specials to his credit, not to mention the nineteen comedy albums he recorded in his lifetime.

At the same time, his personal life was proving to be as turbulent as his childhood, clouded by substance abuse, legal problems, and relationship dramas. There was a tax-evasion arrest in 1974 for which he served ten days in jail. There was his one-year marriage to actress Deborah McGuire in 1977, punctuated by his shooting her car and being ordered into psychiatric treatment after paying fines and restitution. But the most dramatic, frightening, and widely publicized event in his life occurred on June 9, 1980. After several days of free-basing cocaine, Richard poured 151-proof rum on himself and set himself on fire. In flames, he ran out of his house and down the street until the police managed to subdue him, and he spent six weeks in the hospital recovering from burns over 50 percent of his body. It was considered to be a horrible accident at the time, but in his subsequent autobiography, *Pryor Convictions: And Other Life Sentences*, which he wrote with author Todd Gold in 1995, he admitted that it was the deliberate act of a man in an insane drug haze.

In 1981 Richard married actress Jennifer Lee, whom he divorced a year later. Richard's fourth child, Steven, was born in 1984 to his girlfriend Flynn Belaine, whom he married in October 1986 and divorced in 1987, shortly after Richard's sixth child, Kelsey, was conceived—she wasn't born until October 1987, preceded six months earlier by his fifth child, Franklin, whose mother was Richard's girlfriend Geraldine Mason.

In 1986, in the midst of this personal chaos and a career that was still showing no signs of slowing down, Richard Pryor was diagnosed with multiple sclerosis. He continued to work, even after being confined to a wheelchair in the early 1990s, but finally, in 2001, he remarried Jennifer Lee and withdrew with her into the privacy of his home near Los Angeles, where one of his final charitable acts was the establishment of Pryor's Planet for the benefit of animals and their rights and care.

On December 10, 2005, Richard Pryor was rushed to an Encino, California, hospital with Jennifer Lee Pryor at his side. He died at 7:58 A.M. of cardiac arrest, leaving behind an extraordinary body of work and an impact on the world of comedy that will continue to resonate for decades to come.

From Francine

Richard remained earthbound for almost four years in your time, in Los Angeles, which he'd come to think of as home. He wandered back and forth from his Encino house to the backstage areas of the Improv and the Comedy Store, two of the most popular clubs in the area, to watch fellow comedians perform. He suspects that several employees saw, heard, or sensed him there, and that his voice and presence must have been too indistinct to understand. Richard's refusal to acknowledge the tunnel was a deliberate choice on his part, for a common, heartbreaking reason: not for a moment did he believe God would accept him after the flawed, sometimes violent, often self-destructive life he'd lived, especially when he'd been given such an uncommon wealth of gifts. "What a waste," he kept saying. "What a weak, stupid waste."

Finally, on Christmas Day 2008 according to your calendar, Richard's Spirit Guide, Rhima, and his soul mate, a woman named Ashur, retrieved him from his sad, lost state of limbo and brought him Home. His body and mind were too severely debilitated for him to understand where, or even who, he was. And, as happens in cases in which more intensive treatment than cocooning is needed, Rhima and Ashur gently guided Richard past the masses of concerned, loving spirits and animals waiting to greet him and took him directly to the Towers.

When spirits arrive on the Other Side from such extreme circumstances as Richard's physiological illness compounded by his decades of substance abuse, which are beyond the healing therapy that cocooning has to offer, they're embraced by a team of highly advanced physical and psychiatric experts for a form of what you on earth might call "deprogramming." The ailing spirit is led through a slow, compassionate restoration process, at the end of which its body is thriving again and its mind has successfully processed and released its darkness into the white light of the Holy Spirit and clarified the full impact of the powerful, inspiring, and positive legacy it left behind. Richard is still experiencing "deprogramming," surrounded by infinite love and support, and I'm told he's making extraordinary progress.

I'm also told that he's already announced his intention to reincarnate. "Tell everyone I'll be back," he's quoted as saying. "And by the time I'm through, every child will have a safe place to go and someone to believe in them from the minute they're born." He's hard at work on a book called The Vanity of Man in which he's outlining specific plans for finally making the world a safe, nourishing place for the animal kingdom, and he'll be activating those plans when he returns to earth.

Bela Lugosi

The strange, tragic life of Bela Lugosi, known to the world as the man who brought Count Dracula to life on film, began on October 20, 1882, in Lugos, Hungary, near the border of Transylvania. His banker father, Istvan Blasko, and his mother, Paula, named their fourth child Bela Ferenc Dezso and raised him in a Roman Catholic household. At the age of twelve he quit school, studied at the Budapest Academy of Theatrical Arts, performed in provincial theaters beginning in approximately 1903, and went on to join the National Theater of Hungary (1913–19). He also served in the Austro-Hungarian army during World War I and, in 1917, began a three-year marriage to his first of five wives, Ilona Szmick.

After appearing in a number of silent films in Hungary and Germany, Bela immigrated to the United States, settled in New York City, and began touring the East Coast with a small stock company of other Hungarian actors. His first appearance on Broadway was in a 1922 production of *The Red Poppy*. More Broadway shows followed, as well as his first film appearance in a 1923 melodrama called *The Silent Command*.

It was in 1927 that Bela was cast to star in the successful Broadway production of *Dracula*, and he was promptly summoned to Hollywood, where he worked in the new medium of "talkies" and married wife number two, a wealthy widow named Beatrice Weeks, who filed for divorce after four months and named actress Clara Bow as the correspondent.

Universal Pictures released *Dracula*, starring Bela Lugosi, in 1931, and both a major box-office hit and an icon were born. Bela was immediately signed to a contract with Universal, and marriage number three came along, this one in 1933, to a young Hungarian woman named Lillian Arch. Their child, Bela G. Lugosi, was born in 1938, and this marriage lasted until 1953.

Between his remarkable performance as the world's most famous vampire and his thick eastern European accent, which served him well for roles as a horror villain, Bela found it difficult to expand his acting career into a wider variety of roles. The titles alone of his next six films, in which he costarred with fellow thriller movie king Boris Karloff, both exemplified and exacerbated the typecasting that stood in the way of more traditional parts: *The Black Cat, The Raven, The Invisible Ray, Son of Frankenstein, Black Friday,* and *The Body Snatcher.*

In 1936 Universal's new management dropped horror films from its production slate, which reduced Bela to a string of low-budget nonhorror roles and lead roles in some equally low-budget independent thrillers as well as whatever stage roles he could find. His career and earning power predictably declined, as did his own financial stability. He did land and succeed in the coveted role of the hunchback Ygor in *Son of Frankenstein* in 1939 as well as a "normal" and prestigious role in Greta Garbo's *Ninotchka.* But the stardom he'd achieved in *Dracula* seemed to be gone forever.

Adding to Bela's troubles, beginning in at least the late 1930s, was the onset of severe sciatica—compression of the sciatic nerve that causes often extreme, radiating back, pelvic, and leg pain. He became dependent on morphine and methadone and, by the end of the 1940s, when he made the last "A" movie of his career, *Abbott and Costello Meet Frankenstein,* word of his drug dependence had spread throughout the film industry. Work was sparse and undistinguished through the early 1950s, and in 1953 his twenty-year marriage to Lillian Arch ended in divorce. By 1955 his life had declined into obscurity, virtual poverty, and addiction. He voluntarily committed himself to a treatment center in Norwalk, California, and was released later that year.

Hope, such as it was, had arrived in about 1952, though, in the form of a filmmaker named Ed Wood Jr., generally considered to be one of the most artless, incompetent directors in the history of motion pictures. Ed Wood was a Bela Lugosi fan; he tracked him down and offered him parts in upcoming films. Bela was in no mental, professional, or financial position to say no, and the Wood-Lugosi collaboration resulted in a brief series of films so inadvertently ridiculous that they've developed cult followings: *Glen or Glenda?* in 1953, *Bride of the Monster* in 1956, and the impossibly bad *Plan Nine from Outer Space*, released in 1958 after Bela's death.

Bela did find a fifth wife, Hope Linninger, whom he married in 1955, and that same year, after he'd been released from drug treatment, he made one last non–Ed Wood film, *The Black Sheep*, released in 1956. Bela made several personal appearances to promote the film, despite the fact that in the last legitimate movie of his life, he played the part of a mute, without a single line of dialogue.

On August 16, 1956, Bela Lugosi died quietly of a heart attack in his home in Los Angeles. Out of love and respect, Bela Jr. and his mother, Lillian, insisted that he be buried in his *Dracula* cloak as they believed he would have wanted. His body was interred in Holy Cross Cemetery in Culver City, California, and his grave remains a popular site on some of the more cult-oriented Hollywood tours.

From Sylvia

In the early 1980s I was invited by the late, great paranormal investigator Nick Nocerino and a paranormal photographer to accompany them on a trip to explore the Bela Lugosi house. I admit it, I accepted the invitation for one reason: I leapt at every possible opportunity to work with Nick. As for Bela Lugosi, the truth is, I neither knew nor cared much about him. Not only was he a little before my time—*Dracula* was a hit five years before I was born—but I've never made it all the way through any vampire movie without either falling asleep or involuntarily snickering, probably because it's hard to be frightened of something I don't believe exists. My loss, I'm sure, and no fault of Mr. Lugosi's performance. But when Nick, Chuck, and I arrived at the house, I can't stress enough how underwhelmed I was expecting to be, touring the home of a long-dead actor who was best known for a film I didn't enjoy, especially when I was in the midst of a crushing schedule and had a million other things I'd rather have been doing.

It was late evening when our van parked in front of the vacant, sadly rundown property. Nick had done his homework on Bela Lugosi and volunteered to tell me about him while he strapped a lot of incomprehensible equipment on me. I stopped him from saying a word—I prefer to walk into a paranormal investigation "clean," with as little information and as few predispositions as possible.

Once I was fully wired and Nick and Chuck were ready with their amazing battery of devices, we headed toward the main house of the oddly configured compound. The buildings formed a square around a courtyard with a fountain in its center that I imagined might once have been attractive. To the left of the courtyard were stairs that led to a row of rooms accessed by a narrow balcony, creating the effect of a sad motel that had long since gone out of business. The main house was to the right, completely separate from those drab abandoned rooms.

The moment we stepped through the massive doors of the house I felt almost choked by the oppressive distress that still hung in the dead air, some thick aftertaste of depression and hysteria left behind like a force field by someone dark who'd lived there. Nick, Chuck, and I explored every square inch of that house, and while all three of us were resisting an impulse to head back to the car and race to the nearest place we could find where there might be happiness or where it seemed as if someone might have at least laughed once or twice in the last century, we didn't sense a trace of anything paranormal within those walls. There were no ghosts in the house, no spirits, nothing at all to alert the gauges and sensors we were lugging along with us. After a half hour or so we returned to the courtyard, and as we pulled those huge wooden doors closed behind us, I remember taking long deep breaths of fresh air to try to wash that darkness out of my system.

Next we climbed the stairs to those oddly separate rooms across the courtyard. We didn't speak a word to each other, but my guess was that after finding the main house so ghost- and spirit-free, Nick and Chuck were expecting as much as I was that we were about to explore nothing but the same musty gloom we'd just trudged through.

It shocked me that, as we neared the top of the stairs, I was suddenly hit with a wave of panic so strong and overwhelming that, I promise you, I would have turned and run as far and fast as my legs would carry me, if I'd been there alone. Nick recorded my description of the dread I was feeling about whatever was waiting at the top of those stairs, and at my insistence we stopped long enough for me to say a prayer and put a circle of the white light of the Holy Spirit around the three of us to protect us before we stepped onto the narrow balcony and opened the first door.

I was instantly transfixed by the nightmare of horrifying images inside that small room. There seemed to be people everywhere, all of them in black, Goth before it became fashionable. They all had blank, chalk-white faces with hollow eyes and the darkest red lips. They were talking to each other unintelligibly, in a hushed, droning monotone. Three of them were flailing around the room, arms waving wildly, insanely falling into everyone in their path. Four others were lying limp and crumpled on the floor. One of them was slowly and deliberately cutting his arm, letting his blood drain into the glass he was holding, and then passing the glass around the room for everyone to drink from. As each of them took a sip, they swooned into a mirthless euphoria as if they'd just shared some kind of grotesque Communion.

I couldn't move. I couldn't breathe. I couldn't hear, until finally Nick's voice penetrated what felt like a frozen trance, yelling, "Sylvia! Listen to me! Get the hell out of there! Now!" Apparently, according to the gauges strapped all over me, my temperature was spiking in that ice-cold room, I was being assaulted with so much electromagnetic energy that I was on overload, and my pulse was racing out of control. I knew what had held me so psychically captive was my certainty that I'd just witnessed a crowd of earthbound spirits, dark and futile, trapped in a perpetual rite of drugs, despair, and death.

Nick pulled me out of the room and slammed the door, and he and Chuck bolted toward the stairs. My impulse was to bolt right along with them, but I couldn't ignore the energy that was pulling me to a second door just a few feet away. My hand was already on the doorknob when Nick yelled from the bottom of the stairs, "Where are you going?"

"We have to look in here before we go," I called back.

He and Chuck were with me in seconds, protective and concerned for my safety as always, and they were right behind me as I opened the second door and stepped into the pitch-black room. Once my eyes had adjusted I could make out a large horizontal shape that looked as if it might have been an oversized couch against the far wall, but I caught my breath when I realized that no, what I was looking at was a gleaming wooden casket, open to reveal the earthbound spirit of Bela Lugosi himself, wrapped in his signature cape, lying in the satin lining of his coffin, eyes open and empty.

He slowly sat up, and he looked directly into my eyes, as cold and godless as any ghost I've ever seen. "You weren't invited," he said in a hollow voice.

"No, I wasn't," I whispered back. "I'm sorry for the intrusion."

We stepped back out onto the balcony and closed the door. Nick and Chuck were visibly shaken—they hadn't seen or heard what I had, but they'd heard my reply to the lifeless life in that room and felt the dark hopelessness of the energy we'd just confronted. We didn't say a word as we walked back down the stairs to the courtyard. We were all thoroughly depleted, and we sat by the dry fountain for a long time before I finally turned to Nick and said, "Okay. Now you can tell me about Bela Lugosi." He told me the story you've just read, and we held hands and prayed for those poor lost souls before we left.

From Francine

Bela is no longer earthbound. A very short while ago, maybe twenty years in your time, he freed himself, but he turned away from the Other Side and went to the Holding Place instead. He hasn't yet reincarnated.

Chris Farley

Actor and comedian Christopher Crosby Farley was born on February 15, 1964, in Madison, Wisconsin, one of the five children of Thomas Farley, owner of a paving company, and homemaker Mary Anne Crosby Farley. The family was close-knit Irish Catholic, and Chris received his early education in Catholic schools. He graduated from the Jesuit Marquette University in Milwaukee in 1986 after focusing his studies on theater and communications. His professional comedy career got its start at Madison's Ark Improv Theater and Chicago's Improv Olympic Theater. But it was at the famed Second City Theater in Chicago, where Lorne Michaels, creator of television's landmark series *Saturday Night Live*, discovered Chris Farley and signed him to the cast in 1990.

Chris was one of *Saturday Night Live*'s most versatile and innovative comedians, creating a variety of characters and performing hilarious impersonations of such celebrities as Dom DeLuise, General Norman Schwarzkopf, Carnie Wilson, and Rush Limbaugh. He was also part of a group that came to be known as the "bad boys of *SNL*," which included cast mates David Spade, Chris Rock, Adam Sandler, and Rob Schneider, whose off-stage pranks were often as notorious as their onstage comedy.

Between 1992 and 1995 Chris began making cameo appearances in such films as *Wayne's World*, *Coneheads*, and *Billy Madison*. When his *SNL* contract ended after the 1994–95 season, he devoted all his professional energy to films, costarring with his *SNL* cast mate and friend David Spade in the successful comedies *Tommy Boy* and *Black Sheep*. His "bankability" was rewarded with a lead role in the equally successful *Beverly Hills Ninja* in 1997.

Sadly, by now Chris, following in the footsteps of his equally gifted idol John Belushi, was battling severe problems with obesity, drugs, and alcohol. He sought treatment more than a dozen times before attending rehab in 1997, again unsuccessfully. Production of his last film, *Almost Heroes*, was delayed more than once due to his declining health and progressing addictions, and he was in shockingly tenuous shape during his final *Saturday Night Live* guest appearance on October 25, 1997.

Chris Farley, at the age of thirty-three, died in his Chicago apartment on December 18, 1997, from a cocaine- and morphine-related heart attack. His funeral in Madison was attended by more than five hundred friends and family members, who gathered to honor his far too brief life.

From Francine

Chris was distraught and disoriented when he returned Home. Not even the large crowd of friends—including John Belushi and a tall, husky man I believe was his maternal grandfather—could comfort him. A spirit cannot fully experience the sacred peace and exhilaration of life on the Other Side when such pervasive hollow depression has separated it from its faith, its cognitive abilities, and its capacity for joy, and Chris's Spirit Guide immediately took him to the Hall of Wisdom, where he was cocooned.

And then something happened that's very rare here. Chris emerged from being cocooned, quickly realized that he'd been too eager to resume his life to stay as long as he needed, and was cocooned again, with more intensive therapy this time, particularly from one of his closest friends and advisors at Home, a Sikh guru named Amar Das. By the time his second cocooning ended, Chris was fully healed and had evolved into his thirty-year-old visage: a slender, six-foot-tall man with long, jet black hair, and delicate, almost beautiful features.

It will come as no surprise to everyone on earth who knew Chris well that he is a highly advanced soul, a giving, loving light who is much beloved on the Other Side. He is still a devout Catholic, and he's resumed teaching his brilliant classes in world religions. He is also a gifted and very popular classical dance teacher and swimming instructor. He and John Belushi love performing rock-and-roll with a variety of other musicians, including Buddy Holly, Janis Joplin, and Otis Redding, with Chris on drums; and Chris's open-air house on the plains of what corresponds to your North American Midwest is home to any of his world religion students who are in early preparation for new incarnations.

Several hours before Chris's father's body died, Chris retrieved his spirit, escorted him through the tunnel, and brought him Home, where he was cocooned as well. Chris and his father, Tom, were brothers in Switzerland in the late 1600s and deeply devoted to each other, and Chris spoke often of how he felt as if, by remaining obese despite the threat it posed to his health, he could somehow make his equally obese father feel less inappropriate. Tom will return to Chris's house with him when he emerges from the cocooning chamber and resume his work as a film historian.

Chris has no plans to reincarnate, but he does visit his mother and his friend David Spade often.

Eva Gabor

Eva Gabor, the beautiful, utterly delightful actress often referred to as the "talented Gabor," was born on February 11, 1921, in Budapest, Hungary. Her father, Major Vilmos Gabor, a jeweler, and his wife, Jolie, were blessed with three daughters—Zsa Zsa, Magda, and Eva. Eva was a born performer, working as an ice skater and cabaret singer after graduating from the Forstner Girls Institute in Budapest. She and her mother and sisters immigrated to the United States at the outbreak of World War II, and Eva eventually made her way to Hollywood to pursue an acting career. She was quickly signed to a contract with Paramount Pictures and made two films in 1941, *Forced Landing* and *Pacific Blackout*.

After supporting roles in several movies in the 1940s, Eva finally attracted the critical and popular attention she deserved in the 1950 Broadway production of *The Happy Time*. She was inexplicably passed over for the film version, but returned to Hollywood anyway and resumed her movie career, most notably in *The Mad Magician* with Vincent Price and in 1958's Best Picture Oscar winner, *Gigi*, directed by Vincente Minnelli. Her charm and irresistible sense of humor made her a popular television guest as well, especially on such classic game shows as *The Match Game*, *Password*, and *Tattletales*.

It was in 1965 that she truly captured the hearts of the American public, when she debuted as Eddie Albert's wife on the CBS series

Green Acres. Her business acumen inspired her to capitalize on her popularity during the five-year run of *Green Acres* and her long over-due "name value" by forming her own wig company, Eva Gabor International, which continued to thrive long after the series ended.

While Eva's older sister Zsa Zsa was busy making headlines with her brash, contentious behavior and her lengthy string of marriages (the total currently stands at nine), Eva was living a comparatively peaceful life, with only five husbands and one headline-making en-counter with police. In her case, Eva was the victim. In 1964, she was beaten by two gunmen who broke into her Miami apartment and stole her $25,000 diamond ring. (The robbers were ultimately arrested, but the ring was never recovered.)

After her fifth marriage ended, Eva bought and settled into an exquisite home near Sunset Boulevard in Beverly Hills with her five beloved dogs, and for many years she was the devoted companion of her great friend Merv Griffin. She remained close to her mother, Jolie, and her sister Magda, who were living two hours away in Palm Springs by then, but had a difficult, on-again, off-again relation-ship with Zsa Zsa. It was a source of irritation to Eva that she was frequently mistaken for Zsa Zsa, particularly when the two of them were so different in spirit and temperament, and that irritation laid the groundwork for a story Eva delighted in telling about herself.

There was a swimming pool in the secluded backyard of Eva's Beverly Hills home, and Eva was dutiful about swimming laps every morning, in the nude, wearing a large sun hat to protect her alabaster skin from the sun. One morning while she was in mid-lap she was overcome with the feeling that she was being watched. Sure enough, out of the corner of her eye she spotted two workmen from the prop-erty next door who'd made their way to the fence to spy on her as she swam. Finally one of the workmen, unable to contain himself, yelled out, "Hi, Eva!" And without missing a single stroke Eva cheerfully called back, "It's Zsa Zsa!"

Eva loved to work, delighting in the voice-over career that began in 1970 with *The Aristocats* and continued through *The Rescuers Down Under* in 1990, and it was also in 1990 that she happily returned to the screen for the two-hour CBS *Green Acres* revival movie.

In 1995 Eva went on vacation in Mexico and, in a freak accident, fell into her bathtub and broke her hip. She was flown back to Los Angeles and admitted to Cedars Sinai Hospital, suffered respiratory failure, lapsed into a coma, and, just two weeks after she fell, died of pneumonia on July 4. The youngest Gabor was survived by her mother and two sisters—in fact, Jolie was never told of Eva's death, because it was agreed by those who were closest to the family that she wouldn't survive the shock and grief of losing the loving, attentive daughter who brought her as much joy as she brought to everyone else who knew her.

From Francine

While Eva was being mourned by her countless friends on earth, we on the Other Side were euphoric to have her light, her laughter, and her kindness with us at Home again. The throngs of loved ones from her thirty-one incarnations had to wait to welcome her until what seemed like thousands of animals from those incarnations had finished saying hello, and no one was more ecstatic than Eva herself, who never doubted for a moment that she'd be returning to God's arms and a joyful eternity the instant her body took its last breath. In typical style, she spent her time at the Scanning Machine focusing on the great fun and success she had along the way rather than the many times she struggled through family betrayals and career disappointments. She credited her mother with teaching her to be a smart businesswoman, to be responsible with her money, and to never compromise her ability to take care of herself.

There was a time, for example, when her dear friend billionaire Merv Griffin wanted her to sell her Beverly Hills house and move in with him on the top floor of a luxurious hotel he owned. She refused, despite his displeasure. "Give up my house, my most solid investment, my security that I've worked so hard for all my life, to please a man? Mama would have killed me," she says. She laughed as she reviewed another "Mama would have killed me" incident. She was sound asleep early one morning when an earthquake rumbled through Los Angeles. "I jumped out of bed, raced to my closet, took off the T-shirt I was sleeping in, put on a silk peignoir, and went back to bed. Mama didn't raise her girls to be found in a pile of rubble wearing a T-shirt."

From the Scanning Machine she returned to her ecstatic life at Home: a fascinating variety of friends ranging from former U.S. presidents and esteemed actors and actresses to the most modest housekeepers and dressmakers; a Tudor house filled with animals and surrounded by a swimming pool that circles the house like a moat, where she continues swimming laps; devout worship at one of our most ancient and treasured cathedrals in what corresponds to your Italian countryside; and devoted work as a therapist in the cocooning chambers in the Hall of Wisdom. In fact, she was there for both her mother and her sister Magda, to help them through the cocooning process when they returned Home not long after she arrived.

Eva and Merv, who are kindred spirits (her soul mate is an Egyptian man named Nitocris), are almost inseparable now that he's here with her. He's teaching her to play tennis, and the two of them are popular lecturers on the subject of business ethics for those who are preparing to reincarnate and become corporate managers. Merv specializes in the financial aspects of business success, so foreign to many of us on the Other Side, where money doesn't exist, while Eva focuses on returning decency and compassion to corporate priority lists. While she rarely revealed this fact during her lifetime, she says she made it her daily habit, as essential as brushing her teeth, to perform an anonymous act of kindness. She says, "I was a smart businesswoman who looked for ways to conduct my company in that same spirit of quiet, generous giving. Why so many corporations think they have to make a choice between being profitable and being kind I will never understand. Have they never heard of karma?"

She won't be incarnating again, explaining with a smile, "No one ever accused me of not knowing the right time to leave a party."

Gregory Peck

Eldred Gregory Peck, Academy Award–winning actor and humanitarian, was born in San Diego on April 15, 1916. His father, Gregory Pearl Peck, a pharmacist, and his mother, Bernice Ayres Peck, were divorced when the young Gregory was six years old. He lived with his maternal grandmother until, at the age of ten, he was sent to St. John's Military Academy in Los Angeles. He returned home to his father when his grandmother died, and he graduated from San Diego High School before heading on to college, first at San Diego State University and then at the University of California, Berkeley, where he—handsome, six foot three, and strongly built—gained attention as both an athlete and an actor at the university's renowned Little Theater.

After graduating from UC Berkeley, he moved to New York to study at the Neighborhood Playhouse and made his first appearance on Broadway in the 1942 production of *The Morning Star*. Acting jobs were plentiful thanks to World War II, a war in which Gregory Peck (he left his given first name Eldred behind when he headed east) was exempt from military service due to a back injury, while so many of his fellow actors were enlisting and being deployed. Instead, he was quickly recruited by Hollywood, where his first film, *Days of Glory*, was released in 1944, launching a distinguished screen career that didn't end until 1998 with a remake of his earlier classic *Moby Dick*.

Both onscreen and off, he exuded a sense of strength, dignity, and decency. He was very outspoken against racial injustice, the Vietnam War, the nuclear arms race, and even the controversial House Un-American Activities Committee and its infamous search for alleged Communists in the film industry. He took some pride in being named to Richard Nixon's notorious "enemies list" and even more humble pride in the Medal of Freedom presented to him by President Lyndon Johnson. And despite the fact that he was a lifelong practicing Catholic, he was an advocate for women's freedom of choice.

His first marriage, to Greta Kukkomen Rice in 1942, produced three sons before it ended in divorce in 1955. Their first son, Jonathan, who became a television journalist, committed suicide in 1975. Very shortly after Gregory's first marriage ended he married a Paris reporter named Veronique Passani, with whom he had a son and a daughter, and their marriage lasted for the rest of his life.

Gregory's extraordinary half-century career earned him, among other honors, five Academy Award nominations; one Best Actor Oscar, for the 1962 masterpiece *To Kill a Mockingbird;* three Best Actor Golden Globe awards; the prestigious Cecil B. DeMille Award; a Screen Actors Guild Lifetime Achievement Award; the American Film Institute Lifetime Achievement Award; and the Jean Hersholt Humanitarian Award.

During the last years of his life he traveled throughout the world on speaking tours, during which the National University of Ireland made him a Doctor of Letters; he became a founding patron of the University College Dublin School of Film; and he served as chairman of the American Cancer Society. On June 12, 2003, at the age of eighty-seven, Gregory Peck died of natural causes in his Los Angeles home with his wife, Veronique, holding his hand.

From Francine

Gregory was ready to come Home, as his wife will confirm, and he was ecstatic that the first to embrace him was his son Jonathan. While his Catholicism had always taught him that victims of suicide were banished from heaven, his heart and soul had always believed that couldn't be true, so finding his beloved son waiting for him was less a relief than a confirmation.

Gregory was also among the few who, for the most part, enjoyed his time at the Scanning Machine. While there were countless situations he wished he'd handled differently, he was satisfied to see that he never dismissed his significant mistakes with the egocentric defensiveness so common among his peers, but instead made every effort to learn from them. By his own account, he was still amused by his place on Richard Nixon's "enemies list," although they're perfectly amiable when they happen upon each other here, and he took great delight in his performance in and the whole experience of the film MacArthur. *He and Jonathan were both there to greet Gregory's first wife, Greta, when she arrived on the Other Side, and while Gregory and Greta don't spend time together, they have laughed together over their misguided belief that two people so innately, resolutely different from each other could build a successful marriage, and they're fondly grateful to each other for the children they cocreated.*

For the most part, Gregory is as much of a loner here as he was on earth—not unfriendly, just private and appreciative of his own company. He has returned to his position as a quadrant sentry, his house is a small cabin on what corresponds to your island of Fiji, and he never misses a performance of the opera or our popular debates among former U.S. presidents and other world leaders in search of a path to lasting peace on earth. Among his few close friends and tennis partners are his son, his father, and a very short slender blonde female whom he says his family will recognize.

Above all, he is content, grateful for the long, full life he lived and satisfied that he put his chosen life themes—Loner and Builder—to their best possible use. He has no plans to incarnate again.

Spencer Tracy

Spencer Bonaventure Tracy, one of the most gifted and versatile actors of the twentieth century, was born in Milwaukee, Wisconsin, on April 5, 1900, to Irish Catholic truck salesman John Tracy and his wife, Caroline Brown Tracy.

Not an enthusiastic student, Spencer tried but failed to convince his parents to let him quit school at the age of sixteen to go to work. But in 1917 he leapt at the opportunity to quit school, join the navy, and serve his country in World War I. He was discharged without ever leaving the Norfolk Navy Yard, where he first served, and used his military education benefits to enroll in Ripon College with a focus on premed. Joining the debating team at Ripon led to his interest in acting, and when he successfully auditioned for the Academy of Dramatic Arts in New York, he finally found a passion that was exciting and fulfilling enough to make him a good student for the first time in his life.

He met a young actress named Louise Treadwell when he joined a stock theater company, and they fell in love and were married in September 1923. Nine months later their son John was born. They were devastated to discover that he was deaf, but they made it their mission to help him lead a normal, happy life. (In fact, they also made it their mission to help as many others like John as possible and, in 1943, founded the still thriving John Tracy Clinic, an education center for hearing-impaired infants and preschool children.) They also had a daughter, Susie, who was born in 1932.

Spencer was performing in a play called *The Last Mile* in 1930 when the legendary director John Ford discovered him and promptly hired him to costar in Ford's upcoming film *Up the River* with another newcomer named Humphrey Bogart. The Tracy family moved to Hollywood in November 1931, and Spencer appeared in a whirlwind sixteen films during his three-year contract with Fox Films before he was signed by MGM, the most powerful and esteemed studio in the business at the time. It was through his films for MGM that he was able to prove his renowned versatility, moving brilliantly and effortlessly from comedic scripts to dramatic works. To no one's surprise, he made history by being the first to win the Best Actor Oscar two years in a row, in 1937 and 1938.

It was in 1942, while making a film called *Woman of the Year*, that Spencer met, costarred with, and fell in love with Katharine Hepburn, who was to become his partner both onscreen and off for the rest of his life. His Catholicism prevented him from ever divorcing Louise, but she did agree to a discreet, respectful, permanent separation, thanks to which the Tracy-Hepburn affair managed to proceed without bitterness and sensationalism. He reportedly had affairs with a number of other celebrated actresses over the years, but Katharine rode them out, well aware of Spencer's frailties and secure in her knowledge that if she simply stayed out of the way, his compulsive wandering eye would satisfy itself and he'd be back.

Spencer Tracy and Katharine Hepburn made a total of nine movies together, including his last film, 1967's *Guess Who's Coming to Dinner*. By then Spencer's health was seriously compromised from years of alcoholism, diabetes, and recurring heart and lung problems, and his shooting schedule on *Guess Who's Coming to Dinner* was limited to the few hours a day he had the stamina to work. On June 10, 1967, seventeen days after filming was completed, Spencer

Tracy died of heart failure at his Hollywood home, leaving behind a legacy of almost eighty films, seven Academy Award nominations, and two consecutive Best Actor Oscars.

From Francine

Spencer actually remained earthbound for several years after his death. He was frankly too stubborn to leave Katharine, and he was also reluctant to find out whether God would welcome him after a life in which he felt he'd committed more than his share of sins. He visited Katharine relentlessly, trying to get her attention to let her know he was still there, and because he had no idea that he was dead, he couldn't understand why she persisted in ignoring him. She sensed his presence countless times, but her Yankee practicality would never allow her to believe in something as intangible as life after death, and she would scold herself for letting the intensity of grieving the loss of him lead her to indulge in such foolish fantasies.

His mother finally retrieved him and brought him to the Other Side. He was relieved to find himself here after a lifetime of being weighed down with the needless threat of hell, and he was also exhilarated to be rid of a body that had caused him more pain in his last years on earth than he admitted to anyone. He had a difficult time at the Scanning Machine watching the pain his personal emotional conflicts caused those around him.

He was proud of his work as an actor except, he says, when he "caught himself at it," but he regrets that he didn't excel at the most important role he was ever given, the role of father. To make amends, his frequent visits to your dimension are devoted to special-needs children, who see him and enjoy talking to him, and he loves making them laugh.

He spends most of his time here with his soul mate, Katharine. He was one of the first to meet her when she returned Home, and they promptly returned to their secluded house on the shore, where they enjoy writing plays together for themselves and their actor friends to perform. Spencer also writes historical novels with Ernest Hemingway, a friend from several past lives.

He joyfully greeted his son when John came Home not long ago, and the two of them are very much at peace and love building and sailing boats together. Neither Spencer, John, nor Katharine has plans to incarnate again.

Albert Einstein

One of the great minds of the twentieth century and winner of the Nobel Prize in physics in 1921, Albert Einstein was born in Ulm, Württemberg, Germany, on March 14, 1879. His father, Hermann, after a brief career as a featherbed salesman, went on to operate an electrochemical factory, while his mother, Pauline, took care of the middle-class Jewish household. Shortly after Albert's birth the family moved to Munich, where his sister, Maja, was born two years later.

Einstein's uniquely inquisitive mind was evident in what he recalled as the two "wonders" that fascinated him as a child. The first was the compass he came across when he was five and the "invisible forces" that moved the needle. The second, when he was twelve, was his introduction to what he came to call his "sacred little geometry book."

Hermann Einstein moved his wife and daughter to Milan, Italy, in 1894, leaving Albert in a Munich boarding house to finish his education. Six months later, partly because he was miserable and partly because he was facing the prospect of being drafted into the military when he turned sixteen, he ran away and managed to make his way alone to his parents' new home in another country.

He gained admission to the Swiss Federal Polytechnic School in Zurich, where he enjoyed what he remembered as some of the happiest years of his life and met Mileva Maric, his future wife.

He graduated in 1900, and Albert and Mileva were married on January 6, 1903. A daughter, Lieserl, was born to the couple in 1902, before their marriage, and seemingly vanished a year later. Albert is thought never to have seen her, and nothing was written or said about her after 1903. Two sons followed Albert and Mileva's marriage—Hans in 1904 and Eduard in 1910. By then Albert was working as a clerk at the Swiss patent office, a job at which he was so capable that he had plenty of spare time to invest in his ongoing passion for physics.

In 1905, which scholars refer to as his "miracle year," he published four papers in *Annalen der Physik*, one of the world's most respected physics journals. Among his accomplishments in these papers, Albert assembled various pieces of the theory of special relativity developed by other scientists into one whole theory and recognized that it was a universal law of nature. The papers, credited with changing the course of modern physics, captured the attention of the most influential physicist of the time, Max Planck, who developed the quantum theory, and thanks to that attention, Albert became a popular lecturer at international conferences and was offered a series of prestigious jobs in the academic world. He ultimately accepted the position of director of the Kaiser Wilhelm Institute for Physics.

Unfortunately, Albert's growing worldwide renown and immersion in his work had a fatal impact on his marriage. He and Mileva were divorced in 1919, and he later married a distant cousin, Elsa Lowenthal.

An intense backlash against Albert by the growing Nazi movement finally compelled him to leave Germany, and in 1932 he moved to the United States and relocated his work to the Institute for Advanced Study in Princeton, New Jersey, prompting physicists from around the world to flock there to study with him. His brilliant successes were counterbalanced by a series of personal tragedies in the 1930s—his son Eduard was diagnosed with schizophrenia and was institutionalized for the rest of his life; his close friend Paul Ehrenfest committed suicide; and in 1936 his wife, Elsa, passed away from a combination of heart and liver problems.

It's no surprise that a genius so fascinated with "invisible forces" put a great deal of thought into his own religious beliefs, and his writings expressed his faith in a God of harmony and beauty, an "old one" who was the ultimate lawmaker, but not a God who intervened in each of our personal human affairs. He's quoted as saying: "I'm not an atheist, and I don't think I can call myself a pantheist. We are in the position of a little child entering a huge library filled with books in many different languages. . . . The child dimly suspects a mysterious order in the arrangement of the books, but doesn't know what it is. That, it seems to me, is the attitude of even the most intelligent human being toward God."

The impact of Albert Einstein's work is impossible to calculate; his celebrated theory of relativity barely scratches the surface of his accomplishments. He spent his later years in solitude, relying on music for relaxation, and on April 18, 1955, in Princeton, he died of an aneurysm. More than half a century later the results of his genius are still as inspiring, compelling, and motivating as they were during his extraordinary lifetime.

From Francine

The look of blissful awe on Albert's face when he emerged from the tunnel reminded all who saw it of that "little child" he referred to when he described his belief in God. He wept with joy as he rushed first into his mother's open arms and then into the arms of his beloved friend Paul Ehrenfest. (Both his father and his second wife had reincarnated by the time Albert returned Home.) His mentor, Isaac Newton, was there as well, to shake his hand and, with a smile filled with pride, ask Albert if he would please mentor him now, "until we're back on a level playing field again"—Albert had far exceeded Isaac's expectations during his lifetime. Albert is said to have replied, "I simply stood on the shoulders of a giant," a reference to a quotation of Isaac's. He then bowed deeply to the teacher and friend who was so influential in preparing him for this incarnation, which is his third and last. He remarked, "I do much better work here, without the weight of sadness."

As often happens with physicists and other scientists, Albert was almost as mesmerized by the Scanning Machine itself as he was with the lifetime that played out inside it. He continues to visit it regularly, taking full advantage of another of its uses: just as all of us here have unlimited access to the life charts in the Hall of Records, we can also review anyone's lifetime we choose at the Scanning Machine, from the first pharaohs of Egypt or Jesus's disciples to Mozart, Thomas Jefferson, or the doomed residents of Atlantis. For a mind like Albert's, the "mechanics" of what you might think of as the ultimate time machine are irresistible, especially since one of his greatest passions here is to unlock the secrets of time travel for you on earth. He believes that by the 2040s in your years, time travel will be common through what he calls such global "flues" as the Bermuda Triangle, through the infused work of a team that includes Albert, Nikola Tesla, Galileo, and George Hale. One of the recipients of these infusions, beginning in approximately 2018, will be a young man at Duke University whose name is Bernard or Bernhard.

Albert was especially moved by the arrival of his son Eduard, whose exceptional mind was clouded by schizophrenia during his lifetime. After being cocooned, Eduard rejoined his father as a coprofessor at physics and astrophysics seminars designed specifically for spirits who will be incarnating and have charted those sciences as their specialties—"our hands on earth," as Albert calls them. Albert and Eduard live in a Cape Cod cottage in what corresponds to your Provincetown, Massachusetts, and they're avid sailors on their ship called Yanqin, *an Aramaic word for "children." Albert has also reunited with his friend Johann Brahms, whose music he adores, and the two of them enjoy performing Brahms's compositions and other great classical works at small salons throughout the Other Side, with Johann on the harpsichord and Albert on his beloved violin.*

Ray Charles

Brother Ray" Charles, the genius pianist, singer, composer, and bandleader who left an indelible imprint on music, was born Ray Charles Robinson on September 23, 1930, in Albany, Georgia. His father, Bailey Robinson, pieced together what income he could as a railroad repairman, a mechanic, and a handyman, while his mother, Aretha Williams, worked at a local sawmill. Ray was still an infant when the family moved to Greenville, Florida.

The Robinsons were poor, even compared to other black families in the South during the Great Depression, and they were also given more than their share of tragedy early in Ray's life. He was only five when he saw his four-year-old brother, George, drown in a washtub. And he was only seven when, possibly due to glaucoma or an untreated infection, his failing eyesight deteriorated to total blindness.

With Aretha's support, he quickly learned to be capable and independent rather than disabled, and he was promptly enrolled in the Florida School for the Deaf and the Blind in St. Augustine, which he attended from the age of seven until he was fifteen. It was there that his musical gifts were nourished. He was taught composing and reading in Braille. He learned to play the piano, the saxophone, and every other instrument the school had to offer. His young life revolved around studying, practicing, and exploring all the music that moved him, from jazz and the blues to country and gospel.

Ray's mother died in 1945, when he was fifteen. He left school and moved to Jacksonville, where he played piano at the Ritz Theater for over a year before heading on to Orlando, then Tampa, and finally Seattle in 1947. In Seattle, in addition to meeting his lifelong friend and frequent collaborator Quincy Jones, he started recording for the Down Beat label, forming the Maxin Trio with guitarist G. D. McKee and bassist Milton Garrett, and in 1949 their "Confession Blues" reached number two on the R&B charts. Calling himself Ray Charles for the first time, he then joined Swing Time Records and recorded two more hits, which led to a contract with Atlantic Records. His first major hit singles were recorded for Atlantic, including 1954's "I Got a Woman," which he wrote with Renald Richard.

From 1955 until 1959 he had an amazing string of R&B hit singles and albums, with a girl group he recruited and named the Raelettes singing back-up on such classics as "A Fool for You," "Drown in My Own Tears," and "The Night Time (Is the Right Time)." In 1959 he achieved his first "crossover" hit when "What'd I Say" reached number one on the R&B charts, but soared into the top ten on the pop music charts as well. He continued his crossover success when he signed with ABC Records in 1960, releasing hit after hit with such legendary recordings as "Georgia on My Mind," "Hit the Road, Jack," and "Unchain My Heart."

In 1962 Ray crossed over again and helped popularize country music among mainstream listeners with a two-album series called *Modern Sounds in Country and Western Music*. Its first single, a spectacular arrangement of Don Gibson's "I Can't Stop Loving You," not only achieved the number-one spot on both the pop and R&B charts in America, but it also became the number-one record in England.

The "British Invasion," as the 1964 arrival of the Beatles and a stream of other bands from England has come to be known, seriously disrupted the momentum of a lot of American recording artists for several years, and Ray was among them, with a long string of only moderately successful releases through the late 1960s and well into the 1970s. He recorded a breathtaking signature version of "America the Beautiful" in 1972, popularizing the beloved national standard when it was broadcast internationally at the 1980 Olympics. In 1979, Ray Charles's recording of "Georgia on My Mind" was officially proclaimed the state song of Georgia. And in 1985 he was a featured part of an all-star chorus who performed the Michael Jackson and Lionel Richie song "We Are the World" for the USA for Africa charity. He performed at the inaugurations of Ronald Reagan in 1985 and Bill Clinton in 1993, kicking off more than a decade of television and worldwide appearances from Venezuela to France to Italy. And between the years of 1981 and 2004 he received, among other honors, a star on the Hollywood Walk of Fame; induction into the Rock and Roll Hall of Fame, the Rhythm and Blues Foundation, and the Jazz Hall of Fame; the Kennedy Center Honor and a Grammy Lifetime Achievement Award, all in addition to the seventeen Grammy Awards he won throughout his career, five of them presented posthumously.

Everyone he worked with would agree that perfectionism drove every note of every Ray Charles recording session, to the point where he literally let nothing stand in his way. Singer, songwriter, and producer Billy Vera tells the story of delivering the twenty-four-track tape of a $10,000 instrumental session to Ray's Los Angeles studio for Ray to add his vocals. Ray listened and liked what he heard for the most part, but he was sure the saxophone solo should happen eight bars later than it was recorded. While Billy watched in amazement, Ray threaded the tape and cued up the solo. And then, in Billy's words, "I see this blind man take a razor blade to a $10,000 recording, splice in the solo where he thinks it belongs, and sure enough, he was right, it was perfect. And believe me, we all knew Ray too well to try to stop him."

Behind the scenes, Ray Charles's life was as dramatic as his genius. There were two marriages, first to Eileen Williams from 1951 to 1952 and then to Della Howard from 1955 to 1977. From 1950 through 1987 he fathered twelve children by nine different women, including three by his wife Della. It's said that at a family lunch in 2002, Ray presented each of his children with a tax-free check for $1 million.

In 1965 Ray was arrested for a third time for heroin possession. He'd reportedly been addicted to heroin since the mid to late 1950s, and in lieu of serving jail time after the arrest, he checked himself into a rehab clinic in Los Angeles and, by all accounts, emerged free of his addiction. It was during his year on parole in 1966 that his hit single "Cryin' Time" was released.

On April 30, 2004, Ray made his final public appearance, when he was honored by having his Los Angeles music studio dedicated as a historic landmark. Less than two months later, on June 10, 2004, at 11:35 A.M., Ray Charles died of liver cancer at his Beverly Hills, California, home, surrounded by family and friends, including his longtime partner Norma Pinella. His body was interred in the Inglewood Park Cemetery in Inglewood, California. At the time of his death he was survived by his twelve children, twenty-one grandchildren, and five great-grandchildren.

From Francine

Ray regained his eyesight the instant he entered the tunnel, and a huge crowd gathered to greet him when he arrived Home, led by his brother, George, and his mother. It was an especially ecstatic reunion—imagine your first sights after decades of blindness being faces you've longed to see, with the exquisite beauty of Home all around you. And everyone who witnessed it commented on the fact that Ray's tears when he arrived were tears of pure joy, devoid of surprise or relief. While he never made an issue of his faith throughout his lifetime, he always knew with unwavering certainty where he was going when his body died and how much he had to look for-

ward to when he resumed his life on the Other Side. He says it was that certainty that allowed him to make the most of his time on earth. Never fearing what came next, he was able to focus on every moment he lived, often to the point of indulgence, willfulness, and potential self-destruction, he admits, but he's unique in having returned Home with no feeling of having left unfinished business behind.

It was during his time at the Scanning Machine that he recalled all his past lives, both here and on earth, with complete clarity and recognized the extent to which music has always been essential to his spirit; he spent three incarnations as a classical composer and musician and one as an accomplished opera singer in Prague. His lifetime as Ray Charles was his way of influencing other musicians, present and future, as so many historically influenced him along the path of his soul, filling him so completely with creativity, freedom, innovation, passion, and discipline that not even the onset of blindness would discourage him.

He performs here at Home in thrilling concerts with other singers and musicians who are old friends from here and from past incarnations. He continues to "pay it forward," as you put it, by being one of our most prolific composers. He's begun infusing his compositions to a young boy, a musical prodigy. The boy is currently eleven years old, his first or last name is Martin, and he lives in the Macon, Georgia, area. He's already being recognized for his talent as a singer and guitarist. By the time he's in his mid-teens he'll be writing "Ray Charles songs" without knowing where they came from, and four of those songs will be successfully recorded by the time he's twenty-five.

Ray is involved in developing something to do with advancements in computer software that involve composing and transcribing music in Braille, and he is also part of a team of researchers who are exploring the use of stem cells in reversing blindness and diseases of the eye. His primary residence is on the cliffs above what corresponds to the place on earth you call Big Sur. He is always surrounded by a large group of friends with whom he loves playing music, chess, and soccer.

His greatest regret is that he didn't say "no" more often, particularly when it came to heroin. He remembers that when he got involved with drugs, he thought he was simply indulging in the freedom of being able to do anything he pleased, but now he looks back at his addiction as "just another form of slavery."

And he wants Willie Nelson to know that he never heard "Georgia on My Mind" "sung prettier" than when Willie sang it at his memorial service. His incarnation as Ray Charles will be his last.

Michael Jackson

According to *Guinness World Records*, Michael Jackson is the "most successful entertainer of all time." He was inducted twice into the Rock and Roll Hall of Fame. He won fifteen Grammy Awards and twenty-six American Music Awards, including "Artist of the Century," was one of the bestselling recording artists in history, and, through his own efforts and donations, raised more than $300 million for charity. In his brilliant, controversial, and occasionally bizarre time on earth, Michael Jackson became a legend.

Michael Joseph Jackson was born in Gary, Indiana, on August 29, 1958. He was the eighth of Joe and Katherine Jackson's ten children. When Michael was eight years old he and his brother Marlon began singing lead vocals with the family band originally formed by Jermaine, Jackie, and Tito, a band that evolved from the Jackson Brothers into the Jackson Five.

The young singers were signed with Motown Records from 1968 until 1975, then moved to CBS/Epic Records, where they renamed themselves the Jacksons. Michael was the group's lead singer and songwriter by then, and he was also cast in the role of the Scarecrow in the 1978 film *The Wiz*, where he first worked with the renowned Quincy Jones, who arranged the score. Jones and Michael subsequently coproduced Michael's massively successful solo album *Off the Wall* in 1979, and it was also in 1979 that Michael broke his nose and required the first of a highly publicized and often bewildering series of rhinoplasties.

In 1982 Michael's second Epic Records album, *Thriller*, was released. Almost thirty years later it remains the bestselling album in the history of the recording industry. And his utterly mesmerizing live performance on 1983's *Motown 25* special with the rest of the Jackson Five, witnessed by forty-seven million viewers around the world, confirmed his status as an international superstar, one known for his single sequined glove, his haunting, crystal clear voice, and his signature "moonwalk" dance move.

It was during the filming of a Pepsi Cola commercial in 1984 that, due to some mishandled pyrotechnics, Michael's hair was accidentally set on fire, causing second-degree burns and, some believe, the real beginning of addictions to plastic surgery and prescription medications that would plague him for the rest of his life. Unfairly underpublicized was the fact that he donated his entire $1.5 million court settlement with Pepsi to what is now known as the Michael Jackson Burn Center at the Brotman Medical Center in Culver City, California.

While Michael's brilliant recording career continued, his health and his behavior became increasing concerns as the mid-1980s passed into the 1990s. He was diagnosed with vitiligo, which caused blotches of light skin on his body, and the treatments lightened his skin in general, triggering rumors that he was going through a deliberate bleaching process. He was also diagnosed with lupus; his gauntness triggered rumors of anorexia; his dramatically changing facial structure suggested an ongoing series of plastic surgeries, which he denied to the public; and he'd become increasingly introverted and androgynous by the time he bought the 2700-acre Neverland Ranch, his home, zoo, and theme park, near Santa Barbara, California, in 1988. The tabloids seemed to report every bizarre detail of his life without mentioning his almost unprecedented charitable donations, which included millions of dollars to the Heal the World Foundation, which he created to provide food, housing, and medical care to underprivileged children.

In 1993 Michael Jackson was accused of sexually abusing a thirteen-year-old boy. He denied the accusations, the boy and his father settled out of court for a reported $22 million, and the investigation into possible criminal charges was closed due to a lack of evidence. Michael never recovered psychologically or emotionally from the embarrassment and the worldwide sensation the allegations caused in the press.

In 1994 he married Elvis Presley's daughter, Lisa Marie, a marriage that lasted less than two years and was thought by many to be nothing more than an effort to rehabilitate his image. Michael's second marriage, in 1996, was to a nurse named Debbie Rowe, with whom he had two children—Michael Joseph Jr., nicknamed Prince, and Paris-Michael Katherine. They were divorced in 1999, and Debbie Rowe relinquished full custody of the children to Michael. In 2002 Michael's third child was born. He never revealed the identity of the mother and said that the boy—Prince Michael Jackson II, nicknamed Blanket—was the result of artificial insemination.

More accusations of sexual child abuse in 2004 led to an explosive, media-frenzied five-month trial in 2005 that resulted in an acquittal on all charges. Physically and emotionally exhausted from the long ordeal, Michael left the country with his children, spending more than a year on the island of Bahrain at the invitation of Sheikh Abdullah. He returned to the United States at the end of 2006 to attend the funeral of the "godfather of soul," James Brown.

An avalanche of financial problems began in 2005, only some of which were solved with his letting go of Neverland Ranch. He started planning a comeback, and in March 2009 he announced that he would begin his first major concert tour in more than a decade, called "This Is It," starting in London on July 13, 2009. Ticket sales were unprecedented, with all fifty scheduled concerts sold out in a matter of days, and Michael immediately began rehearsing in Los Angeles for what would undoubtedly have been a historic return to the stage.

On June 25, 2009, less than three weeks before his opening night in London, Michael Jackson died of a drug-induced heart attack after collapsing at his rented home in Los Angeles. He was fifty years old. The cause of death is listed as "homicide," and the doctor administering treatment to him on the morning he died has been charged with involuntary manslaughter and is awaiting trial. As a final tribute to the singer, dancer, songwriter, philanthropist, humanitarian, and man unlike any other before or since, more than thirty million people in the United States alone watched Michael Jackson's televised funeral.

From Francine

We've never seen a spirit more ecstatic to be Home than Michael was when he arrived. While he would never have deliberately taken his own life, he'd been ready to be here for quite some time and to be free of a body that was increasingly painful, addicted, and prone to exhaustion. His extraordinary talent combined with a unique emotional fragility created a lifetime in which he was greatly admired, but never felt appropriate and truly didn't understand why he was perceived as odd.

He was met by a tall, ample woman with a sweet round face, but she had to wait to greet him because of the enormous crowd of his beloved animals of all kinds who were there to welcome him. Immediately after this ecstatic reunion Michael did something that's very rare here—he ignored the Scanning Machine and Orientation most rearrivals find helpful in their transition and instead gave a thrilling series of sixteen concerts joined by dozens of transcended musicians, singers, and dancers. He then returned to the life that brings him great joy: entertaining, giving dance instruction, and living among countless animals. He frequently visits his children and his mother on earth. No parent has ever loved his children more, he wants them to know he's watching over them and very proud of them, and he wants the estate he left for them to be fiercely protected on their behalf.

He has nothing to say to or about his father, but he loves the rest of his family and strongly urges his brothers to please tour again as a tribute to him. "Peacefully," he adds with a smile.

His emotional fragility left him more comfortable with children than with other adults, but he is emphatic, from the Other Side, where there is no deceit, no defensiveness, and nothing to lose, that never did he molest or inappropriately touch a child, ever in his life, nor did such a thing ever enter his mind. The mere accusation was a wound that caused him pain until his last day on earth.

By the way, Michael's visage at Home in his happy, healthy thirty-year-old body is exactly how he looked before he began his plastic surgeries and skin treatments.

And finally, a word to Elizabeth Taylor, his most cherished friend on earth. He knows your souls are connected from three past lives together, including two in which you were brother and sister.

Audrey Hepburn

The essence of grace and femininity throughout her acting career, Audrey Kathleen Ruston, the future Audrey Hepburn (only a very, very distant relative of actress Katharine Hepburn, by the way), was born on May 4, 1929, in Ixelles, Belgium, the only child of British banker Joseph Ruston and his second wife, Dutch aristocrat Baroness Ella van Heemstra. Not long after she was born, her father included his grandmother's surname, Hepburn, so that she was raised Audrey Hepburn-Ruston. Audrey was a British citizen despite her birth in Belgium, and she was educated in England during her early childhood. Joseph Ruston, a Nazi sympathizer, left his family in 1935, an event Audrey always referred to as the most traumatic experience of her life. (She managed to locate him decades later, and while there was never a total reconciliation, she supported him financially until he died in 1980.)

In 1939, with World War II threatening, Audrey's mother moved her and her two half brothers to her grandfather's home in the Netherlands, believing they'd be safer from the Germans there. But the Germans soon invaded the Netherlands after all, resulting in the deaths of many of Audrey's relatives. She and her mother struggled desperately just to stay alive, suffering from malnutrition like so many around them. Wanting to help in any way she could, Audrey, a proficient ballerina by then, performed in fund-raisers to support the Dutch war effort.

When the war finally ended, Audrey and her mother went to England, where Audrey was told that, while her ballet skills were brilliant, her above-average height (five foot six) and painfully thin body might prevent her from ever reaching the career pinnacle of prima ballerina. That assessment spurred Audrey into acting, where she could invest her performing experience in an area in which she might find unlimited potential. She successfully auditioned for uncredited theatrical and film roles and, in 1952, was spotted by the French author Colette, whose novel *Gigi* was being translated into a Broadway musical. Colette instantly knew that no one but Audrey should play the lead role in *Gigi*, and she was right. Audrey's performance was critically acclaimed, she won a Theatre World Award, and she was quickly signed by Paramount Studios for the lead opposite Gregory Peck in 1953's *Roman Holiday*, for which she won the Best Actress Academy Award at the age of twenty-four.

Next came *Sabrina*, directed by Billy Wilder and costarring William Holden and Humphrey Bogart. During filming, Audrey had an ill-fated affair with the already married William Holden. She then returned to Broadway to costar with Mel Ferrer in *Ondine* and married Ferrer a few months later. As her talent and timing would have it, in 1954 Audrey Hepburn became one of only three actresses in history to win Best Actress awards at the Golden Globes, the Academy Awards (both of those for *Roman Holiday*), and the Tonys (for *Ondine*) in the same year.

Hollywood and the American public couldn't get enough of this graceful, reed-thin, exquisitely fashionable actress by the mid-1950s, and she was promptly cast in one film after another with the biggest names in the business. There was *War and Peace* with Henry Fonda in 1956, for which she was nominated for a Golden Globe; *Funny Face* with Fred Astaire and *Love in the Afternoon* with Gary Cooper, both in 1957; *Green Mansions* with Anthony Perkins in 1959; and *The Unforgiven* with Burt Lancaster in 1960.

The next decade was no less prolific. To name just a few of her more memorable films and costars in the 1960s: *The Children's Hour* with James Garner and Shirley MacLaine, and *Breakfast at Tiffany's* with George Peppard (for which Audrey was nominated for an Academy Award), both in 1961; *Charade* with Cary Grant in 1963 (for which she was nominated for a Golden Globe); *My Fair Lady* with Rex Harrison in 1964 (for which she was nominated for a Golden Globe); and *How to Steal a Million* with Peter O'Toole and *Two for the Road* with Albert Finney in 1966.

One of Audrey's more intense and difficult films was 1967's *Wait Until Dark*, a disturbing thriller produced by Audrey's husband, Mel Ferrer, as their fourteen-year marriage was disintegrating. Their son, Sean, who was born in 1960, would say later that Audrey stayed in the marriage too long. Ferrer was rumored to have a girlfriend, and it was widely agreed that Ferrer was much too controlling of her and had a terrible temper.

Audrey Hepburn's divorce from Mel Ferrer was final in 1968, and in 1969 she married Dr. Andrea Dotti, an Italian psychiatrist whom she met on a Greek island cruise. Audrey had decided in 1967 to slow down the nonstop pace of her career, and the wisdom of that decision was especially clear during her difficult pregnancy with her and Dotti's son, Luca, who was born in 1970. Sadly, as much as he loved Audrey, Dotti couldn't seem to resist the temptation of other women, and by 1976 Audrey had separated from him and gone back to work, costarring with Sean Connery in *Robin and Marian*. After two Ben Gazzara films and a TV movie with Robert Wagner in the 1980s, Audrey appeared in what was to be her last performance as an actress—the cameo role of an angel in Steven Spielberg's *Always*. By then her divorce from Dotti had been finalized, and she'd begun living with actor Robert Wolders, who was with her for the rest of her life.

Not even at the height of her brilliant success had Audrey's heart forgotten or recovered from the memories of her desperate, malnourished childhood in the Netherlands during the war and the other children around the world who were as trapped as she'd been in seemingly hopeless poverty. She'd worked with UNICEF, the United Nations Children's Fund, for decades, and after *Always* was completed, she decided to devote herself to healing that ache in her heart as best she could. Through her appointment as a goodwill ambassador for UNICEF, she began traveling to the poorest areas in the poorest countries, from Africa to Central and South America to Bangladesh and Vietnam, sparing no effort to bring food, clean water, medical supplies, and some glimmer of hope wherever she went. She was awarded the Presidential Medal of Freedom in 1992 and, posthumously, the Jean Hersholt Humanitarian Award from the Academy of Motion Picture Arts and Sciences.

In October 1992 Audrey was examined in Los Angeles to find the cause of abdominal pains she'd been suffering. On November 1 her doctors discovered abdominal cancer that had been growing over several years. A second surgery on December 1 led to the conclusion that the cancer had spread too far and was inoperable. She was immediately flown to Switzerland, where, on January 20, 1993, Audrey Hepburn died of cancer at the age of sixty-three.

From Francine

No one who knew Audrey on earth will be surprised to hear that she is a Mission Life Entity, a highly advanced soul who is as cherished and admired on the Other Side as she was in her forty-third and final incarnation. Her welcome Home was a massive, joyful celebration; her mother was the first to embrace her, and William Holden, who never stopped loving her, was the second. While she says her death seemed fairly sudden to those closest to her, she wasn't surprised and had made peace with it—she'd had a chronic abdominal problem for more than a year before she was diagnosed. Loved ones from here began making regular visits to her during her second surgery, reminding her of the joy and the important work that were waiting for her, and she was already in the midst of her ecstatic "welcome Home party" by the time her body took its last breath.

Studying her life at the Scanning Machine, with total recall of her chart and her life themes of Caretaker and Builder, filled her with gratitude for the "honor" (her word) of being given two sons she adored "to the fullest depth of my soul." (She hopes they know how proud she is of them and how happy she is that they like each other.) And she felt blessed by the career she so enjoyed and the opportunity to have relationships with such fascinating, desirable men. But nothing moved her quite so much as "the children." Her commitment to them is stronger than ever. Her frequent visits to earth are devoted to third-world countries, where her powerful spirit lends comfort and hope to each child and to those who are continuing her hands-on work. She gathers information on every trip there and returns to advise teams of researchers and developers with whom she's exploring a wealth of possibilities for transforming barren land into rich crop-producing soil. By 2028 in your time they hope to infuse a series of breakthroughs to your geologists, botanists, and environmental scientists that will enable every nation to be self-sufficient in its ability to generously feed its own population, no matter how infertile its land currently seems.

Audrey lives simply in a small community of artists and writers who enjoy gathering with countless other "locals" in a central screening arena to view films from your world, both current and classic. She performs occasional dance recitals at art fairs throughout the Other Side and teaches ballet to those who are gifted in that area and charting it to play an important role in upcoming incarnations.

She has also become a skilled watercolor artist who is illustrating her own book called For of Such Is the Kingdom of God, *from the biblical verse Mark 10:14, which reads: "Suffer the little children to come unto me, and forbid them not: for of such is the kingdom of God." She has entrusted the re-creation of this book on earth to a close friend named Emile, who is reincarnating soon near Vancouver, Canada, and has charted himself to become a successful author before the age of twenty.*

John Candy

The beloved amiable actor and comedian John Franklin Candy was born in Toronto on October 31, 1950, the younger of two sons born to Sidney and Evangeline Candy. Sidney, a car salesman, died of heart disease at the age of thirty-five, leaving five-year-old John and his brother to be raised by the team effort of their mother, aunt, and grandparents. John was a smart, good-natured, popular student and talented football player at Catholic all-boys Neil McNeil High School, but when he was sidelined with a knee injury, he began participating in school theatrical productions, where his confidence in his likeability and talent for comedy grew.

He headed for Centennial Community College, majoring in journalism with the ultimate intention of becoming a sports writer. Drama classes proved irresistible, though, and a very small uncredited role in the 1970 Arnold Schwarzenegger film *Hercules in New York* proved to be a far more powerful lure than classrooms. That same year he left school to pursue a full-time acting career in the potential-packed city of Toronto. He began appearing in local film and television productions, including children's shows in which his natural affability was irresistible. He also became friends with fellow Canadian Dan Aykroyd, and in 1972 they auditioned for a new Toronto branch of Chicago's famed Second City comedy troupe. John's audition made such an impact that he was given the ultimate compliment of an invitation to Chicago to join the core theater, where he worked and became good friends with such other Second City performers as John Belushi, Gilda Radner, and Bill Murray.

He returned to the Toronto outpost in 1976 and balanced his Second City appearances with a late-night Canadian show called *Ninety Minutes Live* and a few low-budget films. In October of that year he helped launch *SCTV* (*Second City Television*), a half-hour sketch-comedy series. *SCTV* began airing in the United States in 1977 and was picked up by NBC in 1981, and during its two-year network run John won two Emmies and a strong following of American fans. He juggled his *SCTV* work with building a film career that included *The Blues Brothers* in 1980, starring his Second City sidekicks Dan Aykroyd and John Belushi, *Stripes* in 1981, and *National Lampoon's Vacation* in 1982. His role in 1984's *Splash*, as Tom Hanks's fun-loving, everyman brother, further established John as a reliable, versatile, enormously appealing character actor.

One of his busiest years was 1985, beginning with a costarring role with Richard Pryor in one of many remakes of *Brewster's Millions* and a silly effort called *Summer Rental*, directed by Carl Reiner. He also executive-produced and starred in a wonderful HBO special called *The Last Polka*. No one was more surprised than John when his hilarious, lovable, successful image propelled him onto *Playgirl* magazine's list of 1985's "Most Desirable Men." By then he was six years into a happy, committed marriage to Rosemary Horbor, whom he married in April 1979 and with whom he had two children, Jennifer in 1980 and Christopher in 1984. But he still appreciated the compliment.

The latter half of the 1980s brought a variety of work that gave John ample opportunity to show off his versatility, from a supporting role in Mel Brooks's sci-fi spoof *Spaceballs* to costarring in a memorably touching role in the comedy *Planes, Trains and Automobiles*. By the early 1990s John's career seemed to be fading. Determined to breathe new life into the industry's perception of him, he broadened his horizons and tackled less on-the-nose roles. His directorial debut came along in 1994, with a Fox TV movie called *Hostage for a Day*, and then he was off to Mexico, where he was costarring in a film called *Wagons East*, unaware that it would be his last.

Obesity relentlessly plagued John throughout his adult life. On one hand, he was painfully aware of his potential for repeating his father's early death from heart disease. He knew intellectually that he was severely compromising his health by carrying more than three hundred pounds on his six-foot-three frame, compounded by an addiction to smoking. He was also in need of surgery to replace a painfully injured hip, but his doctor refused to proceed until he lost weight. As genuinely anguished as he was about his obesity, though, some part of him was also afraid it had become such a part of his persona that he might not be as popular with his fans without it. He finally quit smoking and began losing weight in the months before *Wagons East* started shooting.

Tragically, his efforts were apparently too late. On March 4, 1994, after a long, hard day of filming in the desert heat, John Candy spent a few minutes on the phone with his costars to thank them for their support during some especially challenging scenes, then got into bed, went to sleep, and never woke up, dying of a heart attack at the age of forty-three.

From Francine

John and his father were ecstatic to be reunited when John returned Home, and among the large flock of animals waiting to greet him was an especially giddy English Yorkshire terrier. After his visit to the Scanning Machine, it was decided that John would benefit from being cocooned— his death was so sudden and came so much sooner than he'd consciously expected that once he was here and understood what had happened, he was shocked, a bit disoriented, and filled with regret that his greatest fear had manifested itself: he had left his children without their father, just as his father had prematurely left him.

Once he emerged from being cocooned, he was completely at peace with the Exit Point he'd chosen to take. He'd gone Home at the end of an especially happy day, doing what he loved most, leaving behind a wife and children who knew he adored them and for whom he'd provided well. As it happened, though, their last memories of him are of the wonderfully funny, friendly, playful, loving, light-filled spirit they knew, who is all of that and more on the Other Side now that his cocooning is complete. John loves nothing more than gathering interesting varieties of people for parties and special celebrations. He's thirty years old here, of course, and his visage is that of a man of medium height, dark complected, with a slender, very graceful body. There are few better, more enthusiastic social dancers than John, which makes his parties even more popular. He's also a gifted athlete who especially enjoys baseball and skiing.

He adores his children, he's proud of his wife for being such a dedicated mother to them after he left, and he says he loves the collection of framed photographs.

His "work" here is very much like work he continues on earth. Bear in mind that while all of us are thirty years old here, we return Home at the age we were when our bodies died, and becoming thirty is a process, not an instantaneous event. John's chosen passion is to be among those who help all the newly arrived children make a fearless, happy transition to the Other Side. He also makes very regular visits to children's hospitals around the world, reassuring the children during and immediately after surgery with that warm, loving, infectious joy he emanates everywhere he goes.

Ingrid Bergman

Describing her own remarkable and sometimes controversial life, Ingrid Bergman once said, "I've gone from saint to whore to saint again, all in one lifetime." This astonishingly beautiful and gifted actress was born on August 29, 1915, in Stockholm, Sweden. Her German mother, Friedel, died when Ingrid was three years old, and she was raised by her father, Justus Bergman, a Swedish artist and photographer who was the first to capture her on film and encourage her interest in the arts. Justus passed away when Ingrid was twelve, leaving the child to be briefly cared for by an unmarried aunt until she went to live with her Uncle Otto and his wife and five children during her teenage years.

She graduated from private school in 1933 and, through an audition, won a scholarship to the Royal Dramatic Theatre School in Stockholm, alma mater of the great Greta Garbo. After a year of study there, she was hired by a Swedish studio and impressed audiences and co-workers with her work in a dozen films in Sweden and Germany.

In 1936 Ingrid starred in a Swedish film called *Intermezzo*. Legendary Hollywood producer David O. Selznick fell in love with the film and its star and, in 1939, brought her to Los Angeles to reprise her role in the American remake, *Intermezzo: A Love Story*. By then she'd married dentist and future neurosurgeon Peter Lindstrom in 1937, and she left him and their infant daughter, Pia, at home in

Sweden while she made what she expected to be a relatively brief trip to America to make this one film. Selznick was bright enough not to give her a typical Hollywood makeover, embracing her name, accent, and natural beauty, and when *Intermezzo* became a huge hit in the United States, so did the graceful, warmly shy, exquisitely unenhanced Ingrid Bergman.

She did return to Sweden after *Intermezzo* to satisfy one last film obligation, then came back to America in 1940 for an appearance on Broadway, followed by three fairly successful movies until 1942, when along came a script called *Casablanca* and an actor named Humphrey Bogart. Although Ingrid never considered her portrayal of Ilsa in *Casablanca* to be one of her best performances, she came to accept that it would always be her most talked-about film, a film that had, as she observed years later, "a life of its own."

Next came *For Whom the Bell Tolls,* the screen adaptation of Ernest Hemingway's novel, in 1943, for which she received her first Best Actress Academy Award nomination. The dark, suspenseful *Gaslight* followed in 1944, along with her first Best Actress Oscar. Her role as a nun in 1945's *The Bells of St. Mary's* opposite Bing Crosby made it three Best Actress nominations in a row. From 1945 through 1949 Ingrid went to work for one of her biggest fans in Hollywood, director Alfred Hitchcock, who cast her in *Spellbound, Notorious,* and *Under Capricorn.*

Ingrid's fourth Academy Award nomination was the result of a part she'd yearned for since she arrived in Hollywood, the title role in Walter Wanger's 1948 production of *Joan of Arc.* She'd starred as the tragic heroine on Broadway in *Joan of Lorraine* for twenty-five weeks in 1946 and won a Tony for her performance, and she was ecstatic when the time to portray St. Joan on film finally arrived. It's impossible to calculate how popular the film might have been if its theater showings hadn't been interrupted by the great scandal of Ingrid Bergman's life.

By now Ingrid's husband and daughter had moved to the United States, and she spent as much time as possible with them between films, both in Rochester, New York, where Peter studied medicine and surgery, and in San Francisco, where he completed his internship. America's love affair with Ingrid, her sweet pristine beauty, and the flawless innocence she exemplified onscreen only deepened with her offstage roles as a dedicated wife and mother.

And so it was that the American public seemed to take it as a personal betrayal when the married Ingrid Bergman met, fell in love with, and became pregnant by the also married Italian director Roberto Rossellini. She'd written him a letter to say how much she would love to work in one of his films, and his response was to create a role for her in his 1949 film *Stromboli*. That both of their marriages had been unhappy for a very long time didn't diminish the harsh judgment they faced when their affair became known, and Ingrid's pregnancy while *Joan of Arc* was in theaters across the United States caused a dramatic decline in attendance. Ingrid gave birth to their son, Roberto, before she and Rossellini were able to finalize their respective divorces and legally marry in 1950, which only added to the accusations of Ingrid's immorality. She was even denounced on the floor of the U.S. Senate, where Senator Edwin Johnson of Colorado proclaimed her "a powerful influence for evil."

Ingrid understandably moved to Italy, out of the eye of the outrage against her, and she and Rossellini made five films together there between 1950 and 1955. In 1952 she gave birth to twin daughters, Isotta, a future Italian literature professor, and Isabella, who later became a successful actress and model. Her career didn't show visible signs of international resurrection until 1956, when her film for French director Jean Renoir, *Elena et les Hommes*, was released.

It was also in 1956 that Ingrid finally returned to Hollywood to star in *Anastasia*, for which she won another Best Actress Oscar and made great strides in winning back the affection of America. Her marriage to Rossellini ended in 1957, and in 1959 she married Swedish producer Lars Schmidt, whom she divorced in 1975.

The next ten years were busy and ultimately triumphant for Ingrid Bergman, beginning with a Best Actress Emmy in 1959 for the television adaptation of Henry James's *The Turn of the Screw*. She gave critically acclaimed theatrical performances in London in 1965's *A Month in the Country*, and in an American production of *More Stately Mansions* in 1967. She further won back film audiences in 1968 with her performance in the Goldie Hawn vehicle *Cactus Flower*.

In 1974 Ingrid Bergman received the rare compliment of a third Academy Award, for Best Supporting Actress in the Sidney Lumet film *Murder on the Orient Express*. Her seventh Oscar nomination came in 1978 for *Autumn Sonata*, directed by a man to whom, despite many rumors to the contrary, she was not related, the esteemed Ingmar Bergman. The beautiful film, shot in Norway, was one of her finest performances and, as it turned out, her last feature.

Her final appearance as an actress was the 1982 miniseries *A Woman Called Golda*, in which she starred as Israeli prime minister Golda Meir. She won a Best Actress Emmy for her stunning portrayal. Sadly, it was presented posthumously; her daughter Pia accepted it on her behalf. It was widely known in the industry that Ingrid's health was failing. She'd been diagnosed with breast cancer, and it was spreading. What wasn't so widely known was how far it had progressed.

On August 29, 1982—her sixty-seventh birthday—Ingrid Bergman lost her seven-year battle with breast cancer. Her body was cremated in London, where she died, and her ashes went home to Sweden, where some were scattered in the sea and the rest were interred beside her parents.

From Francine

Ingrid was greeted by her parents before she'd even emerged from the tunnel. She lingered at the Scanning Machine and in Orientation, very methodical in her determination to learn all she could from the lifetime she'd just left behind and make peace with it. She knew she felt no guilt about the Rossellini scandal, because at no time did it feel like a choice to her. Instead, it seemed to her that she was participating in an inevitability, against her wisdom and logic, but something she had to demand of herself, regardless of scandal and public censure, whether she understood it or not.

What became very clear to her after reviewing her lifetime repeatedly at the Scanning Machine and with the help of her Orientation counselors is something that so many learn, to their surprise and relief, when they return Home: what they charted for themselves often has a purpose greater than what might have been apparent on earth. When Ingrid met Rossellini and found herself prepared to abandon everyone and everything she knew and compromise her reputation, to be with him, she mistakenly believed at the time that their passionate love for each other was the reason he had seemed so inevitable to her. That belief turned to confusion when that passionate love and their marriage began dying and it became clear she would not be spending the rest of her life with him.

The confusion ended when, on the Other Side, she was able to reflect on that lifetime and the chart she wrote before she was born: Rossellini's overwhelming importance to her was nothing more and nothing less than the fact that only he could give her the exact three children she charted to bring into the world. And of course Rossellini charted Ingrid for the same reason. Only secondarily was it about the magnetic attraction between the two of them. That attraction existed purely because they recognized each other on sight from the pact they'd made before they incarnated, that together they would create Roberto, Isotta, and Isabella. Once they'd satisfied that mutual purpose, there was no further reason for their relationship.

Ingrid and Rossellini occasionally see each other here at social events, particularly the ballet and art exhibits. They're pleasant, as we all are to each other, but there is no special connection between them. It's interesting that Ingrid is as innately drawn to directors here as she was in her lifetime. She, Alfred Hitchcock, and Carlo Ponti, old friends from Home, are frequently together again as usual.

Like so many actors, by the way, Ingrid's visage on the Other Side is identical to the physical image she had on earth. Picture her as you knew her at the age of thirty and you'll know exactly how she looks now, with the added light of peaceful bliss radiating from her, as it does from all of us.

She says she was very discouraged when the lump in her breast was discovered and she was first diagnosed with breast cancer. Even though her doctors reassured her that they had caught it very early, she knew when her arm began to swell that she would be taking advantage of this Exit Point and heading Home, with her intended purposes on earth accomplished. She urges her daughters, particularly Isabella, to be religiously vigilant about their health, not only through regular mammograms, but also by CAT scans every two years.

Ingrid's chosen passion here is in Orientation, where she specializes in working with girls who come over in their early teens, particularly trauma cases and suicides related to pregnancies and bullying, for which her most recent lifetime prepared her so effectively. She has no desire to incarnate again.

John Lennon

One of the founding members of the historically influential rock band the Beatles, John Lennon was a singer, songwriter, writer, artist, and peace activist who, in his forty years on earth, became a legend. John Winston Lennon was born on October 9, 1940, in Liverpool, England, during a World War II German air raid. His father, Alfred Lennon, was a merchant seaman in the war and was rarely at home with his wife, Julia, and their infant son. Complicated dissension between his parents resulted in John's living with his mother's sister, Mimi Smith, and her husband, George, for the majority of his childhood, although his mother visited almost every day and remained an integral part of his life. (Alfred left when John was five and didn't reappear in his life for another twenty years.) It was Julia who bought John his first guitar in 1957, taught him to play the banjo, and introduced him to American rock-and-roll records. Her death on July 15, 1958, after being hit by a car, devastated John, who was then seventeen.

John was a brilliant and witty, but undisciplined student at the Liverpool College of Art after graduating from Quarry Bank High School, and he dropped out before his senior year. He and his future wife, Cynthia Powell, met at Liverpool College in 1957 and were married August 23, 1962, shortly after she discovered that she was pregnant with their son, Julian, who was born on April 8, 1963.

In March 1957 John started a band called the Quarrymen. At their second concert, July 6, 1957, John met a young singer and musician named Paul McCartney and invited him to join the group. John and Paul began writing songs together, and Paul convinced John to let fourteen-year-old George Harrison play lead guitar for the band; Stuart Sutcliffe, a friend of John's from art school, joined in as the Quarrymen's bassist. A series of band name changes followed, finally resulting in unanimous agreement on "The Beatles." The band achieved some popularity at a variety of clubs in Liverpool and in Hamburg, Germany. But not until they performed at the Cavern Club in Liverpool on November 9, 1961, after Stuart Sutcliffe had left the group and subsequently died and drummer Pete Best had been replaced by Ringo Starr, did the historic lightning-in-a-bottle phenomenon of the Beatles take shape. Record-store owner Brian Epstein saw the performance and convinced them to let him manage them, and his instincts effectively overcame his lack of experience. On May 9, 1962, Epstein successfully convinced producer George Martin to sign the Beatles to EMI, and their first album *Please Please Me* promptly became the number-one album in England.

By January 1964 the Beatles' second album, *Introducing . . . the Beatles*, reached number one in America, and John, Paul, George, and Ringo "crossed the pond" for their legendary appearances on *The Ed Sullivan Show*, which catapulted them to international superstardom and triggered what came to be known as the "British Invasion": the arrival of the Beatles and such other English rock bands as the Rolling Stones, the Animals, the Kinks, the Dave Clark Five, Herman's Hermits, and many more.

The Beatles shot their first film, *Hard Day's Night*, in 1964, and John's two books, *In His Own Write* and *A Spaniard in the Works*, were published that same year. The Beatles' second film, *Help!*, was released in 1965, and their insane whirlwind of touring finally ended with their August 29, 1966, concert in San Francisco's Candlestick Park.

Drug experimentation was as popular with the Beatles as it was with the youth in general in the 1960s, and its influence became apparent in their subsequent albums, particularly *Sergeant Pepper's Lonely Hearts Club Band*, which is widely regarded as the greatest rock album in history. Brian Epstein's death of an accidental drug overdose on August 27, 1967, was a shocking blow to the Beatles, and after filming the critically unpopular *Magical Mystery Tour* and recording the soundtrack album, the Beatles traveled to India to lose themselves in the transcendental meditation craze under the instruction of the Maharishi Mahesh Yogi. They returned to England to film *Yellow Submarine* and record *The Beatles*, more popularly known as *The White Album*.

By now there was little if anything left of John's marriage to Cynthia, and they were divorced in 1968. In November of that year John attended an art opening at London's Indica Gallery and met Japanese artist Yoko Ono. They became virtually inseparable from that fateful meeting on and were married in Gibraltar on March 20, 1969.

John and Yoko's instantaneous partnership exacerbated the tension that was already plaguing the Beatles. John and Yoko created their own version of peace protests, spending days at a time in bed giving filmed interviews and forming the Plastic Ono Band to record the ultimate pacifist anthem "Give Peace a Chance." In September 1969 John officially announced that he was leaving the Beatles, just as their last album *Abbey Road* was released.

In 1971, after recording his critically acclaimed *Imagine* album, John moved to the United States with Yoko, where they were greeted almost immediately with efforts by the Nixon administration to have them deported. The excuse was John's conviction in England in 1968 for marijuana possession. The reality, revealed in subsequent papers as a result of the Freedom of Information Act, was that the administration wanted to punish John and Yoko for their activism against the Vietnam War. Nixon resigned in 1974, and in 1976 John was granted permanent residency in America.

John and Yoko separated in 1973, sending John on a drug-and-alcohol-hazed trip to Los Angeles, an eighteen-month "lost weekend" that ultimately resulted in their reconciliation. On John's thirty-fifth birthday, October 9, 1975, Yoko gave birth to their son, Sean, and John made the choice to stay home in New York to be a full-time father and househusband. But in 1980 he returned to the recording studio for his hit album *Double Fantasy*, which included the haunting single *Starting Over*.

On the night of December 8, 1980, less than a month after the release of *Double Fantasy*, John Lennon was shot to death by deranged fan Mark Chapman in front of the Dakota in New York, where he was happily living with Yoko and Sean. The impact on the world he left behind extends far beyond his music, as everyone who was touched by his life continues to *Imagine*.

From Francine

John is a well-loved, highly regarded force of nature here, and while we were surprised by his sudden arrival, we were euphoric to welcome him. He, on the other hand, was angry and disconsolate from the circumstances of his death when he emerged from the tunnel, and not even the embrace of his cherished mother could comfort him. He was immediately taken to the cocooning chamber by his Spirit Guide, named Gregory, where he was spiritually and emotionally healed for approximately five years in your time. By then he was thriving and excited to return to his life on the Other Side after his time at the Scanning Machine, about which he expressed his profound regret at his neglect of his first wife and particularly his son Julian. "I can offer a million reasons but no excuses," he says. "It wasn't for lack of love for him, that's for sure. It had more to do with my being a self-involved, out-of-control pain in the ass for many, many years. I adore both my sons, and I'm so proud of them. And to Paul, Elton, and the other men who stepped up to be better fathers to Julian than I was, I'm deeply and eternally grateful."

John now reflects that he had many premonitions of an early death and never believed he would live to be an old man, which might explain why he tried to "squeeze several lifetimes into one," until Yoko, he says, "gave me the boundaries that kept me from completely self-destructing, and Sean came along to finally put my priorities in their proper place."

His life here is, in many ways, a continuation of his last incarnation. He's deeply spiritual and a great student of both Buddhism and Hinduism. (He and George Harrison are often seen meditating and taking long, pensive walks together, now that George is Home as well.) He's brilliantly witty and continues writing books for his own amusement. He continues performing and writing music, often collaborating with his friend Harry Nilsson. He prefers living simply, his "house" consisting of nothing but a modest bedroom with what I'm told is an extraordinary video and audio system. He's invariably barefoot and dressed in robes. And his passionate pursuit of peace on earth, which existed long before his most recent incarnation and will continue until it's accomplished, is expressed through his very popular lecture series and valued participation in an ongoing peace congress of former world leaders. "We infuse our solutions constantly," John says, "but they can't be received by small, closed minds."

Diana Spencer, Princess of Wales

One of the most celebrated women in the history of the British royal family, Diana Frances Spencer was born on July 1, 1961, at Park House in Sandringham, England, to Edward Spencer, titled Viscount Althorp, and his first wife, Frances. Diana's parents were very acrimoniously divorced when she and her two sisters and brother were young, and when Frances left for London with her new lover, Peter Kydd, Edward was granted custody of the children. In 1975 Edward inherited the title "8th Earl Spencer," which afforded Diana the title "Lady" Diana Spencer, and the earl and his children moved to the ancestral Althorp mansion. A year later he married Raine Cartland, daughter of romance novelist Barbara Cartland. By all accounts Lady Diana didn't like her new stepmother, which brought her enjoyment of living in her father's home to an end.

Diana's academic success, both in England and in Switzerland, was less than stellar. She was a shy below-average student, but she was gifted at ballet and sports. She moved to London when she finished her formal education and, guided by her love of children, became a kindergarten teacher.

During her early childhood at Park House, Diana and her siblings occasionally played with two of her "landlady's" children, Prince Andrew and Prince Edward, the younger sons of Queen Elizabeth, from whom Edward Spencer was leasing the mansion. In

1977, sixteen-year-old Diana became reacquainted with her former playmates' older brother, Prince Charles, heir to the British throne. He was entering his thirties and under pressure from his family and the public to settle down and find a suitable princess. He'd had a lengthy relationship with Camilla Parker Bowles, whom the royal family didn't consider acceptable—unlike Diana, she had no aristocratic lineage, she was married, she wasn't a Protestant, and she was no longer a virgin. In fact, many believe that Camilla Parker Bowles, who became Charles's second wife, had a hand in selecting Diana as the prince's bride.

On July 29, 1981, in London's St. Paul's Cathedral, the shy, beautiful twenty-year-old Lady Diana Spencer became Her Royal Highness the Princess of Wales, marrying Prince Charles in a spectacular ceremony broadcast to an audience of approximately a billion viewers around the world. (Among the thirty-five hundred invited guests were Camilla Parker Bowles and her husband, Andrew Parker Bowles, who happened to be a godson of Charles's mother, Queen Elizabeth.) Within the next three years Princess Diana gave birth to the couple's two sons, "an heir and a spare," Prince William Arthur Philip Louis and Prince Henry Charles Albert David (who's come to be known as Prince Harry).

The marriage was unhappy from the beginning. Diana found the rigors of her royal duties to be both overwhelming and confining, and the world press had become virtually obsessed with everything about her, from her brilliant sense of fashion to her obvious hands-on adoration of her two little boys. She began devoting more and more time to her own passionate charitable causes, which included needy children, AIDS victims, the impoverished homeless, and the crusade against landmines.

She also went through more than her share of emotional challenges, struggling with depression and bulimia and more than one suicide attempt. Both she and Prince Charles were unfaithful in the marriage—Charles's longtime affair with Camilla Parker Bowles continued, and Diana reportedly had a series of affairs, many of which became embarrassingly public. Finally, in December 1992, the separation of the prince and princess was formally announced, and their divorce was finalized in 1996.

Diana's great worldwide popularity continued after the divorce, as did her devotion to her two beloved sons. She was probably the most photographed woman in the world both during and after her marriage, and she used the spotlight brilliantly to call attention to her international charitable pursuits. She had little if any privacy, so that in 1997, when she became involved with Egyptian producer Dodi Al-Fayed, the couple was relentlessly photographed and reported on by the worldwide tabloid press.

In Paris, on the night of August 30, 1997, Diana and Dodi climbed into their limousine with their driver, Henri Paul, and Dodi's bodyguard, Trevor Rees-Jones, outside their hotel. The paparazzi immediately gave chase, and in the Pont de l'Alma tunnel a devastating collision occurred. Dodi Al-Fayed and Henri Paul were pronounced dead at the crash site. Trevor Rees-Jones was severely injured, but survived. Diana was raced by ambulance to Pitié-Salpêtrière Hospital, where, despite hours of extraordinary efforts to save her, she was pronounced dead at 4:00 A.M. on August 31, 1997.

The funeral of Diana, Princess of Wales, was held on September 6, 1997. The procession started at Kensington Palace and ended at Westminster Abbey. Diana's casket was immediately followed by her sons, Prince William and Prince Harry; Diana's brother, Charles Spencer; Prince Charles; Diana's former father-in-law, Prince Philip; and representatives from each of the 110 charities Diana had supported throughout her adult life. The televised funeral of the "people's princess" was watched by an estimated two and a half billion shocked, saddened mourners in every corner of the world she affected so deeply.

From Francine

Diana's life themes were Caretaker and Builder, and like so many Mission Life Entities who make the decision to experience an incarnation on earth, her widely publicized lifelong battle with depression was virtually inevitable. Earth is one of the most challenging and troubled of all the occupied planets in the universe, a shock to spirits as intensely sensitive as Diana. She accomplished everything she intended during that incarnation, although she's the first to say that she sometimes accomplished it with "startling imperfection." Her first incarnation will also be her last.

Diana arrived on the Other Side depleted, disoriented, and grieving such a sudden departure from her beloved sons. She was welcomed and embraced by her maternal grandmother and by scores of animals and loved ones from Home and then immediately cocooned for what in your time was several years until she was her joyful, reverent, focused self again. She is still as soft-spoken as ever, with a beautiful visage identical to her appearance on earth, fairly solitary as she's always been, preferring to study and meditate rather than socialize. She's returned to her work in one of our medical research centers specializing in pediatric diseases and disorders. One of her great joys is traveling to civilizations on other planets and returning with reports on any of their advancements that can contribute to the constant efforts on the Other Side to treat, cure, and eradicate threats to the health of the earth's children.

Diana knows that William is going to be an inspiration to his country when he becomes the next king of England. She also continues her work on earth, not only spending time with critically ill children in hospitals around the world, but also joining legions of spirits from Home who flock to sites of natural and human-made disasters to comfort the youngest victims and, when there are fatalities involved, taking them to the blissful safety of God's arms on the Other Side. Diana has always been enchanted by the fact that, almost without exception, children and animals don't return Home through a tunnel when they die, but instead cross a beautiful footbridge that leads them to the same vast meadow that welcomes everyone else. (*Children and animals can find it jarring to find themselves in a tunnel. Crossing a footbridge, on the other hand, makes sense to them, allowing them to understand how and why they traveled from one dimension to the other.*) Never does a child or an animal traverse the footbridge unaccompanied by the spirit world, and Diana is one of their most loyal, loving companions as they make that journey.

She says that although she was clearly ill-suited to many of the expectations of royalty, she is deeply grateful for the platform her title made possible for her passionate causes around the world and, above all, for the honor of being the mother of the two sons "*who taught me what it feels like to love someone to the core of your soul.*" She speaks constantly about how proud she is of them. And she has nothing at all to say, by the way, about the collision that ended her lifetime.

Acknowledgments

To my smart, beautiful agent, Jennifer DeChiara, who gives new meaning to the words loyalty and integrity . . .

To my friend and assistant, Linda Rossi, for everything, but particularly for the hours and hours she spent interviewing Francine and making this book possible . . .

To my editor, Nancy Hancock, and the whole team at HarperOne for their tireless diligence every step of the way . . .

To my husband and best friend, Michael Ulery, for his love, patience, kindness, and support every minute of every day . . .

And of course to Francine, my source of information and guidance from the instant I arrived on this earth . . .

. . . my eternal, heartfelt gratitude.

Sylvia